D0822474

DEMOCRATIC POLITICS
AND
POLICY ANALYSIS

Hank C. Jenkins-Smith

UNM Institute for Public Policy
University of New Mexico

Brooks/Cole Publishing Company
Pacific Grove, California

For Liz.
For where we've been,
and where we're going.

Brooks/Cole Publishing Company
A Division of Wadsworth, Inc.

Printed in the United States of America
10 9 8 7 6 5 4 3 2 1

Library of Congress Cataloging-in-Publication Data
Jenkins-Smith, Hank C.
    Democratic politics and policy analysis / Hank C. Jenkins-Smith.
      p. cm.
    Includes bibliographical references.
    ISBN 0-534-12702-9
    1. Policy sciences.   2. Democracy.   I. Title.
H97.J46   1989
320'.6--dc20   89-17426
                                                 CIP

Sponsoring Editor: *Cynthia C. Stormer*
Editorial Assistants: *Mary Ann Zuzow, Cathleen Sue Collins*
Production Editor: *Ben Greensfelder*
Manuscript Editor: *Robert E. Baker*
Permissions Editor: *Carline Haga*
Interior and Cover Designs: *E. Kelly Shoemaker*
Art Coordinators: *Sue C. Howard, Cloyce Wall*
Interior Illustration: *Graphic Arts*
Typesetting: *Dharma Enterprises*
Printing and Binding: *Malloy Lithographing, Inc.*

PREFACE

This is a book about the relationship between applied public policy analysis and democratic politics. The topic is urgent because policy analysis is increasingly—and formally—intertwined with the making of public policy in modern politics. From the standpoint of the norms of democratic politics, important charges have been leveled at policy analysts, claiming that the application of policy analysis undermines, distorts, or overburdens the policy-making process. From the perspective of the policy analyst, on the other hand, the question is whether the potential benefits of policy analysis can survive the vicissitudes of politics without being a mere handmaiden to the politically powerful or, alternatively, simply ignored and irrelevant.

Since the rise of policy analysis over the past two decades, the assessments of the role of analysis have oscillated between "belief and doubt."[1] Analysis has alternately been deemed irrelevant or outrightly harmful by its critics and a godsend by its advocates. Both critics and advocates have mobilized evidence —primarily in the form of case studies—backing their claims. The intent of this book is to analyze these claims and counterclaims in a way that is of use to students, scholars, and practitioners of both politics and policy analysis.

The goals of this book are to clarify the fundamental bases of public policy analysis—what I call the policy analysis paradigm—and to address, with a focus on the premises of the critiques regarding the role of analysis in demo-

---

[1] See Martin Rein and Sheldon White's "Policy Research: Belief and Doubt," *Policy Analysis*, 3(2) (Spring 1977), pp. 239–271. Also see Henry Aaron's *Politics and the Professors: The Great Society in Perspective*, (Washington, DC: Brookings Institute, 1978).

cratic politics, various themes critical of policy analysis. In so doing, a model of policy analysis and its political context is developed and applied to a set of federal energy policy cases. The first case is an in-depth study of strategies of analytical debate in a highly charged dispute over energy export policy in the early 1980s. Then an array of cases are applied that, while primarily concerned with energy issues, cover a broad range of the significant "policy contexts" in which analysis is applied. Finally, a conclusion is reached regarding the implications of policy analysis for democratic politics and the effects of politics on the practice of policy analysis.

For course work, this book should be of use in advanced undergraduate- and graduate-level courses in public policy analysis, public policy processes, and public administration. For those whose strength is in the area of policy analysis, this book's greatest offerings are the treatment of the criticisms of policy analysis (chapter 3), and the integration of analysis with the politics of policy making (chapters 4 through 7). For those with less background in policy analysis, the discussion of the philosophical and technical underpinnings of policy analysis (chapter 2) is also essential: a general understanding of the concept of efficiency is necessary for any reasoned assessment of the intended and the de facto roles of public policy analysis.

The model of policy analysis in the political context (chapter 4) is intentionally designed to facilitate application across the full gamut of policy contexts. Thus I would encourage instructors and students to apply the model to new areas to test its propositions and to extend, enrich, and (where warranted) revise the model. While the book is written at an advanced level, the basic concepts are fully defined in the text and pinpointed in the index.

In writing a book of this scope, it is probably inevitable that many debts, intellectual and otherwise, will be incurred. The primary argument of this book was extensively influenced by Ted Bluhm, Paul Sabatier, and David Weimer. Many others have read and provided useful comments on all or parts of the book, including Richard Barke, Marshall Hoyler, Bruce Jacobs, Roger James, Liz Jenkins-Smith, Steve Minihan, Jill Clark, Robert Bartlett, and Peter deLeon. Others provided invaluable time and data in the form of the personal interviews employed in the case studies described in chapters 5 and 6. Bob Baker's thorough copy editing greatly improved the manuscript, and Ben Greensfelder kept production flowing smoothly. Finally, I wish to thank Cindy Stormer and Linda Stark of Brooks/Cole for their encouragement and assistance in bringing this project to completion. To all these individuals, and the many others who helped in innumerable ways, I express my heartfelt thanks! Blame for any errors, omissions, or other faults, however, rests completely (well, almost) with Paul Sabatier.

Hank C. Jenkins-Smith

CONTENTS

PART THREE
THE PRUDENTIAL PRACTICE OF
POLICY ANALYSIS   201

CHAPTER 1

Democratic Politics
and Policy Analysis:
Harmony or Tension?

Policy analysis, as a set of techniques and criteria with which to evaluate public policy options and select among them, has been widely promoted since the 1960s as a tool to rationalize the development and implementation of public policy. The proponents of analysis—from presidents of the United States to practitioners of the art—have touted analysis as the means to greater efficiency and equity in allocation of public resources. Democratic politics will be improved, it is said, by a more accurate translation of the preferences of American citizens into public policy.

In nearly equal measure, however, the widespread use of policy analysis in public policy formulation has been roundly condemned as destructive to the norms, institutions, and practices of American politics. Analysis, it is argued, will result in the transfer of power to a new, unrepresentative, and narrow technical elite. Furthermore, critics charge that the application of policy analysis will serve to seriously distort the expression of public preferences because of flaws in both the underlying theory of value and the techniques employed by the policy analyst. Other critics see the primary source of the threat of analysis in the generation of overwhelming strains on the political process and institutions. In this view, both the cognitive capabilities of decision makers and the institutional processes through which political power is fragmented and (in some measure) coordinated in American politics are placed in jeopardy.

Particularly perplexing for those of us who would assess these competing contentions is that both the proponents *and* the various critics of policy analysis are able to marshal theoretical and empirical evidence to support their arguments. Each can point to contingencies in the application of policy analysis that seem to bear out their hopes or fears. How can the general plausibility of the threats and promises of analysis for our political processes be assessed?

These are matters that must concern any student, practitioner, or scholar of policy analysis. For those of us who do (or who plan to do) policy analysis, the belief that we are "doing good" is a central professional motivation. Yet when one looks to the literature on the debate over the threats and promise of policy analysis, one is struck by the eerie quality of the dialogue: the proponents and critics of policy analysis seem more often than not to talk *past* one another, generating images of analytical perfection (wherein all citizens' preferences are accurately measured and reduced to a single comparable metric of benefits and costs) that compete with specters of *analysis from hell* (in which analysts usurp political power, mangle preferences, or reduce venerable political institutions to ruin by the very weight of the analytical complexity they generate).[1] It is no wonder that new entrants to the debate ignore their adversaries, or that many students and practitioners of policy analysis ignore the debate altogether. But that is a tragedy, because analysis has become, for better or worse, an integral part of the workings of our political institutions. Its implications for our democratic processes are of urgent concern to us all.

I should make clear that I do not enter this particular debate with clean hands. As a student, practitioner, and teacher of policy analysis, and now as director of a public policy research institute, I have remained convinced that analysis does indeed have a great deal to offer policy makers and citizens in

---

[1] Contrast Edith Stokey and Richard Zeckhauser's *A Primer for Policy Analysis* (New York: W. W. Norton and Co., 1978): 151, and Allan Williams' "Cost–Benefit Analysis: Bastard Science? And/Or Insidious Poison in the Body Politick?", eds. Robert Haveman and Julius Margolis *Public Expenditure and Policy Analysis,* 2nd ed. (Chicago: Rand McNally, 1977), with Irving Horowitz's "Social Science Mandarins: Policymaking as a Political Formula," *Policy Sciences,* vol. 1 (1970), pp. 339–360, or Edward Banfield's "Policy Science as Metaphysical Madness." Robert Goldwin (ed.) *Bureaucrats, Policy Analysts, Statesmen: Who Leads?* (Washington, DC: American Enterprise Institute, 1980).

democratic societies. And yet both practice and study of analysis have also convinced me that, on occasion at least, public policy analysis *is* in tension with important norms of democratic practice. This book, as a result, makes a self-conscious argument about the characteristics, potential costs, and benefits of policy analysis that in some measure reflects these discordant convictions. Throughout, this argument is based as solidly as possible on empirical evidence concerning the pattern of demand for, provision of, and response to policy analysis in our political institutions; and I have sought to address that evidence directly to the normative boasts and condemnations of analysis.

My intent is to systematically evaluate the validity of the conflicting claims about the place and effect of policy analysis in American politics. In particular, I attempt to assess the praise and damnation of analysis in light of its practice *in context* over the range of contingencies of the policy process. The chapters of Part One seek to clarify the underlying foundations of, and claims for, policy analysis in theory and the perceived threats for democratic politics should such analysis be widely applied. The characteristic elements of policy analysis—with emphasis on the theoretical underpinnings and techniques of efficiency analysis—are distilled and clarified in chapter 2. The implications of these characteristic elements, and of the claims made for policy analysis by its proponents, for the practice of American politics are highlighted. In chapter 3, the primary themes critical of policy analysis are pulled together from a broad array of sources and perspectives. The specific threats posed by analysis are developed in a manner designed to facilitate subsequent assessment of their validity in light of a conceptual model of the practice and process of policy analysis. Specifically, what does the theme of criticism presume about the context in which analysis is applied, and about the constraints and incentives with which the policy analyst is confronted? As it turns out, the presumptions implicit within the different critical themes are quite at odds with one another.

In Part Two, I develop a conceptual model of policy analysis *as applied* in political institutions, and provide tests and elaboration of the model through a series of case studies. Chapter 4 presents the model of the process of policy analysis, arguing that the characteristics of the application of analysis—and the uses to which it is put—must be understood as an interactive process within the cluster of specialized policy experts, government officials, lobbyists, reporters, and others who work closely in the issue area. Characteristics of the policy-issue context—the intensity of conflict, the level of analytical uncertainty attending the issue, and the nature of the political forum—systematically affect the tendency toward, and constraints on, particular kinds of uses of policy analysis. Chapter 4 also examines the kinds of professional roles, here called "styles" of policy analysis, promoted for policy analysts and explores the applicability and effect of these styles within the varying issue contexts.

Chapters 5 and 6 apply the model of the process of analysis to a set of detailed case studies on the use of energy policy analysis in the federal government. First, the use of policy analysis within a bureaucratic debate among an array of federal agencies over oil export policy is examined in detail. Particular attention is given to the styles of analysis adopted by the various protagonists and to the strategies employed in advocacy of particular policy options by those protagonists. Second, a series of cases—including analytical debates over natural gas regulation, domestic refinery policy, and the size of the Strategic Petroleum Reserve—are reviewed with attention to the attributes and implications of analysis when applied in varying policy contexts.

Part Three weaves together the themes of praise and criticism of policy analysis with the exploration of the use and characteristics of analysis in practice. Under what circumstances—what configurations of attributes of the policy context—do the threats perceived by the critics of analysis hold greatest plausibility? Are instances of such contexts likely to occur with sufficient frequency, and with enough breadth, to threaten democratic political processes? If not, are there particular regions of the policy process in which such threats *do* hold greater validity?

On the whole, I will argue, the threats anticipated by the critics of analysis have not been realized. Analysis has been *transformed* as it has been integrated into the political process and dispersed among its halls and denizens. Except perhaps in rare instances, policy analysis has not been applied as prescribed by the policy analysis paradigm outlined in chapter 2. Rarely does policy analysis acquire significant independent influence in the shaping of public policy, although on occasion, policy analysis *can* alter the beliefs of policy makers. Furthermore, the interactive and often iterative process of analysis serves to limit the potential for unbridled distortion of the expression of values and beliefs on the part of any particular analyst.

Rather than indict policy analysis generally, the criticisms of policy analysis hold greatest force when applied to the use of analysis in specific contexts. When the forum for analytical debate is open, and many contending sides have cause and resources to mobilize analysis, the threats to democratic process are slight; when applied in less visible and less open fora, however, and particularly when the issue under review is subject to domination by particular political interests, advocacy analysis may do most to distort policy and mislead decision makers. It is in such contexts that the criticisms that policy analysts wield undue influence and distort the expression of citizen preferences holds greatest force.

I will argue that the most general institutional effect of policy analysis is its surprising tendency to inhibit political initiatives, thereby reinforcing the policy status quo. Critics who fear that the mobilization of analysis will lead to radical change in policy and political institutions should be reassured.

If anything, the provision of another tool with which to resist political initiatives serves to *reinforce* the decanting and slowing of political power that for liberal democrats is so essential. Participatory democrats, on the other hand, will find little to celebrate; though policy analysis poses little threat to direct decision makers, its tendency to inhibit change on larger issues may reduce the ease with which popular expression can work its way through the policy process to create new public policy.

It is not necessary to conclude, however, that policy analysis is inevitably a mere handmaiden to the exercise of power politics. In a policy context of moderate conflict, on analytically tractable issues, and when employed in a forum dominated by similarly trained policy analysts, policy analysis can be expected to make a substantial contribution to the ways that policy elites perceive policy issues and options. Of course, most policy contexts are neither completely hospitable to the provision of analysis nor wholly conducive to the use of analysis as a political resource.

Based on this assessment, how should policy analysis be practiced to mitigate the apparent threats of analysis while still allowing provision of useful advice and information to decision makers? How can the practitioner adapt to the systematically varying context in which he or she plies the trade? In what ways can analytical resources be most effectively, and least threateningly, applied?

A primary concern of this volume is to develop a conceptual framework that allows the policy analyst to distinguish among the various types of policy contexts and to anticipate the probable efficacy of various styles for the practice of analysis within those contexts. I will argue that arming policy analysts with such a framework provides a possible resolution to this problem. Prudent analysts can constructively tailor the practice of policy analysis to the contingencies of the policy context. Recognizing that within some contexts there exist unresolvable tensions between the practice of analysis and the norms of democratic governance, I will describe a style of policy analysis that will permit the analyst sufficient flexibility to adapt to the varying policy context while limiting and counteracting potential threats and abuses of analysis.

Given the contentious nature of the debate over the harmonies and tensions between policy analysis and democratic politics, I anticipate that much of the argument contained in these pages will spark rejoinder, modification, and I hope, extension and further tests of the hypotheses it contains. Indeed, much of this book is a response to what others have written and argued. Should such rejoinders be made, I will claim success, for my intent is to push the debate in the direction of bridging the empirical work on the role of policy analysis in policy making—and on policy change in general—with the theoretical and normative concerns about the role of public policy analysis in a democracy.

PART ONE

THE FOUNDATIONS OF POLICY ANALYSIS: THREATS AND PROMISES

CHAPTER 2

The Policy Analysis
Paradigm

What is it that is praised and criticized as policy analysis? How can it be characterized in a way that renders examination of the implications of its use for American politics—if not a straightforward exercise—at least a manageable problem? What are the characteristics of the analysis and advice provided that make it distinctive from, for example, the prescriptions for the Good Polity in the writings of the ancient Greek theorists? Perhaps no definitive characterization is available, for the scope and content of policy analysis remain matters of extensive debate among both theorists and practitioners.[1]

---

[1] Illustrative of the divergence of views on the characterization of policy analysis are the reflections of Aaron Wildavsky in *Principles for a Graduate School of Public Policy*, (Berkeley, CA: University of California at Berkeley, 1977), and those of Mark Moore in "Statesmanship in a World of Particular Substantive Choices," in *Bureaucrats, Policy Analysts, Statesmen: Who Leads?*, ed. Robert Goldwin, (Washington, DC: American Enterprise Institute, 1980), pp. 20–36. Wildavsky, in particular, seems to celebrate the myriad of approaches taken to policy analysis in the various schools of public policy, and purposefully leaves the content of his own approach open-ended.

Yet if analysts are not in full agreement on the uses to which they are to put their tools, an examination of the core methods and techniques of policy analysis indicates that there exists, if not unanimity on its characterization, at least a set of characteristics that, owing to their force, clarity, and deep grounding in the theories underlying policy analysis, may be called a "dominant paradigm" in the field.[2]

For purposes of this chapter, the primary techniques of policy analysis are accepted at face value, as are the definitions of value, public interest, and decision criteria from which those techniques are derived. The intent is not to erect a "straw man," but rather to address the *normative and logical implications* of policy analysis as derived from the primary analytical techniques. Many, perhaps most, policy analysts embrace these implications, but more important for our purposes is that the key "threats" and "promises" of policy analysis for democratic government are typically cast in terms of the implications of policy analytical techniques. To understand the dialogue between proponents and critics of policy analysis, it is critical that the underlying normative bases of analysis be teased out of the technical core of analysis. Even more, assessment of the threats and promises of policy analysis, and its place in American policy making, requires that these normative bases and their implications be made explicit.

In the sections that follow, the core of the policy analytic approach—the conception of choice grounded in utility theory and employing the criterion of economic efficiency—is described in some detail. In addition, the origins and techniques for application of the efficiency criterion are given sufficient attention to illustrate the normative basis and implications of efficiency as the primary grounding principle in policy analysis.[3] The more technical elements of the descriptions of efficiency and its development are reserved for the exhibits in this chapter.

_____ 2.1 _____

CHARACTERIZING POLICY ANALYSIS

I have argued that efficiency analysis and the efficiency criterion of choice make up the core of policy analysis. For that reason, much of what policy

---

[2] I am, of course, not the first to speak of a dominant paradigm in policy analysis: see Aaron Wildavsky, *Speaking Truth to Power,* (Boston: Little, Brown, 1979). Also see his "The Political Economy of Efficiency: Cost–Benefit Analysis, Systems Analysis, and Program Budgeting," *Public Administration Review*, 26(2) (December 1966), pp. 292–310.

[3] Though the primacy of the efficiency principle in policy analysis, and its basis in theory, may seem obvious to some readers, recent attempts to come to grips with the apparent tensions between democratic politics and the principles of efficiency have neglected the theoretical idea of efficiency altogether. See for example, Douglas Yates' *Bureaucratic Democracy* (Cambridge, MA: Harvard University Press, 1982), and M. E. Hawkesworth's *Theoretical Issues in Policy Analysis* (Albany, NY: SUNY Press, 1988).

analysts learn and do, and much of the substantive knowledge employed, is deliberately excluded from the characterization of policy analysis made here. This exclusion may appear to doom this characterization of policy analysis to inaccuracy because policy analysis appears to be eclectic: it makes use of techniques developed in the fields of economics, mathematics, statistics, operations research, and systems dynamics, among others, to provide decision makers with advice in the formulation of public policy. In applying those techniques, the analyst may draw on knowledge from fields such as sociology, political science, welfare economics, law, organization theory, the physical and biological sciences, and elsewhere. Policy analysis must take the analyst wherever the policy issue leads, making analysis the multidisciplinary activity par excellence.[4]

Despite the apparent cacophony of activities involved in policy analysis, the logic of analysis imposes an order on these activities and bends them to a uniform purpose: to determine which policy (if any) provides the largest net gains in social welfare. Examining how social welfare is defined and how it is estimated will take up much of this chapter. At heart the procedure is derived from the model of rational individual decision making, wherein the individual, with a given set of preferences, limited resources, and using the knowledge at his or her disposal, takes the action likely to maximize his or her individual utility.[5] Thus, in the style of the rational decision maker, the policy analyst is to use a range of analytical techniques and multiple fields of knowledge to engage in a number of distinct procedures or steps, including: (1) identifying the "problem" to be resolved, (2) specifying the goal(s) to be sought through public policy, (3) identifying or inventing the available policy alternatives, (4) estimating the effects of each of the alternatives, both favorable and unfavorable, (5) imputing values in a single, commensurable metric to those effects, and (6) choosing the "best" policy alternative according to an explicit decision rule.[6] The

---

[4] See Martin Landau, "The Proper Domain of Policy Analysis," *American Journal of Political Science*, vol. 21 (May 1977), p. 419; and Duncan MacRae, Jr. and Dale Whittington, "Policy Analysis as an Applied Social Science Discipline," *Administration and Society*, 6(4) (February 1975), pp. 363–388.

[5] For a development of the assumption of rationality in individual choice, see William H. Riker, and Peter C. Ordeshook, *An Introduction to Positive Political Theory* (Englewood Cliffs, NJ: Prentice Hall, 1973), Chapter 2, and Herbert Simon, *The Science of the Artificial* (Cambridge, MA: MIT Press, 1969). For an introduction to the application of the rational choice approach to public decision, see Edith Stokey and Richard Zeckhauser, *A Primer for Policy Analysis*, (New York: W. W. Norton and Co., 1978), Chapter 3.

[6] Many such lists of steps are enumerated in the policy analysis literature, each quite similar to the list presented here. See, for example, Stokey and Zeckhauser, *A Primer of Policy Analysis*, pp. 5–6; David Nachmias, *Public Policy Evaluation: Approaches and Methods* (New York: St. Martins Press, 1979) pp. 12–18; Alice Rivlin, *Systematic Thinking for Social Action* (Washington, DC: Brookings Institute, 1971), pp. 3–5. The Graduate School of Public Policy at the University of California at Berkeley propounds a version of the above list called the "eightfold path," which seeks to give somewhat greater emphasis to the role of analysis in *creating* policy alternatives. For a critique of this restrictive "problem solving" approach, see Martin Rein and Sheldon White, "Policy Research: Belief and Doubt," in *Policy Analysis*, 3(2) (Spring 1977), pp. 239–271.

techniques and fields employed are thus intended to be steps in a rational procedure for making public choice. If, as is typically the case, the government policy is to result in some change in human condition or behavior, the analyst requires knowledge about that condition or behavior. In addition, the analyst may require behavioral models that indicate the change likely to result from government action. Furthermore, where problems are more complex, the analyst may employ more sophisticated quantitative models to determine the relationship between various possible government actions and the desired policy outcomes. All of these activities, however, are steps in the direction of discovering—among the options available—the policy that best serves "society's" interests. It therefore follows that the criterion that determines the best or optimal choice serves as both the logical and normative core of policy analysis: logical because it indicates what knowledge is required and what techniques are applicable, and normative because it prescribes the best policy.

In the analysis of the optimal allocation of things valued in society (which is the quintessential problem of policy analysis), the problem is generally conceived by policy analysts as being concerned with two components: one concerns the attainment of an equitable *distribution* of valued things in society, and the other concerns the attainment of an *efficient* satisfaction of individual wants given the distribution of valued things.[7] Each of these components provides criteria that may serve as the normative core of policy analysis. Yet, from the standpoint of the policy analytic framework, equity criteria suffer from the lack of a solid analytical basis and from a lack of consensus on the appropriate formulation of such criteria, while the efficiency criterion is well grounded in the analytical framework and provides a normative standard that is both well understood and widely accepted.

Limitations on the use of equity criteria.   Normative criteria based on the distribution of values in society are necessarily derived from a conception of distributive justice.[8] Such criteria must address how scarce valuables are to be allocated among groups or individuals. Policy analysts, borrowing from mainstream welfare economics and working from a strictly individualistic utilitarian framework, have typically declined to propose an explicit normative standard for the distribution of value. In an evolution to be described later in this chapter, analysts have become heirs to a tradition that has concluded

---

[7] A still broader conception of "public sector management" adds economic stabilization as a further relevant concern. See Richard Musgrave, *The Theory of Public Finance* (New York: McGraw-Hill, 1959), Chapter 1.

[8] There are numerous theories of distributive justice that could provide a normative criterion for policy analysis. One of the most widely known of such theories can be found in John Rawls' *A Theory of Justice* (Cambridge, MA: Harvard University Press, 1971), which stands as a justification of the redistributive social programs of the 1960s and early 1970s. An opposing criterion,

that, given the limits of what can be "objectively" and unambiguously identified as "improvements" in social welfare, analysts can say little regarding the superiority of one efficient distribution of values over another. The techniques and methods employed in policy analysis thus give analysts no independent *analytical* base from which to propound the supremacy of any distribution of values.

Given the lack of a criteria of distributive justice readily derived from the dominant analytical framework, should analysts seek to employ a distributive criterion they must rely for their normative standard on some source outside that framework. As a practical matter, many competing distributional criteria are available for use in public policy formulation, and an impartial analyst is left in a position of attempting to display the expected results of the policies that would be optimal under some range of contending standards.[9] Furthermore, though the analyst may be unable to assess the competing standards on grounds of distributive justice from within the analytic framework, he or she is able to assess the effects of each of the equity standards in terms of the efficiency of the distribution of values that results. The analyst is able to specify, for example, the effects that a given scheme of redistribution of wealth may have on the work incentives of the participants.[10] But perhaps most illustrative of the favored place of efficiency relative to equity criteria is the argument that analysts should treat redistribution of wealth as a "good," like other goods, that can be valued.[11] If the value of an increment of redistribution can be determined by, for example, determining people's "willingness-to-pay" for it, redistribution can be included like any other good provided by government within the framework of an efficiency analysis. In this way, assuming that the hurdles in the way of discovering how much people value

---

providing for a much more restricted role for government, can be found in Robert Nozick's *Anarchy, State and Utopia* (New York: Basic Books, 1974.)

[9] The complexity and ambiguity resulting from inclusion of such standards may also restrict the breadth of applicability of policy analysis. Thus Duncan MacRae, Jr., and Dale Whittington argue in a very perceptive article that "The price of formal rationality [traditional benefit–cost analysis] is that some wrong decisions will be made. The price of substantive rationality [in which appropriate social equity considerations are made] may be that no expert advice at all will be available for some of these decisions." See their "Assessing Preferences in Cost–Benefit Analysis: Reflections on Rural Water Supply Evaluations in Haiti," *Journal of Policy Analysis and Management*, vol. 7, no. 2 (Winter 1988), pp. 246–263; p. 260.

[10] Perhaps the most thorough, though still inconclusive, study of this nature is contained in Joseph A. Pechman and P. Michael Timpane, eds., *Work Incentives and Income Guarantees: The New Jersey Negative Income Tax Experiment* (Washington, DC: Brookings Institute, 1975).

[11] According to A. Myrick Freeman, III, "Under plausible assumptions about individuals' utility functions, namely interdependence, it can be shown that individuals could increase their utility by contributing to government enforced tax and transfer systems." "Project Evaluation and Design with Multiple Objectives," *Public Expenditure and Policy Analysis*, eds. Robert H. Haveman and Julius Margolis, 2nd ed. (Chicago: Rand McNally, 1977), p. 242.

redistribution could be overcome, equity criteria would be subsumed under the criteria of efficiency.[12]

In response to attempts to integrate equity concerns into the framework of efficiency, a number of practitioners and theorists have countered that such attempts will necessarily result in disagreement and may discredit the use of policy analysis altogether. One widely used text in policy analysis contends that, if policy analysts attempt to mingle equity and efficiency analyses through employment of such techniques as distributional weights or other equity criteria, then the result of analyses will necessarily be arbitrary. The weights chosen

> [W]ill vary with the political climate and are likely to cause squabbles among economists themselves, and between economists and the public. To the extent that economists did not reject the principle of employing such weights but participated in the struggle to establish one set of weights rather than another, cost–benefit analysis as a technique could become discredited.[13]

Others have held that attempts to collapse equity concerns together with efficiency concerns, in order to make them commensurable, merely cloud the issue and bury personal judgment and bias under an impenetrable thicket of numbers.[14] The implication is that policy analysts should do what they know how to do, efficiency analysis, and leave the equity concerns of policy to others.

To recapitulate, equity criteria concerning the distribution of values are external to the dominant framework of policy analysis; given the lack of consensus on appropriate equity criteria, analysts are limited to assessing and displaying the results of equity criteria supplied by others, or to reviewing the efficiency implications of various equity criteria—or at most, barring technical difficulties, the analyst may reduce the equity criteria to a component of efficiency analysis. To many analysts the difficulties of including equity considerations suggest that such considerations be left to others.

Efficiency analysis suffers far less from such limitations. As shall be described below, efficiency analysis falls squarely within the tradition of

---

[12] When offering this technique for analysis of distributional programs, it is usual for the proponent of the method to rely on the valuation of elected officials, rather than on the public at large, to determine the value of redistribution as a good. See Freeman, ibid. Also see Harold M. Hochman and James D. Rogers, "Pareto Optimal Redistribution," in *American Economic Review*, 59(no. 4) (September 1969), pp. 542–557; and Otto Eckstein, "A Survey of Public Expenditure Criteria," in the Universities-National Bureau for Economic Research's *Public Finances: Needs, Sources, and Utilization*, (Princeton, NJ: Princeton University Press, 1961), pp. 439–504.

[13] E. J. Mishan, *Cost–Benefit Analysis*, 3rd ed. (Boston: George, Allen and Unwin, 1982).

[14] See, for example, Otto Eckstein, "A Survey of Public Expenditure Criteria," p. 449, and Peter O. Steiner, "The Public Sector and the Public Interest," in Haveman and Margolis, *Public Expenditure and Policy Analysis*, pp. 62–64.

policy analysis as it has developed from the utilitarian theorists of the eighteenth century. Though disputes remain, the basic criteria of efficiency are widely agreed upon among economists and policy analysts, eliminating the necessity to choose among competing normative standards. Because the concept of efficiency is well defined, and because a broad consensus exists on the proper formulation of an efficiency criterion, no "outside" specification of the criterion from clients is required. Moreover, it is the concept of efficiency that ties together the disparate elements of analysis; it imposes a logic on the collection of data, valuation of outcomes, and comparison of and selection among alternatives. Finally, the conception of efficiency provides a coherent normative standard that can be applied, in the abstract at least, across the full range of activities in which government engages. It is with little exaggeration, therefore, that the concept of efficiency can be said to provide the logical and normative core of policy analysis.

—————— 2.2 ——————
DEVELOPMENT OF UTILITY THEORY

The concept efficiency did not spring forth, fully formed, from the brow of Zeus. Rather, the concept has evolved over the past two centuries, beginning as a key element of a reformist (and quite radical) political movement and undergoing transformation toward an ever more technical and "content-free" analytical concept. Yet the current form owes much to its early makeup, and the place accorded efficiency analysis in policy making is much in line with the early vision.

Central to the concept of efficiency is the theory of utility developed by economists from foundations first laid by Jeremy Bentham late in the eighteenth century. Bentham declared the "season of fiction" to be at an end and called for enlightened formulation of public policy based on the principles of utility.[15] According to Bentham, an experience provides utility when it produces "benefit, advantage, pleasure, good, or happiness," or when it prevents "mischief, pain, evil, or unhappiness."[16] All individual behavior could be understood as the pursuit of utility, based on a hedonistic calculus designed to maximize pleasure and minimize pain. The value of an act or experience was to be defined in terms of the pleasures and pains it brought to individuals; individuals were thus the ultimate arbiters of value.

---

[15] In Jeremy Bentham, *Fragment on Government,* in *The Collected Works of Jeremy Bentham,* eds. J. H. Burns and F. Rosen (New York: Oxford University Press, 1983), pp. 393–501; p. 441.

[16] In Jeremy Bentham, *Introduction to the Principles of Morals and Legislation,* eds. J. H. Burns and H. L. A. Hart (London: Athlone Press, 1970), p. 12. Utility generally is discussed on pp. 11–16.

For Bentham the concept of utility was rich in substantive content. The chief dimensions of utility were (1) intensity, (2) duration, (3) certainty or uncertainty, and (4) propinquity or remoteness. Also important were fecundity (meaning the likelihood that the pleasure or happiness would be followed by more of the same) and purity (meaning the likelihood that the pleasure would *not* be followed by pain).[17] Bentham lists no less than twenty-six categories of pleasures and pains making up the "simple" roots of utility to which all specific pains and pleasures can be reduced, including (but not limited to) sense, wealth, skill, amity, good name, power, piety, benevolence, and association.[18]

Having named the categories and dimensions of utility, Bentham then specified the factors influencing the quantity of utility that an individual would derive from a particular experience. While the sources of pain and pleasure may be common to all men, the amounts of utility received by individuals from a given source will not be uniform. Bentham argued that an individual would gain utility based upon his or her "quantum" of sensibility, a factor that varies from person to person. The quantum of sensibility, in turn, is affected by a host of factors—primarily education—that serve to "bias" the sensibilities of both body and mind.[19]

Much like economists who followed him, Bentham employed money as a common metric in the measurement of pleasures. He argued as follows: imagine two pleasures, between which one is indifferent, one of which may be purchased with money and the other not. Because one is indifferent between them, the pleasures must be equal.

> But the pleasure produced by the possession of money, is as the quantity of money that produces it: money is therefore the measure of this pleasure. But the other pleasure is equal to this; the other pleasure therefore is the money that produces this: therefore money is also the measure of that other pleasure.[20]

Furthermore, while money can be used to value pleasures, the value of money itself *decreases* as the amount of money held increases—a phenomenon later dubbed the decreasing marginal utility of money. As Bentham argued, ". . . the quantity of happiness produced by a particle of wealth (each

---

[17] Ibid., pp. 38–41.

[18] Ibid., Chapter 5. Especially intriguing is Bentham's catalog of the types of pleasures to be gained from viewing a country scene in the footnote in ibid. on pp. 49–50.

[19] Ibid., pp. 51–69.

[20] Elie Halevy, *La Formation du radicalisme philosophique* (Paris: Germer Bailliere, 1901), p. 410, as cited in George Stigler, "The Development of Utility Theory," in his *Essays in the History of Economics* (Chicago: University of Chicago Press, 1965), pp. 66–155.

particle being of the same magnitude) will be less and less at every particle. . . ."[21]

For Bentham, the development and use of utility theory in the formulation of public policy rested on an unresolved ambiguity. On one hand, Bentham held that it would be impossible to determine with any exactitude the quantity of utility that an individual obtained from an experience or to compare the gains or losses of utility of any two individuals. On the other hand, unless one *could* compare the utilities of individuals the utility calculus would provide little aid to the formulation of public policy. The solution, for Bentham, was simply to *assume* utilities to be comparable. The assumption was justified as providing a useful tool for legislators that would be, at worst, far better than any basis for legislation that failed to take utility into account. In the words of Bentham's disciple, Etienne Dumont,

> Differences of character are inscrutable; while the diversity of circumstances is such that they are never the same for two individuals. Unless, therefore, we begin by eliminating these two considerations, it will be impossible to arrive at any general conclusions. But, although any one of our propositions may be found false or inexact when applied in a given case, this should not lead us to doubt their theoretical accuracy or their practical utility. It is sufficient to justify our propositions if (a) they approach more nearly to the truth than any others that can be substituted for them, and (b) they can be employed more conveniently than any others as the basis for legislation.[22]

Based on his elaborate utility calculus, Bentham called for the state to employ legislation to pursue "the greatest good for the greatest number."[23] By this Bentham meant the establishment of public policy that would increase the sum of the utilities of the individuals that make up society. An illustrative example employing his calculus concerns the distribution of wealth in society. Based on his conception of the diminishing marginal utility of money, Bentham determined that the greatest aggregate utility from the wealth of society would be obtained by evening out the distribution of wealth; gains in utility from giving money to the poor would more than offset losses in utility from taking money from the rich. On further reflection, however, Bentham determined that the loss of utility sustained from weakening the security of property, resulting from taxing the rich, would offset any gains made through the

---

[21] In Jeremy Bentham, *Works of Jeremy Bentham* (Edinburgh: Tait, 1843), vol. 3, p. 229, as cited by Stigler, "The Development of Utility Theory," p. 73.

[22] Etienne Dumont, *Bentham's Theory of Legislation,* trans. by Charles Atkinson, (London: Oxford University Press, 1914), p. 134.

[23] In Burns and Rosen, eds., *The Collected Works of Jeremy Bentham,* passim.

redistribution of wealth. Therefore the utility calculus could not support legislation to equalize wealth in society.[24]

A central weakness in Bentham's calculus was its inability to compare the utilities of different individuals in prescribing legislation for the greatest good. Could we be sure that the loss of utility due to weakening the security of property would outweigh the gains to be had from a more equal distribution of wealth if we were unable to compare the respective gains and losses sustained by different individuals? Alternatively, could we even be sure that a more equal distribution of wealth would result in larger aggregate utility? Might not the rich have had sufficient opportunity to partake of education and other factors affecting their "sensibilities" to pain and pleasure such that their loss would be felt far more acutely than the gains of the poor, notwithstanding the diminishing marginal utility of money? The utility theorists following Bentham struggled with the problem presented by the incomparability of individual utilities and generally rejected Bentham's contention that utilities could be assumed comparable.

Building from foundations laid by Bentham, utility theorists have broadened and generalized the theory of utility, effectively purging it of the substantive form and content specified by Bentham. Late in the nineteenth century, political economists Stanley Jevons, Leon Walras, and Carl Menger, among others, altered Bentham's formulations to focus on the satisfaction to be obtained from the possession of individual goods.[25] Among these early theorists the concept of diminishing marginal utility—holding that the increment of utility gained from possession of an added unit of a good declines as the number of units possessed increases—was deemed a general law of utility.[26]

---

[24] In Dumont, *Bentham's Theory of Legislation,* pp. 157–162. One observer ties the early rise of policy analysis to the activities of Benthamite reformers in nineteenth century Britain, when Bentham's techniques were applied to health care issues. See Rudolf Klein's "The Rise and Decline of Policy Analysis: The Strange Case of Health Policymaking in Britain," *Policy Analysis,* 2(3) (Summer 1976), pp. 459–475.

[25] The primary works are, Stanley Jevons, *Theory of Political Economy,* 4th ed. (London: Macmillan, 1911), Leon Walras, *Elements d'économie politique pure* (Paris: Pichon and Durand-Auzais, 1926), and Carl Menger, *Grundsatze der Volkswirtschaftslehre* (Vienna: Braumuller, 1871). For a lucid summary of the contributions of these "early marginalists" see Stigler, *The Development of Utility Theory.* Also see Jacob Oser and William C. Blanchfield, *The Evolution of Economic Thought,* 3rd ed. (New York: Harcourt, Brace, Jovanovich, 1975), pp. 220–241.

[26] For these theorists the measure of utility gained from the last unit of the good obtained, the so-called "marginal unit," must be equal to the money value of the price paid for it. Prices, in turn, were seen simply as the rate of exchange by which the good under consideration could be traded for other goods. Utility maximizing individuals would spend their available resources such that the gain in utility from expenditure of the last dollar would be the same for all types of goods; that is, utility is maximized when:

$$MU_1 = MU_2/P_2 = MU_3/P_3 = \ldots = MU_n/P_n$$

where MU_2 is the utility gained from possession of the last unit of good 2, and P_2 is the price or exchange rate of good 2 for good 1. It was assumed that, should the price of one good fall relative

Furthermore, most early marginal utility theorists held total utility of the individual to be derived from simple summation of the utilities gained from the goods possessed by the individual.

This formulation, however, ignored complementary and substituting goods that, when consumed, change the utility to be gained by consumption of other goods. This problem led theorists to specify a more general formulation of the individual's "utility function," that would allow for utilities to be affected by such relationships among goods.[27] The general utility function eliminated the need to assume diminishing marginal utility for consumption of individual goods in order to assure equilibrium in economic trades; indeed, diminishing marginal utility was shown to be neither a necessary nor sufficient condition for achievement of equilibrium conditions.[28] Still later developments of utility theory, based on the concept of indifference schedules (see exhibit 2-2), took a further leap toward generality; the conception of individual utility itself that had underlaid the development of utility theory was abandoned as too "metaphysical" and restrictive. As Vilfredo Pareto wrote early in this century,

> The entire theory [now] rests on a fact of experience, that is to say, on the determination of the quantities of goods which constitute combinations that are equivalent for the individual. The theory of economic science thus acquires the rigor of rational mechanics; it deduces its results from experience, without the intervention of any metaphysical entity.[29]

The development of utility theory has thus been marked by a progressive development away from the substantively grounded, limited theory of utility proposed by Jeremy Bentham; successively, interpersonal comparisons of utility, additive individual utility functions, the requirement of diminishing marginal utility, and even the "metaphysical" conception of utility itself have been shed in favor of increasingly general propositions. Yet, despite the increasing generality of the theory, the prescriptive "legislative" role of utility theory envisioned by Bentham has been preserved.[30] That prescriptive role is embodied in the concept of economic efficiency.

---

to all others, more of that good would be purchased—becoming the familiar law of demand in economics.

[27] Francis Edgeworth developed the more general utility function in *Mathematical Psychics,* (London: Kegan Paul, 1881).

[28] Stigler, *The Development of Utility Theory,* pp. 98–100.

[29] Vilfredo Pareto, *Manuale di economia politica* (Milan: Piccola Biblioteca Scientifica, 1919), pp. 160, 169, as cited in Stigler, *The Development of Utility Theory,* p. 126.

[30] Bentham would surely be quite comfortable with the modern concept of "hedonic damages," applied by economists in death-related lawsuits. The idea is to measure the "value of life" that stems from the joys of living; what is the dollar loss attributable to the ending of a person's life? One guru of hedonic damages, Stanley V. Smith, argues that the value of a life may be as high as $12 million, but puts the "reasonable" range at between $500,000 and $3.5 million. See Paul M. Barrett, "Price of Pleasure: New Legal Theorists Attach a Dollar Value to the Joys of Living," *Wall Street Journal,* vol. CXIX, no. 114 (December 12, 1988) p. A-1.

———— 2.3 ————
THE CONCEPT OF EFFICIENCY

Efficiency analysis is applicable whenever one regards a system in which individuals seek cooperatively to satisfy their wants. Thus it is equally applicable (in principle) to political and economic systems. It is assumed at the outset that the system is made up of individuals, and that each of these individuals has an ordinally ranked set of wants or "preferences." "Society" is thus strictly an aggregation of individuals, and social welfare is no more or less than the aggregation of the welfare of the individuals that make up the society. As stated by a leading economist,

> [I]n Western economics, economic welfare is almost always related to individual welfare; it is postulated that there can be no welfare other than what accrues to individuals. This is a rejection of the organic theory of the state: the state as an entity enjoys no welfare, only the people that compose it.[31]

The normative heart of the concept of efficiency derives straight from Bentham: a social system or policy ought to be designed to maximize the satisfaction of individual wants, subject to certain limitations on the analyst's ability to specify what constitutes an "improvement" in overall want satisfaction. Thus efficiency analysis, like Bentham's calculus of pleasure and pain, is based solidly on an individualistic and utilitarian view of human activity.

The problem addressed by efficiency analysis concerns the opposition of individual wants and the limited means available to satisfy those wants. An economic or political system can be regarded as a mechanism for adjusting the myriad of competing individual wants to available means. The question asked by efficiency analysis is, how well does a particular system (method for making choices) or policy (a given choice or set of choices) for the allocation of society's resources satisfy individual wants? The answer is necessarily limited because of the premise that each individual holds a possibly unique schedule of preferences; without omniscience it is impossible to determine whether satisfaction of one individual's wants adds more to total well-being (or social welfare) than would satisfaction of some other individual's wants. Rather than confront the problem of the incomparability of individual utilities directly, the criterion of efficiency provides a way around this problem.

In a society of limited resources, and in which individuals compete for those resources in order to satisfy wants, improvement of a single individual's well-being can occur either (1) without reduction (and perhaps with improvement) in the well-being of others, or (2) with a concomitant decrease in the well-being of others. In the latter case, due to the assumed incomparability of individual utilities, it is impossible to determine whether society as a whole is

---

[31] Eckstein, "A Survey of Public Expenditure Criteria," p. 441.

made better by the change. In the former case, when one person's gain is not offset by the losses of others, the sum of the individuals' welfare can unambiguously be said to have increased. This represents a clear-cut increase in the efficiency with which wants are satisfied.

Pareto optimality.   The strict criterion of efficiency, often called Pareto optimality, is met when a system allocates resources in such a way that no further reallocation of goods can increase any individual's utility without diminishing the utility of others. Put otherwise, all individuals are made as well-off as possible to the point that any increase in the well-being of one must decrease the well-being of someone else. If at any time any individual can be made better-off without reducing the well-being of others, the system is not operating strictly efficiently.[32] A given policy is efficient in this strict sense if it increases the well-being of at least one individual without diminishing that of others. It is important to note that there exists no uniquely efficient allocation of resources; beginning from any less than optimal distribution of wealth, movement toward efficiency can be achieved by distributing the added increment of well-being in countless ways among the members of society. Thus, many Pareto optimal solutions exist, differing according to the distributions of goods achieved.

A more thorough and somewhat more technical description of Pareto efficient solutions is provided in exhibit 2-1.

The Kaldor-Hicks criterion.   Unbending application of the strict Pareto optimality criterion would impose rather severe restrictions on government action: no action, no matter how beneficial it might be to the community as a whole, could be taken that diminished the well-being of even one individual. In the extreme, even an action required to maintain the viability of the community (say, maintenance of law and order) would violate the criterion if any person, on the basis of his or her own assessment of the effect of the action on his or her utility, determined that the action would leave them worse off than would no action at all. But clearly much of government action does just that: policies of income redistribution, progressive taxation, use of eminent domain for the construction of highways and dams, and price-support programs for

---

[32] The development of the concept of efficiency in this chapter refers primarily to efficiency in exchange among consumers. It is important to also recognize the application of efficiency in production: briefly, in economic terms, efficiency in production means production on the "production possibilities frontier"—meaning the maximum output given the available material inputs and technology—at the point at which the marginal rate of transformation of one good into another is equal to the ratio of the prices of those goods. See Michael Intriligator, *Mathematical Optimization and Economic Theory*, 2nd ed. (Englewood Cliffs, NJ: Prentice-Hall, 1971), pp. 178–189. Also see Robert Y. Awh, *Microeconomics: Theory and Applications* (New York: John Wiley & Sons, 1976), pp. 161–210.

agricultural products, to name just a few, improve the lot of some at the expense of others. The applicable criterion, then, would be one that would allow assessments of the efficiency of policies that do increase the welfare of some at the expense of others.

The use of such a criterion would seem to run up against the problem of the comparison of individual utilities—the problem avoided through the use of the strict criterion of efficiency—because one must weigh the gains of some in society against the losses of others. The solution takes the form of a weak criterion of efficiency, sometimes called "Kaldor-Hicks criterion."[33]

The Kaldor-Hicks criterion allows redistributions that increase *net* welfare such that those who gain from the distribution could compensate those who lose, restoring the losers to their prior level of well-being, while the winners retain enough of their gains to be better-off than they would have been without the redistribution. In this case individuals' utilities need not be compared; as long as a common value of the good redistributed is available, such as the money value of the gains and losses to the individuals involved,[34] it is possible to determine just how much of the improvement to the gainers must be given in compensation to the losers to assure that no one is worse off than they would have been without the redistribution. Thus, the criterion specifies that a system that results in an allocation of goods from which subsequent redistribution could result in *net* increases in social well-being is not efficient. Furthermore, in the comparison of policies, the relevant criterion is: which policy option serves to create the largest net gain in social well-being?

Although the Kaldor-Hicks criterion requires that a policy result in net gains in social well-being, it does not require that the gains actually be redistributed in a manner that offsets the losses of those harmed by redistribution. The principle requires only that such a compensation *could* have been made, and that net social gains be left over. It is enough to show that, in the aggregate, sufficient value has been created to more than offset the losses entailed. No guidance is offered by the criterion as to whether or how compensation should be made; such decisions are beyond the scope of efficiency analysis and must be made on the basis of other criteria.

The Kaldor-Hicks criterion is the central normative standard in the policy analysis paradigm. The criterion is applied most widely as the decision rule for benefit–cost analysis. Benefit–cost analysis is essentially concerned with

---

[33] This discussion draws heavily from the classic paper by J. R. Hicks, "The Foundations of Welfare Economics," *The Economic Journal*, 49(196) (December 1939), pp. 696–712.

[34] Specification of gains and losses to different individuals in money terms does not directly imply a comparison of individual utilities because one need not assume that the value of an added (or subtracted) dollar is the same for all individuals. Because money *does* measure the relative market value of whatever is gained or lost in terms of all other goods that have prices, once the money value of a loss is specified it is known how much money compensation is required to increase the losers' ability to obtain enough other goods to compensate for the original loss.

whether a policy generates more social benefits than social costs, and if so, what level of program expenditure provides optimal results. The steps in benefit–cost analysis include:

1. identification of the project or projects to be evaluated;
2. determination of all impacts, favorable and unfavorable, present and future, on all of society;
3. valuation of those impacts, either directly through market values or indirectly through shadow price estimates;
4. calculation of the net benefit—total value of positive impacts less total value of negative impacts; and
5. application of the decision rule: selection of the project that produces the largest net social benefits.[35]

The decision rule employed is a straightforward application of the Kaldor-Hicks criterion; if gains in social well-being are in excess of losses incurred, those who gain from the program could compensate those who lose and still retain net benefits, and the program should be undertaken. Still another widely used technique, cost-effectiveness analysis, is a truncated form of efficiency analysis. This technique asks only which policy achieves a given objective at least cost, or which one achieves most of a desired objective at a fixed cost. These techniques, and the methods of estimation and projection that make them possible, constitute the primary tools of the trade for the public policy analyst. At its core, then, policy analysis as generally practiced is applied efficiency analysis.

_____ 2.4 _____

EFFICIENCY AND MARKET PRICES

The use of competitive market prices has come to be one of the cornerstones of efficiency analysis in public policy. The reasons for the affinity of market analysis and public policy are several: ideological persuasion surely plays a part along with technical and theoretical reasons.[36] The chief theoretical link

---

[35] See, e.g., Stokey and Zeckhauser, *A Primer for Policy Analysis,* pp. 136–138. Also see Mishan, *Cost–Benefit Analysis,* passim.

[36] An eloquent case for greater reliance on "voluntary" means of production and exchange on libertarian grounds can be found in Freidrich A. Hayek, *The Road to Serfdom* (Chicago: University of Chicago Press, 1972) and *Individualism and Economic Order* (Chicago: University of Chicago Press, 1948). Another libertarian defense of greater reliance on markets and less on collective action can be found in Nozick, *Anarchy, State and Utopia.* An alternative and less dogmatic justification for markets is made by Arthur Okun, *Equality and Efficiency: The Big Tradeoff,* (Washington, DC: Brookings Institute, 1975). Here the productive force of the market, which has "proved to be an efficient organizer of production in practice as well as in theory," is raised in defense of markets (p. 50).

of competitive markets to efficiency analysis, however, lies in the Pareto efficient properties of free market outcomes.

One of the earliest and most important applications of utility theory was termed the "theorem of maximum satisfaction," holding that competitive market allocations of value will be Pareto efficient.[37] In brief, the theorem states that utility maximizing consumers will adjust consumption patterns such that the ratio of the gains in utility for possession of the last unit (marginal utility) of any two goods is equal to the ratio of the prices of those goods.[38] Because consumers face common prices, the ratio of the marginal utilities for any two goods will be the same for all persons.[39] This is precisely the condition in which consuming individuals will, through voluntary market exchange, have achieved a Pareto optimal allocation of available goods.[40] Thus Leon Walras could proclaim:

> Production in a market governed by free competition is an operation by which the [productive] services may be combined in products of appropriate kind and quantity to give the greatest possible satisfaction of needs within the limits of the double condition that each service and each product have only one price in the market, at which supply and demand are equal, and that the prices of the products are equal to their costs of production.[41]

Pareto's conditions for the theorem of maximum satisfaction have, of course, been extended; it is now recognized that all significant costs and benefits of a good must be captured by its price (e.g., the price must cover the

---

[37] See Walras, *Elements d'économie,* p. 231, as described in Stigler, *The Development of Utility Theory,* pp. 94–97. The discussion of efficiency is paraphrased from that provided by James M. Henderson and Richard E. Quandt in *Microeconomic Theory* (New York: McGraw-Hill, 1958), pp. 87–88.

[38] Assuming that consumers face common prices for n available goods, and each acts to maximize utility by purchase of those goods within a limited budget, each consumer will contrive to purchase each of the n goods until the ratio of the gains in utility for possession of the last unit ("marginal utility") of any two goods is equal to the ratio of the *prices* of those two goods. That is to say: $(\delta U_m/\delta x_i)/(\delta U_m/\delta x_j) = p_i/p_j$, where U_m is total utility of person m, x_i is the quantity of good i consumed, and p_j is the price of good j.

[39] This can be expressed as: $(\delta U_m/\delta x_i)/(\delta U_m/\delta x_j) = (\delta U_n/\delta x_i)/(\delta U_n/\delta x_j)$, where m and n are any two consumers, and i and j are any two goods.

[40] Note that this condition is equivalent to the consumers' condition that the indifference curves (which are often called "marginal rates of substitution") are tangent in the Edgeworth diagrams discussed in exhibit 2-1; for a given distribution of the two "goods," the ratios of the marginal utilities of guns and butter for Ron and Jim (shown by the *slopes* of their indifference curves) were the same only when the curves were tangent. When the curves were tangent, Ron and Jim were on the Pareto "contract curve"; no subsequent improvement could be made in the well-being of either party without reducing that of the other. A symmetrical proof exists for the Pareto optimality of free markets for the production of goods and services by competitive firms. See Henderson and Quandt, ibid.

[41] Walras, *Elements d'économie,* p. 231, as cited in Stigler, *The Development of Utility Theory,* p. 97.

costs incurred by pollution generated in producing or consuming the good), information about all significant aspects of the good must be freely available, and it must be costless for participants to make trades in the market.[42]

The Pareto optimal quality of competitive price gives it a special role in the valuation of goods produced and resources utilized in public programs. Market price indicates the efficient valuation of a good, in money terms, relative to other goods in the economy. The valuation of all such goods in terms of money is, of course, necessary in order to be able to compare the costs and benefits of public policy in a common metric. However, a difficulty arises for those frequent cases in which no market price exists for the various benefits and costs of the policy: how are policy analysts to compare the value of goods that are not priced—or that are not believed to have competitive prices in the market? For example, how would the analyst compare the value of reduced risk of deaths in auto accidents with that of the increased costs of travel time resulting from the imposition of the 55 mile per hour speed limit, neither of which "goods" are directly priced in the market? Alternatively, how would an analyst quantify the benefits—or more likely the costs—of allocation schemes for petroleum products during periods in which oil supplies are disrupted, as they were in the 1973 and 1979–1980 "oil crises"?

The answer is through the use of "shadow prices." When no market price is available for the goods and resources under consideration, or when available prices are not deemed to meet the requirements of the perfectly competitive market, shadow price estimates of competitive market prices are to be used. As stated by one economist:

> The basic question asked by the analyst when he searches for shadow price is: what would the users of the public output be willing to pay? The analyst tries to simulate a perfect and competitive market for the public output, estimate the price which would have resulted, and accept this as the shadow price.[43]

Thus the analyst estimates what individuals *would* have been willing to pay for the good had it been available in a competitive market, using such estimating techniques as: (1) interpolation from the prices of similar goods, (2) treatment of the good provided by the public program as intermediate to the production of other goods that have market prices, and valuation of the intermediate good according to its marginal contribution to the final goods, and (3) estimating the value of the good created by the public program to be equal to the reduction in costs to society that would result from existence of

---

[42] See Otto A. Davis and Morton I. Kamien, "Externalities, Information, and Alternative Collective Action" in Haveman and Margolis, *Public Expenditure,* pp. 82–104. Also see Kenneth Arrow, "The Organization of Economic Activity: Issues Pertinent to the Choice of Market Versus Nonmarket Allocation," ibid., pp. 67–81.

[43] Julius Margolis, "Shadow Prices for Incorrect or Nonexistent Market Values," ibid., p. 204.

the good.[44] Using such techniques to calculate shadow prices for goods and resources without competitive market prices is a crucial step in the application of the Kaldor-Hicks criterion through benefit–cost analysis. Benefit–cost analysis thus attempts to work from market prices, or estimated market prices, in order to assure that the resources used and benefits produced by public programs are valued as they would be under an efficient allocation of resources.

Another important market-based technique employed in valuation of public policy options involves the calculation of expected changes in "economic surplus" attributable to the option. Economic surplus is composed of two elements: (1) the value to consumers of the good in excess of what they must pay to get it, and (2) the difference between the price a producer receives for a good and the actual costs of production. Whenever a policy affects price, consumer demand, or production costs, economic surplus is altered. In part the alteration reflects transfers of surplus between groups of producers and consumers; it also reflects net changes in the amount of economic surplus generated. These net changes are treated as equivalent to changes in social benefits because of the policy, and can thus be used to indicate the dollar value to society of a particular policy option. A more detailed description of this technique is provided in exhibit 2-2.

In addition to the central role of market prices in the valuation of goods and resources in benefit–cost analysis, markets are used as guides to determination of the *appropriateness* of government action. If competitive markets generate an efficient allocation of resources, government should "intervene" into such allocations only when the market deviates in some way from the purely competitive model. Among the conditions most prone to arise as reasons for government action are the following:[45]

1. the industry faces ever increasing returns to scale;
2. relevant market information is not believed to be freely available to producers and consumers;
3. the existence of "public goods," meaning goods for which consumption by one person does not exclude consumption by others. Lighthouses and national defense are familiar examples;
4. there are significant "spillover" costs or benefits from production and consumption; and
5. one or more actors in a market are believed to hold "monopoly power."

---

[44] Ibid., pp. 213–219.

[45] Taken from Davis and Kamien, "Externalities, Information, and Alternative Collective Action," Haveman and Margolis, *Public Expenditure and Policy Analysis*. Also see Arrow, "The Organization of Economic Activity," ibid.

When the first condition arises, as for example may be true for transmission of electricity or provision of local telephone service, it is least costly to limit the number of providers. Because this may create monopoly power conditions, it has been usual for government to regulate such industries. Occurrence of the second condition is particularly a problem when (a) the market information is difficult to understand and (b) the consequences of misinformation can be disastrous, as is true with respect to the purchase of pharmaceuticals. Sales of drugs are, accordingly, regulated. Where the third condition arises, the private market will not provide the public good in optimal amounts. In such cases, the government typically provides the good, as with national defense. The fourth condition occurs whenever production of goods imposes costs or provides benefits not captured by the price of the good. The various forms of pollution are the most celebrated examples, as illustrated by the acid rain debate now in progress. Fifth, when a buyer or seller holds "market power" he or she is able to unilaterally alter the price of the good. U.S. antitrust laws are specifically designed to limit occurrences of such conditions, and regulations are designed to limit abuse when monopoly conditions are unavoidable.[46]

In all these cases, then, the appropriateness of government action is justified by some "failure" in the market. The growth of the literature on market failure over the past century has, from the perspective of efficiency analysis, *increased* the range of legitimate government intervention into the allocation of goods and services as the known sources of market failure have proliferated.[47] In more recent years, however, more attention has been given to the perceived failure of government action—particularly the failure of regulation—to improve the situation when markets fail.[48] Just as the development of understanding of market failure *increased* the scope of appropriate government action, the literature on "government failure" suggests that the perceived scope for intervention in the interest of efficiency has narrowed once again.

---

[46] For the best and most exhaustive treatment of market failure, see David L. Weimer and Aiden R Vining, *Policy Analysis: Concepts and Practice* (Englewood Cliffs, NJ: Prentice-Hall, 1989), chapter 3.

[47] For a few of the better known works on this area, see: F. H. Knight, "Some Fallacies in the Interpretation of Social Cost," *Quarterly Journal of Economics,* vol. 38 (1924), pp. 582–606. A. A. Young, "Pigou's Wealth and Welfare," *Quarterly Journal of Economics,* vol. 27 (1913), pp. 672–686. T. Scitovsky, "Two Concepts of External Economics," *Journal of Political Economy,* vol. 62 (1954), pp. 143–151. R. H. Coase, "The Problem of Social Cost," *Journal of Law and Economics,* vol. 3 (1960), pp. 1–44. K. A. Arrow, "The Organization of Economic Activity," Haveman and Margolis, *Public Expenditure and Policy Analysis.*

[48] See, for example, Roger G. Noll, *Reforming Regulation: An Evaluation of the Ash Council Proposals* (Washington, DC: Brookings Institute, 1971); Charles Wolf, *Markets or Governments: Choosing Between Imperfect Alternatives* (Cambridge, MA: MIT Press, 1988); and Weimer and Vining, op. cit., chapter 4. For recent criticism of specific governmental programs and regulations, see any issue of *Regulation,* published by the American Enterprise Institute, Washington, DC.

--------- 2.5 ---------
EFFICIENCY CRITERION:
PRESCRIPTION OF THE PARADIGM

I have argued that the dominant paradigm of policy analysis finds its roots in utility theory, as developed from the utility calculus of Jeremy Bentham and as employed in the analysis of the efficiency of public policies. Efficiency is employed as a metavalue; efficiency is the pursuit of value maximization— and takes as given the particular values pursued by citizens or public officials. I have also argued that the frequent usage of the theory of competitive markets in policy analysis stems largely, though perhaps not exclusively, from the Pareto efficient properties of the purely competitive market. The use of such techniques as benefit–cost analysis derive from the more general concept of efficiency; benefit–cost analysis is an application of the Kaldor-Hicks crite-rion, declaring a policy efficient if it generates net social benefits.

How well does the content of the curriculum in public policy analysis schools bear out this argument? In a broad review of public policy curricula, a leading scholar noted that among the "subset of existing arts and sciences and professional fields" from which the policy curriculum was synthesized, foremost was

> . . . microeconomics, the intellectual source of the optimization techniques introduced with such apparent success into [Secretary] Robert McNamara's Defense Department—and subsequently blessed by [President] Lyndon Johnson as a resource for the government as a whole.[49]

Regarding specific curricular content, microeconomics—and benefit–cost analysis—are clearly central: in a nationwide survey of public policy pro-grams, microeconomics was found to be a required core course in all but a very few. Many schools add a specific required course in benefit–cost analysis or "applied microeconomics."[50] In evaluating the role of microeconomics in public policy programs, the reviewer argued that:

> Through its normative focus on efficiency, microeconomics teaches the student to seek opportunities for resource allocations that can, at least potentially, make everyone better-off.[51]

---

[49] Donald Stokes, "Political and Organizational Analysis of the Policy Curriculum," *Journal of Policy Analysis and Management,* vol. 6, no. 1 (Fall 1986), pp. 45–55; pp. 45–46.

[50] Lee S. Friedman, "Public Policy Economics: A Survey of Current Pedagogical Practice," *Journal of Policy Analysis and Management,* vol. 6, no. 3 (Spring 1987), pp. 503–520. The survey was of all degree-granting public policy programs that were institutional members of the Association for Public Policy Analysis and Management.

[51] Ibid., p. 518.

The content of the most widely used textbooks on public policy analysis further bears out the prominence of efficiency analysis: the discussion of efficiency, of benefit–cost analysis, and their application to policy problems generally take up the bulk of such texts.[52] The empirical evidence thus supports the argument that efficiency analysis and its application constitute the core of the policy analysis paradigm.

This should not be taken to say that efficiency provides the only criterion employed in analysis—indeed, as I will point out later, in practice analysts sometimes ignore efficiency altogether. What is argued here is simply that efficiency analysis is deeply imbedded in the *approach* and the techniques of policy analysis, and that the relatively undisputed definition and centrality of the efficiency criterion make it the essential and most prominent characteristic of the policy analysis paradigm. For these reasons, while analysis in practice frequently departs from the prescription of the paradigm, the prescription itself serves as the basis for the claims made on behalf of analysis and for much of the criticism leveled at analysis.

_____ 2.6 _____
POLICY ANALYSIS AND POLITICS IN TENSION

The policy analysis paradigm is itself a partial political theory. Deriving its conception of value from radically individualistic utilitarianism, the paradigm adopts the efficiency criterion—maximization of net gains in social (i.e., aggregated individual) welfare—as the central guide for choice of public policy. Other bases of value, such as rights or equity, are either reduced to the terms of efficiency or act as parameters within which the efficiency criterion is employed. Within such limits, the approach and technique of analysis are designed to accurately translate citizen preferences into public policy. Because these elements of the paradigm are explicitly political, in that they bear fundamentally on the allocation of value in society, the paradigm has strong implications for the appropriate form and process of government.

One proponent of the policy analysis paradigm has described at some length the ideal form of government appropriate to full implementation of the

---

[52] See, for example, Weimer and Vining, *Policy and Analysis: Concepts and Practice;* Stokey and Zeckhauser, *A Primer;* and Nachmias, *Public Policy Evaluation: Approaches and Methods.* A leading text that takes an "alternative approach," Garry Brewer and Peter deLeon's *The Foundations of Policy Analysis* (Pacific Grove, CA: Brooks/Cole, 1983), still gives prominent place to these concepts—despite the explicit alternative spin.

[53] See Robert H. Haveman, "Policy Analysis and the Congress: An Economist's View," *Policy Analysis,* 2(2) (Spring 1976), pp. 235–250. Also see Roland McKean, "The Unseen Hand in Government," *American Economic Review,* vol. 55 (June 1965), pp. 496–505.

policy analysis paradigm.[53] All participants would know and agree to all ultimate objectives of policy maximization of citizen welfare and would be able to make necessary trade-offs among objectives. Full information would be obtained by participants, involving benefit–cost analyses of all options, resulting in a shifting of resources among programs to assure that the marginal benefits of such programs remain equal. Most importantly, the makers of public decisions must be provided with proper incentives to maximize social welfare; the legislative process should resemble a "smoothly functioning market system." In legislatures as in markets, the full set of costs and gains of any decision—as these are experienced by individual citizens—would be brought to bear on the decisionmaker.

> Considering legislative decisions, this implies the need for a political process in which the full set of impacts of a decision on all citizens—the poor and minority groups as well as those with vested power—be somehow registered with decision makers.[54]

The overall attempt is to create institutions and processes that serve to better map the preferences of *all* citizens into public policy. Much of the recent effort to reform the budgetary process, such as the institutionalization of Planning, Programming, Budgeting System (PPBS),[55] Zero Based Budgeting (ZBB), and more recently Executive Order 12291, which calls for systematic benefit–cost analysis of all "major" regulations,[56] has sought to implement pieces of this ideal of government.

The urge for institutions and processes that better map citizen preference into public policy leads to considerable friction between the ideals of the policy analysis paradigm and perceptions of American politics-as-usual. Because politics in practice often appears resistant to the application of analysis, proponents of the policy analysis paradigm tend to view politics with some disdain. One policy analyst, lamenting the minimal attention given policy analysis in Congress, writes:

> In short, because of the characteristics of the legislative process and the structural characteristics of Congress itself, objective policy analysis does not automatically find a warm reception in the legislative branch. Except in unusual circumstances, analysis directed at isolating policy alternatives that

---

[54] Haveman, "Policy Analysis," p. 239.

[55] See Allen Schick, "The Road to PPB: The Stages of Budget Reform," in *Perspectives on Budgeting*, ed. Allen Schick (Washington, DC: American Society for Public Administration, 1980), pp. 46–67.

[56] See William West, "Institutionalizing Rationality in Regulatory Administration," *Public Administration Review*, 43(4) August 1983, pp. 326–334, and V. Kerry Smith, ed. *Environmental Policy Under Reagan's Executive Order: The Role of Benefit–Cost Analysis* (Chapel Hill, NC: University of North Carolina Press, 1984).

serve the general interest will fail to dominate the power and pleas of special interest advocates. *Without major reform of the operation of Congress,* the probability is not high that an increased flow of analytic studies directed at Congress will play a significant role in improving legislative decisions.[57]

Nonetheless, policy analysis is seen by many as a partial corrective to the deficiencies of politics as practiced. In the words of two proponents of the policy analysis paradigm:

> One of the great virtues of the benefit–cost approach is that the interests of individuals who are poorly organized or less closely involved are counted. (This contrasts with most political decision making procedures.) Even when pushed by powerful interest groups, projects whose benefits do not outweigh their costs will be shown to be undesirable. The benefits and costs accruing to all—to the highway builders, the environmentalists, the "little people," the users and providers of services, the taxpaying public—will be counted on a dollar-for-dollar basis. Benefit–cost analysis is a methodology with which we pursue efficiency and which has the effect of limiting the vagaries of the political process.[58]

The use of analysis, then, is seen by its proponents as in tension with the norms and practice of American politics, and as providing the vehicle for reform in both the policies selected and the procedures for selecting them.[59]

Out of these tensions grow both the promise of the policy analysis paradigm as an enhancement of democratic characteristics of American politics, and the perceived threats to the norms and operation of American politics. The promise is that, through widespread utilization of techniques based on the criterion of efficiency in the formulation of public policy, we will achieve a better translation of the preferences of citizens into public policies. Needless to say, that promise holds considerable democratic appeal. Critics, however, argue that should the proponents of the policy analysis paradigm be successful in working their reforms, dire threats to norms and operation of democratic politics will be realized. It is to those threats—what they are, the premises behind them, and their plausibility—that the next chapter is addressed.

---

[57] Haveman, "Policy Analysis," p. 248. Emphasis added.

[58] Stokey and Zeckhauser, *A Primer,* p. 151.

[59] Several observers see in the policy paradigm considerable *antipathy* to politics in general. According to these observers, proponents of analysis have adopted the notion implicit in the "end of ideology" euphoria of the 1960s that the messy business of politics can be replaced by objective *management* of public issues. See James B. Rule, "The Problem with Social Problems," *Politics and Society,* 2(2) (Fall 1971), pp. 47–56; Sylvia Fries, "Expertise Against Politics: Technology as Ideology on Capitol Hill," *Science, Technology and Human Values,* vol. 43 (Spring 1983), pp. 6–15; and Max Nieman, "The Ambiguous Role of Policy Analysis and an Illustrative Look at Housing Policy," (paper presented at the annual meeting of the Western Political Science Association, Sacramento, CA, April, 1984).

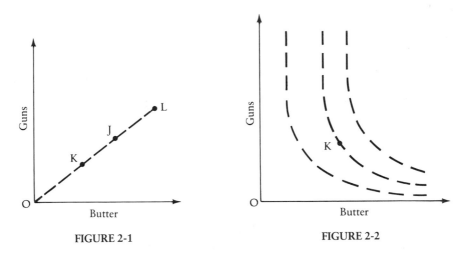

FIGURE 2-1   FIGURE 2-2

_____ EXHIBIT 2-1 _____
EFFICIENCY IN VOLUNTARY EXCHANGE

The concept of Pareto efficiency, described in section 2.3, can be illustrated
with the use of a device called the Edgeworth diagram. The diagram represents
the changes in ordinally ranked levels of utility of two (or more) individuals,
originally endowed with some quantity of two kinds of goods (or bundles of
goods), when the goods are exchanged (or reallocated). Adequate description
of the diagram requires a brief digression into the geometric method of
depicting ordinal rankings of utility in a two-product "utility space."[60]

Imagine for illustrative purposes an individual who gains well-being from
the possession of two kinds of goods. Both goods are "private goods":
possession and consumption of the good by one individual excludes possession and consumption of the good by other individuals. The goods can take
any form (tangible, intangible, discrete, continuous, or whatever) as long as
they exist in limited supply and can be possessed in various quantities; for now
assume them to be guns and butter—though resalable presidential pardons
and religious indulgences would do just as well. Our individual (call him Jim)
gains some level of utility from any combination of guns and butter and
generally prefers more of either good to less. The quantities of guns and butter
can be shown, as in figure 2-1, in a two-dimensional space with guns represented on the vertical axis and butter on the horizontal axis.[61] Utility within

---

[60] For a description of the formal theory underlying the concepts discussed in the following
paragraphs, see W. Hildenbrand and A. P. Kirman, _Introduction to Equilibrium Analysis:
Variations on Themes by Edgeworth and Walras_ (New York: American Elsevier, 1976), especially Chapter 1.

[61] To be precise, figure 2-1 is the northeast quadrant of a Cartesian space, representing the area
in which the values for both coordinates are equal to or greater than zero.

the space is represented ordinally by distance from the origin; any mix of goods in the space, say point *J*, provides more utility than would a mix anywhere on the ray between the origin and point *J*. Thus *J* provides more utility than *K*, but less than *L*.

Jim is assumed to be able to compare the utility he receives from any two combinations of guns and butter. In comparing two points in the space, Jim will be able to tell whether one or the other points is preferred, or whether he is "indifferent" between them. Using these comparisons, it would be possible to find all those combinations of guns and butter that would provide Jim with the same level of utility as would point *J*; we would say Jim is indifferent among all these points. Connecting all these points creates an "indifference curve," as shown in figure 2-2. For the sake of clarity, the indifference curves shown are convex to the origin. In practical terms, this means that Jim prefers some mix of guns and butter to an extreme case of all one and none of the other. Furthermore, if Jim is indifferent between two mixes, he will prefer the average of the two to either one of them. While this assumption seems valid in many cases, one need not assume strict convexity of indifference curves to derive many of the basic results of the theory of consumer behavior. All mixes of goods below and to the left of the indifference curve are inferior (for Jim) to those on the curve; all those above and to the right are preferable to those on the curve. As indicated in figure 2-2, Jim could assemble a number of indifference curves of varying distances from the origin, thus creating an "indifference map" of his preferences among the full range of possible mixes of guns and butter.

In figure 2-3 we introduce a second actor, Ron, who also values possession of guns and butter, and we limit the availability of guns and butter. As before, Jim's preferences are represented by indifference curves that are convex to the origin (point *O*). But now Ron's preferences are shown as well, originating from the upper right corner in figure 2-3 (point *O′*). Ron's preferences are represented in the same manner as Jim's, except that his indifference map has been rotated 180 degrees and superimposed on top of Jim's. Because the availability of guns and butter is now fixed, the distance *OX* (or *YO′*) represents the total supply of butter, while *OY* (or *XO′*) shows the total supply of guns. Any point in the space thus represents a potential distribution of the total supply of guns and butter between Jim and Ron. For example, point *K* in figure 2-3 shows a distribution in which Jim has *OA* butter and *OB* guns while Ron has *O′a* butter and *O′b* guns.

Turning back to the question of efficiency, how can it be determined if a particular distribution of guns and butter between Jim and Ron is efficient? Beginning from point *J* in figure 2-4, Jim will prefer any mix of guns and butter above or to the right of the indifference curve on which *J* is a point, as shown by the area shaded by vertical lines. Ron, on the other hand, will prefer any point below or to the left of the indifference curve on which *J* is a point, as

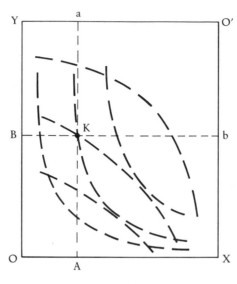

FIGURE 2-3

shown by the horizontal shading. The overlap of these two areas, the "lens" made by the two interfacing indifference curves, shows the set of redistributions of guns and butter that will improve the position of one or both persons while making neither worse off. Point *K*, for example, improves Ron's position while leaving Jim indifferent to his prior position. Likewise, point *L* improves Jim's position while leaving Ron as well-off as he was before but no better. Thus, point *J* is "Pareto inefficient" because it can be improved upon without making anyone worse off. Any redistribution to a point in the lens will increase efficiency.

Notice that, should the initial distribution of guns and butter be at point *E*, no redistribution could be made that would not diminish the well-being of either Jim or Ron. Such a point is "Pareto efficient." Pareto efficient points will occur where Jim's and Ron's indifference curves are tangent, such as points *E*, *F*, *G*, and *N*.[62] Were all such points identified and connected, they would form the "contract line," the set of points from which no cooperative improvement could be made. In an efficient system of distribution, allocations would always be on the contract line; an efficient policy will always move the participants into the lens area as shown in figure 2-4.

---

[62] Technically, the slope of the indifference curve at any point shows the "marginal rate of substitution" of guns for butter at a given point while utility is held constant. Where the two persons' indifference curves are tangent, their marginal rates of substitution are equal. In this situation the two persons' *relative* valuation of the two goods, for very small changes in the mix of goods held, are equal. This condition characterizes the outcome of an efficient allocation of valued things.

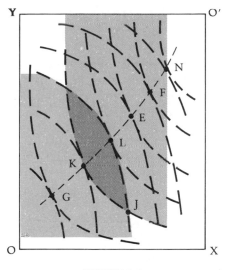

FIGURE 2-4

It was noted in chapter 2 that given an initial inefficient distribution of valued things, there are many possible efficient reallocations that could be made. Referring again to figure 2-4, beginning from distribution *J, any* reallocation that moved onto the contract line between points *K* and *L* would provide an efficient solution. On the basis of the efficiency criterion alone, however, there is no way to determine whether one of these solutions is superior to another; according to Edgeworth, the exact placement on the contract line will be determined by "higgling dodges and designing obstinacy, and other incalculable and often disreputable accidents."[63] Furthermore, the efficiency criterion takes no account of the initial starting position; such "endowments" of wealth are taken as given. In figure 2-4, point *N* is just as efficient—though perhaps not as egalitarian—as point *L*.

The usefulness of the Edgeworth diagram stems from its illustration of the meaning of efficiency in very general terms. The strict criterion of efficiency would hold that a reallocation of things of value should be undertaken if the new distribution resulted in placement in the lens of increased efficiency—or better still, on the contract line. The criterion says nothing about which of the possible efficient allocations should be made. A movement away from the contract line is ruled out as inefficient. Thus, movement in figure 2-4 from point *L* to point *J* violates the efficiency criterion, though it may well satisfy some other criterion for public decision making.

---

[63] Francis Edgeworth, *Mathematical Psychics* (London: Keegan Paul, 1881), p. 46, as cited in George Stigler, *Essays in the History of Economics* (Chicago: University of Chicago Press, 1965), pp. 104–105.

____ EXHIBIT 2-2 ____
ECONOMIC SURPLUS IN EFFICIENCY ANALYSIS

One of the more widespread uses of market theory in efficiency analysis involves the concept of "economic surplus," initially developed by Alfred Marshall to assess gains or losses in the utility of consumers and producers resulting from changes in market conditions.[64] Building from the works of earlier utility theorists, Marshall argued that changes in utility derived from market operations could be analyzed by estimating market supply-and-demand relationships and assessing how changes in these relationships affect "consumers' surplus" and "producers' surplus."

In the theory of competitive markets, price is assumed to be set by the cost of producing the last unit of the good (referred to as the "marginal cost") for which a purchaser can be found. Utility, for a given consumer, is assumed to be represented by the amount of money that consumer is willing to pay to get a unit of the good. The area under the demand curve thus represents the total utility that consumers would gain from consumption of the good.

Assuming that the quantity of the good demanded increases as the price drops, as shown by demand curve DD in figure 2-5, and that price is set competitively at price P, all purchasers but the very last one (the one who buys the "Qth" good) would have been willing to pay more than the competitive price rather than go without the good. All consumers but the one who buys the Qth good can thus be said to gain a "surplus" of utility over and above

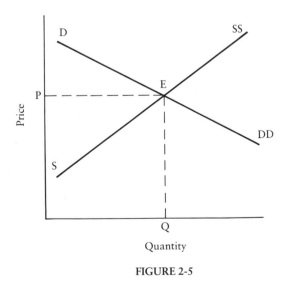

FIGURE 2-5

[64] See Alfred Marshall, *Principles of Economics* (London: Macmillan, 1890).

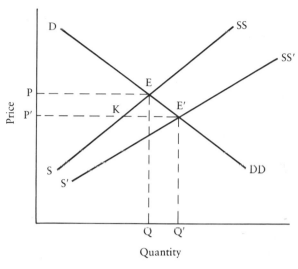

FIGURE 2-6

the price paid for the good. In figure 2-5 this surplus is represented by the triangle *PDE*—the area under the demand curve and above price.

Producers of the good, on the other hand, can make added profit from producing more of the good as long as the price received for the good is greater than the "marginal cost" of producing the next unit. Thus, assuming that marginal costs rise as more of the good is produced, as shown by supply curve *SS* in figure 2-5, producers of all but the last unit (the *Q*th unit) will receive a price higher than was required to induce them to produce it. Area *SPE,* below price and above the marginal cost (supply) curve, represents this "surplus" of value to producers. Together consumers' and producers' surplus are referred to as *economic surplus,* representing the value provided to society by production and consumption of the goods in excess of the costs of production of the goods. The policy concern, applying the potential Pareto criterion, is to take those actions that result in *net* increases in economic surplus.

Use of Marshall's concept of economic surplus in efficiency analysis can be illustrated by example. Imagine a country that has long forbidden import of a commodity—say corn—with the result that domestic farmers produce corn in the quantity price relationship shown by supply curve *SS* in figure 2-6. Domestic demand *DD* results in market equilibrium at *E* with price *P*. Now imagine that the restrictions on corn imports are removed, resulting in a new total corn supply curve *SS',* as shown in figure 2-6. New equilibrium price *P'* and quantity *Q'* would result. In view of the new domestic situation, is the government policy of permitting imports of corn efficient?

Consumers' surplus has grown from an original amount *PDE* to *P'DE',* an increase of *P'PEE'.* Domestic producers' surplus, however, has declined from *SPE* to *SP'K,* a decline of *P'PEK.* Clearly, employing the strict Pareto optimality criteria, the change could not be called efficient. But using the Kaldor-Hicks criterion, consumers would be able to pay producers *P'PEK* and *still* have a net gain of area *KEE'.* Thus, by the Kaldor-Hicks criterion, the policy is efficient.

Armed with these tools, the utility theorist would be able to assess whether a government-induced change in price, demand, or supply would result in a net increase or decrease in economic surplus. Later theorists have significantly revised Marshall's initial formulation; in particular, it is now recognized that the demand curve used to assess the effects of changes in prices must also reflect changes in the marginal utility of money due to the fact that changes in price will alter the real income of consumers.[65] Numerous technical criticisms of the approach have been made, primarily contending that we lack adequate measures of the effect of price changes on the consumer's marginal utility of money.[66] Despite ongoing theoretical disputes over the validity of economic surplus analysis as a measure of changes in social utility,[67] economic surplus is among the most widely employed bases of efficiency analysis. Perhaps in the end, Bentham's reasoning in justifying his own utility calculus will be revived for economic surplus:

> It is sufficient to justify our propositions if (a) they approach more nearly to the truth than any others that can be substituted for them; and (b) they can be employed more conveniently than any other as the basis of legislation.[68]

---

[65] J. R. Hicks was responsible for this adjustment of the theory, and thus the "Hicksian income compensated demand curve" replaces the "Marshallian demand curve" in most modern analyses. See J. R. Hicks, *A Revision of Demand Theory* (London: Clarendon Press, 1956).

[66] For criticisms of the use of economic surplus see Paul A. Samuelson, *Foundations of Economic Analysis* (Cambridge, MA: Harvard University Press, 1947) and I. M. D. Little, *A Critique of Welfare Economics* (London: Clarendon Press, 1957).

[67] Defenders of the use of utility theory include Allen Herberger, "Monopoly and Resource Allocation," *American Economic Review,* vol. 54, (May 1954), pp. 77–87; R. D. Willig "Consumers' Surplus Without Apology," *American Economic Review,* vol. 66, (September 1976), pp. 589–597; and Jerry A. Hausman, "Exact Consumers' Surplus and Deadweight Loss," (unpublished manuscript, June 1980).

[68] Etienne Dumont, *Bentham's Theory of Legislation,* trans. by Charles Atkinson, (London: Oxford University Press, 1914), p. 134.

CHAPTER 3

The Threats of
Policy Analysis

The policy analysis paradigm, as abstracted from the foundations of the central techniques of policy analysis, provides a partial theory of democratic policy making. That theory is optimistic; it promises to improve the mapping of individual preferences into policy—encompassing the preferences of the "little guy" as well as those of the well-financed political lobby. In the tradition of Western liberalism, this form of decision making would rely more on the expressions of individual citizens and less on political representatives. The techniques of analysis would play a central role in collection and aggregation of individual preferences, and therefore, the information and advice of the analyst would become crucial and influential in the policy-making process. Though not all practicing policy analysts aspire to these ends, the expression of this "ideal" democracy can be found in the foundations of the analytical techniques, and in the writings of the proponents of these techniques. Furthermore, as indicated in the previous chapter, the inefficiency and disorder of politics grates on the sensibilities of many analysts, leading them to call for reform that more closely approximates the ideal. The PPBS, ZBB, and like movements were of this type.

Given the overtly political implications of the paradigm, it should come as no surprise that it has been the subject of extensive criticism for its effects on political processes and policy outcomes. A survey of this criticism reveals that it originates from across the spectrum of normative political persuasions and encompasses quite a range of perceived threats to the proper functioning of democratic political systems. In many ways the criticism of the policy analysis paradigm is difficult to disentangle from the literature predicting and lamenting the rise of technocracy; the emergence of policy analysis and its associated techniques as a visible factor in the formulation of public policy might be taken as confirmation of the dire predictions of the anti-technocrats. Therefore much of the criticism directed specifically at the policy analysis paradigm is in fact anti-technocratic in nature. For this reason the basic themes of the anti-technocracy literature are included in this chapter's examination of the possible threats to democratic politics posed by the policy analysis paradigm.

The intent of this chapter is to analyze the more persistent themes within this critical literature in order to render its contentions amenable to evaluation in light of the claims made by—and implicit in—the policy analysis paradigm and the practice of policy analysis within the context of modern politics.

The cacophony of critiques of the policy analysis paradigm, its disparate parts often bearing little in common other than their rejection of the policy analytic approach, makes straightforward evaluation of the criticisms a rather cumbersome task. In the interest of clarity and tractability, I will examine the critiques of the policy analysis paradigm through review of the dominant *themes* evident in the literature. Three broad themes capture the range and thrust of the critical literature: (1) technical policy analysts will, by virtue of their knowledge and expertise, obtain significant unrepresentative power within democratic political systems, (2) the rise of technique as a major force in policy formulation will result in the distortion of the expressed preferences of the citizens, and (3) the advent of technical policy analysis as a major force in the policy process has introduced new institutional and organizational strains that threaten to overwhelm the democratic process. Within each of the major themes there are, of course, significant divergences on important points among the various critics. These divergences will be mapped, and in each instance, a set of questions will be raised that bear on the validity of the critique: does the force of the critique depend on the actual application of the techniques and norms of the policy analysis paradigm—or at least some significant part of them—in policy formulation? If so, the validity of the critique rests on the perceived *influence* of the analysts as purveyors of the policy analysis paradigm. The reasonableness of the assumed level of influence will be assessed in later chapters. If, on the other hand, successful application of the policy analysis paradigm is not presupposed, by what mechanism do policy analysts constitute a threat?

Before commencing this enterprise, one disclaimer is warranted. The themes and subthemes of the criticism of policy analysis examined here are not intended to be taken as an exhaustive and exclusive categorization of all possible criticisms: not exhaustive because only the major criticisms in the literature have been selected, largely on the basis of their premises that democracy or the institutions of democracy are somehow threatened by the attempted application of the policy analysis paradigm. Some of the criticisms of the far political left and right are therefore given less attention than might otherwise seem warranted. The themes and subthemes explored here are not exclusive; as will be seen, the various kinds of threats depicted by the critics of the policy analysis paradigm intertwine and interact, often with the result that a given attribute of the practice of analysis is implicated in more than one of the major threats to democratic practice.

_____ 3.1 _____
THE THREAT OF TECHNOCRATIC CONTROL

The projection that a technically and scientifically sophisticated elite will wrest power (or already has wrested power) from the hands of the politicians is a venerable one, with eloquent proponents stretching back to Bacon and Saint-Simon.[1] Though the theme has many variants, the common thread holds that, as technology progresses and mankind's reliance on the fruits of technology increases, knowledge and technical expertise will grow in importance as a resource for political power. Eventually this particular power base will eclipse the more traditional ones of coercion, wealth, and charisma. Politicians, being mere lay persons, will not understand the elaborate technical underpinnings of society and its engines of well-being, and will therefore be more of a hindrance than a help in advancing the interests of society through public policy. Thus, as stated by one leading democratic theorist:

> [D]espite all talk to the contrary, we are moving toward *less* power of the people. The obvious reason for this is that a maximum of popular power is possible only in simple societies whose leadership-tasks are relatively elementary. As the mechanisms of social and economic life become more and

---

[1] For a sampling, see Francis Bacon, *New Atlantis,* in *Selected Writings of Francis Bacon,* ed. Hugh G. Dick (New York: The Modern Library, 1955); Henri de Saint-Simon, *Social Organization, the Science of Man and Other Writings,* ed. and trans. Felix Markham (New York: Harper & Row, 1964); and F. W. Taylor, *The Principles of Scientific Management* (New York: Harper & Row, 1947).

more complex, interlocking, and pre-ordained, the expert's opinion must acquire much greater weight than his vote as an elector.[2]

For a significant number of writers, the trend would be a good one: the transfer of power from the bumbling, inept politicians to the hands of the efficient, dispassionate scientist–technicians would lead to social harmony and physical abundance—toward a technological utopia.[3] Others, more relevant to this chapter, have taken a less optimistic view of this transition, seeing in it a drift toward a technocratic Brave New World.

By what processes will the technical expert rise to political prominence? In common, critics of technocracy envision the process as part of a larger change in advanced societies; the infusion of "technique," and the norm of efficiency, into social as well as industrial management. Max Weber, for example, saw the rise of the expert as a part of the advance of the "rational bureaucratic structure of domination."[4] Natural forces of development within modern societies—including the growth of demand for, and scope of, government action—lead rulers to rely ever more heavily on the efficient workings of bureaucratic organizations staffed and headed by experts. Initially, political rulers would turn to bureaucratic organizations as instruments of power.

> Bureaucracy is *the* means of carrying 'community action' over into rationally ordered 'social action.' Therefore, as an instrument for 'societalizing' relations of power, bureaucracy has been and is a power instrument of the first order—for the one who controls the bureaucratic order.[5]

In early stages of development the ruler is able to keep the power of the bureaucratic experts in check; the ready availability of aspiring experts, and the ability to play one expert against another, maintains the ruler's control over his or her experts.[6] Over time, however, the experts and the organizations in which they became ensconced "continued to exist in the face of changing rulers,"[7] and they seek to "increase the superiority of the professionally

---

[2] Giovanni Sartori, *Democratic Theory* (Detroit, MI: Wayne State University Press, 1962), p. 405.

[3] Bacon, *New Atlantis,* Taylor, *Scientific Management,* and Saint-Simon, *Social Organization,* looked for improvement in the lot of mankind to result from the ascension of the technocrat. Another important author, and one who actively urged the transition of power onward, was Thorstein Veblen. See his *The Engineers and the Price System* (New York: The Viking Press, 1954). A more recent book that captures the zeitgeist of this movement, without the overt political content, is Daniel Boorstin's *The Republic of Technology* (New York: Harper and Row, 1978).

[4] Max Weber, *Structures of Power* in *From Max Weber: Essays in Sociology,* trans. and ed. by H. H. Gerth and C. Wright Mills (New York: Oxford University Press, 1946), pp. 196–244.

[5] Ibid., p. 228.

[6] Ibid., pp. 235–236.

[7] Ibid., p. 237.

informed by keeping their knowledge and intentions secret."[8] The result, according to Weber, is that gradually the expert's power vis-à-vis the politician becomes "overtowering":

> The 'political master' finds himself in the position of a 'dilettante' who stands opposite the 'expert,' facing the trained official who stands within the management of administration. This holds whether the 'master' whom the bureaucracy serves is a 'people' . . . or a parliament. It holds whether the master is an aristocratic, collegiate body . . . or a popularly elected president . . .[9]

A more recent critic of technological developments in modern society, Jacques Ellul, follows Weber in arguing that the rise of the expert to dominance is an outgrowth of a larger phenomenon: the "technicization" of society.[10] As the technical means for achieving social and economic ends become more complex and effective, expert technicians assume a more central role in providing politicians with information and analysis upon which decisions can be based. Ostensibly, technicians remain passive political actors; they represent no constituency, and once they indicate to politicians the possible technical "solutions" to social and economic "problems," they retire from the field. But the reality is that politicians become wholly dependent on the experts' advice:

> There is generally only one logical and admissible solution. The politician will then find himself obliged to choose between the technicians' solution, which is the only reasonable one, and other solutions, which he can indeed try out at his own peril but which are not reasonable. . . . In fact, the politician no longer has any real choice; decision follows automatically from the preparatory technical labors.[11]

Echoing Weber, Ellul further argues that "every advance made in the techniques of enquiry, administration, and organization in itself reduces the power and the role of politics."[12]

Both Weber and Ellul find in the rise of the bureaucratic expert a tendency toward concentration and centralization of power. According to Weber, the provision of expert advisors will enhance the more centralized and bureaucratized power of the executive, while diminishing that of the legislative

---

[8] Ibid., p. 233.
[9] Ibid., pp. 232–233.
[10] Jacques Ellul, *The Technological Society* (New York: Vintage Books, 1964).
[11] Ibid., pp. 258–259.
[12] Ibid., p. 259.

bodies.[13] Within the bureaucracy, power becomes ever more centralized in the hands of the expert–technician. Even among administrators, the intellectual gulf between the few technicians, who understand the requisite techniques, and the greater number of executive functionaries who are "hacks who understand nothing about the complicated techniques they are carrying out," becomes unbridgeable.[14] Coupled with the growing concentration of power in the bureaucracy, the ineffectual bumblings of the elected representatives become a blockage to the efficient pursuit of social policy by the expert–technicians. Thus the cumbersome operation of democratic control becomes inoperable and intolerable to those who exercise the technical monopoly.

> Technique shapes an aristocratic society, which in turn implies aristocratic government. Democracy in such a society can only be a mere appearance.[15]

What will be the result of this transition to technocracy? Though there is considerable disagreement regarding the exact nature of the world dominated by the "rational bureaucratic order," there is consensus that it will be far from the utopia envisioned by Bacon and Saint-Simon. The "dystopian"[16] world will be characterized by an ever-increasing regimentation, with "ever-new work for the clerks, an ever-new specialization of functions, and expert vocational training and administration. All this," Weber tells us, "means caste."[17] The spontaneity and passion of free men are gradually squeezed into the regular, orderly, reliable behavior of men in mass society. Ellul, among the most pessimistic, foresees a "total technical society"— epitomized by the rational technician in the bureaucracy.[18] In a fully developed technical society, technique (defined as the collection of available means for achieving given ends) becomes an end in itself, indifferent to all human values. The internal logic of technique—the drive for efficiency in all human activity—drains human ends of meaning, leaving a bloodless yet satiated society populated by the likes of Nietzsche's "last man." Says Ellul:

> We shall have nothing more to lose, and nothing to win. Our deepest instincts and our most secret passions will be analyzed, published, and exploited. We shall be rewarded with everything our hearts ever desired. And the supreme

---

[13] Weber, *Structure of Power*, p. 234. Also see p. 239, wherein Weber notes Bismarck's "attempt to realize the plan of a 'national economic council' as a means of power against Parliament." Defending its interests, Parliament rejected the proposal. The attempt, and failure, to implement such initiatives as PPBS are a similar phenomenon.

[14] Ellul, *The Technological Society*, p. 275.

[15] Ibid.

[16] Bernard Gendron labels theorists who fear the emergence of Aldous Huxley's Brave New World as "dystopians" in *Technology and the Human Condition* (New York: St. Martins Press, 1977).

[17] Weber, *The Structure of Power*, p. 71.

[18] Ellul, *The Technological Society*, pp. 246–247.

luxury of the society of technical necessity will be to grant the bonus of useless revolt and of an acquiescent smile.[19]

Not all the dystopian theorists envision the easy and contented drift into a Brave New World dominated by a technological aristocracy. Karl Mannheim foresaw the drives toward impersonal social and economic efficiency as an end value in organization and administration, but the realization of that value would result in a society of alienated, frustrated individuals who, seeking scapegoats, would clamor for a fascistic form of government.[20] Likewise, Friedrich Hayek contends that the end result of technocratic "social planning" will be a collectivist or totalitarian state with little room for individual liberty.[21] Commonly, however, the threat posed to democratic society is seen to include (1) the rise of the unrepresentative technocrat to power, accompanied by (2) the distortion or erosion of important human values, and (3) the centralization of power under a bureaucratic, technocratic elite.

A strand of the technocratic critique that takes specific aim at the policy analysis paradigm shares the gloomier view of Ellul and Hayek. In this view, the policy analyst, under the umbrella of positivistic science, pretends to hold scientific answers to political problems.[22] The acceptance and application of the policy analysis paradigm ". . . subtly sustains the displacement of politics by science,"[23] which serves to truncate the democratic political process and "concentrates power in the hands of the self-certifying technocrats."[24]

The usefulness of the dystopian critique, for our purposes, is that it carries the criticism of the policy analysis paradigm bearing on the *power* of the technical expert to its logical extreme. It makes clear the linkage presumed to lead to political dominance by the technocratic elite, and permits evaluation of that linkage. The dystopian theses hold in common that: (1) the increasing

---

[19] Ibid.

[20] Karl Mannheim, *Man and Society in an Age of Reconstruction* (London: Paul Trench, Trubner, 1940).

[21] See Friedrich A. Hayek's *The Road to Serfdom* (Chicago: University of Chicago Press, 1972) and *Individualism and Economic Order* (Chicago: University of Chicago Press, 1948).

[22] See M.E. Hawkesworth's *Theoretical Issues in Policy Analysis* (Albany, NY: SUNY Press, 1988). Hawkesworth argues that policy analysts may be well aware that their work has only a flawed "scientistic" basis, but they cling to positivism through "a cynical and willful adherence to distortions that promote political advantage." (p. 109).

[23] Ibid., p. 188.

[24] Ibid. What makes Hawkesworth's critique particularly interesting is that she constructs it from an epistemologically based rejection of the veracity of the social sciences. The sciences in general are but "one fallible cognitive practice among others" (p. 188). Since, she argues, we have discovered no scientific covering laws capable of prediction in the social/political world, we cannot base policy analysis on a positivistic science. In attempting to do so, the policy analyst treats "contentious claims" about the social world as if they were "truth."

demand for, and complexity of, information and analysis needed for political management will make the politician ever more dependent on expert advice, (2) the control of the politician over his expert advisor will be eroded because the techniques employed by the experts assume that the "one best answer" will be a function of *techniques*—not the individual expert (i.e., advice by different experts will not result in meaningfully different policy options), and (3) the efficient development and implementation of complex policies will require an ever-increasing centralization of control and authority. Implicit are the assumptions [in (2) above] that all sufficiently schooled expert analysts will be able to arrive at "one best solution" in a given instance, and that effective constraints will exist to assure that analysts do not provide politicians with politically expedient advice in return for personal influence or whatever favors politicians may bestow.

In assessing the contentions of the dystopian critics, it is important to keep in mind that, with few exceptions, the phenomena described are *projections* toward which society is moving. We should not, therefore, expect to find these projections fully developed. An assessment is necessarily concerned with the *plausibility* of the dystopian claims and the current *trends* in the use and influence of analysis. Nonetheless, available data suggest that analysts are far from achieving the status of all-powerful technicians, and that the likelihood of obtaining that status appears slim.

At first blush, a survey of recent trends in the employment of analysts and expenditures on analysis would seem to provide ample support for the dystopian thesis. On the expenditure side, the federal government was estimated by the General Accounting Office to have increased outlays on non-defense program analysis by 500 percent between 1969 and 1974; by 1976, federal expenditures on the somewhat broader category of "social research and development" were estimated to have reached $1.8 billion.[25] The rise in employment of analysts by government has also proceeded apace, spreading from defense and water resources to social programs in the 1960s and 1970s. A recent study of the utilization of analysis estimated that, in the Washington D.C. area alone, analysts working in the natural resource area numbered nearly 5,000.[26] The rapid proliferation of energy-policy analysis, responding to the urgency of the "energy crisis" of 1973–1974, has probably provided the most dramatic evidence of the rising demand for analysis, leading to a

---

[25] Statistics taken from Genevive Kelezo, *Program Evaluation: Emerging Issues of Possible Legislative Concern Relating to the Conduct and Use of Evaluation in the Congress and Executive Branch* (Washington, DC: Congressional Research Service, Library of Congress, 1974); and Laurence Lynn ed., *Knowledge and Policy: The Uncertain Connection* (Washington, DC: The National Research Council, 1978).

[26] Christopher Leman, *Some Benefits and Costs of the Proliferation of Analysis in Natural Resource Budgeting*, Discussion Paper, D-101, (Washington, DC: Resources for the Future, December 1982), pp. 6–7.

series of major studies and countless minor analyses over the past decade.[27] Cumulatively, these partial statistics indicate that demand for analysis has grown extensively, and that the number of analysts involved in proposing and reviewing policies has increased. So far, then, the argument of the dystopian critics seems valid.

Growing employment and expenditures do not translate directly into growing political influence, however. Repeated studies have shown that, despite the increased provision of analyses, those analyses have little direct effect on policy formulation.[28] One survey of those studies concluded that "The recent literature is unanimous in announcing the general failure of evaluation to affect decision making in a significant way."[29] Reviewing the energy analyses done throughout the 1970s, one insightful scholar notes that, though issues marked by high levels of uncertainty and large political stakes are precisely those that create a significant demand for analysis, those are also the issues for which "analysis is most likely to be disputed or ignored."[30]

The lack of apparent success in influencing policy has led many theorists to revise the technocratic notion that analysts provide essential advice that is used to "solve problems." One perceptive critique describes this widespread belief as a "problem solving myth" that diverges from the actual uses to which analysis is put.[31] The actual uses of analysis, it is argued, tend to be more overtly political in nature; in social-policy areas, analysis has served to "contain" program growth by adding to the "nothing works" refrain—even though the analyses are technically and substantively inconclusive; analysis has served to build up power bases, through establishment of agency expertise and data bases, in emerging issue areas; and analysis has served a "policing function" useful in controlling the behavior of program–agency bureaucrats. Most prevalent, however, is the contention that a primary use to which analysis has been put is the *legitimation* of policy choices made by politicians.[32] In this role, the analyst is employed for the aura of dispassionate,

---

[27] For a review of the major energy analyses provided through the decade, see Martin Greenberger, et al., *Caught Unawares: The Energy Decade in Retrospect* (Cambridge, MA: Ballinger, 1983). Some of the less publicized policy analyses performed in recent years are provided as case studies in chapters 5 and 6 of this book.

[28] For a summary of that literature, see Michael S. Goldstein, et al., "The Nonutilization of Evaluation Research," *Pacific Sociological Review*, 21(1), January 1978, pp. 21–44.

[29] S. Groose, *Evaluations of the War on Poverty* (Washington, DC: General Accounting Office, 1969), as cited in ibid., p. 23.

[30] Greenberger, et al., *Caught Unawares*, pp. 282–284.

[31] Martin Rein and Sheldon White, "Policy Research: Belief and Doubt," *Policy Analysis*, 3(2) Spring 1977, pp. 239–271.

[32] Jeffrey Straussman, *The Limits of Technocratic Politics* (New Brunswick, NJ: Transaction Books, 1978), pp. 139–143; James Marver, *Consultants Can Help: The Use of Outside Experts in the U.S. Office of Child Development* (Lexington, MA: Lexington Books, 1979), chapter 1; and Guy Benveniste, *The Politics of Expertise* (Berkeley, CA: Glendessary Press, 1972).

objective rationality that he or she can impart to politically motivated policy initiatives. The analyst's contribution is largely symbolic.

Taken further, the legitimation function of analysis overturns the dystopians' fears; rather than usurping the power of the politicians, the analysts merely serve to *reinforce* the power of those already possessed of political clout. Describing analysts as "mandarins," or "The Great Justifiers," one review contends that, in the "more nearly empirically verifiable" model of the role of analysis, decision makers (a) choose policies based on political considerations, and *then* (b) search for rationalization and justification of that choice, using analysis only "to prove beyond a shadow of a doubt the legitimacy of the course of decisionmaking decided upon in some political back room . . ."[33] Critics of the left, such as Herbert Marcuse and Andre Gorz, have argued that expert technicians act to preserve the domination of the wealthy business class;[34] the efforts of the expert–advisor serve to soften the rough edge of capitalist domination, thereby prolonging it.[35] Other theorists of the left have argued that the expert–technician is at heart a conservative, a servant of the capitalist state.[36] In this line of thought, the rise of the sophisticated techniques of analysis, and the extensive employment of consultant analysts by governments at all levels, ". . . lend the authority of technico-logical justification to regulations which may serve certain industries better than the commonweal."[37]

The perception of policy analysts as mandarins, at best mere legitimizers of choices made by others, draws support from the research noted above showing analysis to make little *direct* and independent contribution to policy formulation. An alternative line of research, however, based on a more permissive definition of influence, does find independent influence exerted on policy by analysis. This view holds that analysis has an *indirect* effect on the formulation of policy; though few observers can point to specific analyses that have influenced a given policy choice, the more general and persistent conclusions of policy analyses become widely diffused among the policy community concerned with the affected issue area. The new concepts and information

---

[33] Irving Horowitz, "Social Science Mandarins: Policymaking as a Political Formula," *Policy Sciences*, vol. 1 (1970), pp. 339–360.

[34] Herbert Marcuse, *One Dimensional Man* (Boston: Beacon Press, 1964), pp. 1–18; and Andre Gorz, *A Strategy for Labor* (Boston: Beacon Press, 1964), pp. 120–125.

[35] Gorz contends that the technicians will be willing partners in a new socialist order—once they are shown a genuine alternative to the capitalist state. Ibid., p. 125.

[36] Jean Meynaud, *Technocracy*, trans. by Paul Barns, (New York: The Free Press, 1969), pp. 187–188.

[37] Ida Hoos, *Systems Analysis and Public Policy: A Critique* (Berkeley, CA: University of California Press, 1972), pp. 241–247.

become the revised common wisdom of the policy community.[38] This "enlightenment" model of analysis holds that:

> [Research] provides the intellectual background of concepts, orientations, and empirical generalizations that inform policy. As new concepts and data emerge, their gradual cumulative effect can be to change the conventions policymakers abide by and to reorder the goals and priorities of the practical policy world.[39]

Thus the diffusion and cumulation of information may influence the direction and content of policy, even though no direct link to specific analyses is evident. Analysis thus becomes a potent ingredient in the "marketplace of ideas."

With respect to the dystopian critics' fear that analysts, as carriers of the policy analysis paradigm, will emerge as dominating technocratic elites, these findings provide little support and at the same time, no conclusive refutation. The dystopians claim only that the dominance of the technocrat is *emerging*, not that it has already been achieved. Thus far, the evidence depicts no clear trend toward greater influence by policy analysts or their techniques, despite the profusion of analysts and their studies in the bureaucracy. Perhaps, then, the accumulation of that influence awaits the other development projected by the dystopians: the heightened centralization and homogeneity of policy advice.

The dystopians could find both theoretical and empirical justification for their fears that the practitioners of the policy analysis paradigm will lead to an increasing centralization of control over policy formulation. As described in chapter 2, effective translation of citizens' preferences into policy would require considerable planning. Furthermore, *efficient* policy formulation would require that the marginal contribution to social utility of each program (that is, utility obtained from the last dollar spent on each program) be identical. Thus, all government programs would need to be compared and marginal adjustments in expenditures made where marginal utility differed. This function of comparing all policies, with authority to shift funds among alternative programs, would almost certainly require a centralized office for program and budget review, separate from and with authority over the various program offices. Programmatically, attempts to install the policy analysis paradigm into governmental processes have made explicit the intent to centralize budgetary authority; budget reform programs such as PPBS would, in ideal form, centralize budget authority in order to improve plan-

---

[38] Carol Weiss, "Research for Policy's Sake: The Enlightenment Function of Social Research," *Policy Analysis*, 3(4) (Fall 1977), pp. 531–545; Nathan Kaplan, et al. *The Use of Social Science Knowledge in Policy Decisions at the National Level* (Ann Arbor, MI: Univ. of Michigan, Institute for Social Research, 1975).

[39] Weiss, "Research for Policy's Sake," p. 544.

ning, management, and control.[40] Not only would the increasing role of the techniques of the policy analysis paradigm centralize control within the executive branch, it would also enhance the power of the executive branch relative to that of the legislative branch. According to one proponent of policy analysis, the use of analysis strengthens the position of executive officials, which ". . . means reducing the power of congressional committees and sub-committees which have direct lines of communication with and influence over individual operating units."[41] In this way, attempts to institutionalize the policy analysis paradigm, like earlier proposals for budgetary reform in the more traditional literature of public administration,[42] have carried a distinct tendency toward centralization and concentration of authority in the executive branch.

But the budgetary reforms such as PPBS have seldom matched the promotional claims of their proponents. Following its official promulgation in the federal government by President Johnson in 1967, the elements of PPBS were never fully transplanted from defense to civilian agencies.[43] Indeed, even in defense, where PPBS scored its most apparent success, ". . . it was only after [Secretary of Defense] McNamara gave the analysts command over the central programming and budgeting systems that PPBS became a working reality."[44] Such a transfer of authority was not possible in civilian agencies, where control over the levers of policy and the budget has traditionally been more dispersed.[45] Traditional patterns of budgeting, reflecting ingrained and institutionalized patterns of politics, resisted the transformations required for PPBS.[46] Particularly in Congress, which stood to lose in the transfer of control to the executive branch, resistance was high.[47] The result was the official abandonment of PPBS in September of 1971 by the federal government. Though vestiges of PPBS remain, and several recent initiatives by the Office of Management and Budget (OMB) have again sought to "rationalize" public

---

[40] Allen Schick, "The Road to PPB: The Stages of Budget Reform," in *Perspectives on Budgeting,* ed. Allen Schick, (Washington, DC: American Society for Public Administration, 1980), p. 49.

[41] Charles Schultze, *The Politics and Economics of Public Spending* (Washington, DC: Brookings Institution, 1968), p. 94. Schultze argues that this will prove a beneficial shift of power.

[42] See Herbert Kaufman, "Emerging Conflicts in Democratic Public Administration," in *American Political Science Review,* 50(4) (December 1956), pp. 1057–1073.

[43] Allen Schick, "A Death in the Bureaucracy: The Demise of Federal PPB," in *Public Expenditure and Policy Analysis,* eds. Robert Haveman and Julius Margolis 2nd ed. (Chicago: Rand McNally, 1977), pp. 556–576.

[44] Ibid., p. 559. Also see Alain Enthoven and Wayne K. Smith, *How Much is Enough?* (New York: Harper and Row, 1971).

[45] Aaron Wildavsky, *The Politics of the Budgetary Process,* 3rd ed. (Boston: Little Brown, 1979).

[46] See Schick, "A Death in the Bureaucracy," *American Society,* for a catalog of the causes of PPBS failure. Also see Wildavsky, *Politics of the Budgetary Process,* pp. 193–202.

[47] Schultze, *Public Spending,* p. 94. Also see Charles O. Jones, "Why Congress Can't Do Policy Analysis (or Words to that Effect)," *Policy Analysis,* 2(2) (Spring 1976), pp. 251–264.

programs through centralized control,[48] the centralized ideal of PPBS has not been realized. Perhaps most indicative of this failure has been the *dispersion* of analysts throughout Congress and the various executive program offices and departments, rather than their concentration in a budget bureau as called for in PPBS.[49] Because of this dispersion, not only has analysis failed to achieve the centralization so useful for the implementation of the policy analysis paradigm, but also it has come to serve as a resource employed by all sides in the policy and budgetary struggles.

Though the dispersion of analysts throughout the bureaucracy addresses the dystopian concern over centralization of control over policy, it does not directly confront the *possibility* of dominant influence by the analysts.[50] The dystopians argue that (a) the increasing demand for policy advice coupled with (b) the uniformity of the advice provided will assure that the analysts' advice is followed; if there is "generally only one logical and admissible solution," as Ellul argues, politicians will have little choice.[51] If, on the other hand, various analysts provide a range of substantively different policy advice, politicians will be able to pick and choose among analytically defensible options, or play one analyst against another; the lack of consensus among analysts would serve to reduce the influence of analysis on the substantive content of policy.

Which scenario best portrays the prospective use of analysis? Claims made by the proponents of the policy analysis paradigm indicate that some, at least, believe analysis will eventually be capable of providing the one best solution to policy problems concerning allocations of value. Note the optimism of one leading policy economist:

> [U]nder full employment conditions, with the marginal utility of money the same for all individuals, and with perfect markets and no external economies or diseconomies in production or consumption, prices are perfect measures of benefit.[52]

When these conditions are not met, such techniques as shadow price estimates are used. Given the current state-of-the-art, adequate estimation of shadow prices remains difficult; thus, "While in principle it is always possible to

---

[48] Executive Order 12291, issued in February 1981, requires that federal agencies produce benefit–cost analyses of all "major regulations." See William West, "Institutionalizing Rationality in Regulatory Administration," in *Public Administration Review*, 43(4) (August 1983), pp. 326–334.

[49] Christopher Leman, *Some Benefits*.

[50] Note that the failure to impose a centralized system of analysis makes the comparison of various policies, and their respective marginal contributions to social utility, very difficult to accomplish.

[51] Ellul, *The Technological Society*, p. 258.

[52] Otto Eckstein, "A Survey of Public Expenditure Criteria" in *Public Finances: Needs, Sources, and Utilization,* Universities-National Bureau for Economic Research (Princeton, NJ: Princeton University Press, 1961), pp. 439–504.

measure the change in utility of individuals, . . . in practice this is an enormous task and shortcuts must be devised."[53] The dystopians would agree, contending that it is only a matter of time, as better techniques are developed, until the shortcuts will be abandoned in favor of the genuine article.

In order to assess the claim (and fear) that analysts can provide the one best solution, it is important to clearly delineate the conception of the *process* of analysis implicit in the claim. That view of process, aptly dubbed the "problem solving myth" of policy analysis, holds that the analyst confronts a clearly defined problem, and can identify the set of optimal means for achieving publicly specified goals.[54] The role of the analyst is thus to evaluate the alternative means to achieve the stated goals and provide policy makers with advice concerning the best option.[55] Thus analysis and policy analysts are to be neutral and apolitical.[56]

The most critical flaw in this view of the process and provision of policy analysis stems from its presumption that the specification of goals can be separate from the process of analysis. A wealth of literature has provided ample evidence that analysis *necessarily* shapes the ends, as well as the means, of public policies.[57] The reason is that problems rarely if ever enter the policy process as fully defined phenomena. Political issues, as patterns of events with meaning for human values, are properly seen as emerging from a policy "primeval soup": a mixture of public and official attitudes and beliefs concerning the issue.[58] In that process, many actors and groups may compete to impose interpretations of meaning for social values on that pattern of events—to define the important dimensions of the problem and its implications for society. Only when an interpretation of a social problem exists does it make sense to ask citizens what they might be willing to pay to ameliorate it. In the energy debates of the 1970s, for example, the debate between proponents of the "hard" and "soft" energy paths was at heart an argument

---

[53] Ibid., pp. 449–450.

[54] In keeping with the policy analysis paradigm, these goals would be derived from a solicitation (via existing prices or surveys) of citizen preferences.

[55] Many primers and "how-to" texts on policy analysis describe the steps in analysis described here. See chapter 2 of this sudy for an extended discussion.

[56] For a lucid discussion of the problematic claim that the basis of the policy analysis paradigm is value-neutral and objective, see David Paris and James Reynolds, *The Logic of Policy Inquiry* (New York: Longman, 1983), chapters 4 and 5; also see the following section of this chapter.

[57] This literature is vast; for a sampling, see Richard Nelson, *The Moon and the Ghetto* (New York: W. W. Norton, 1977); Martin Rein and Sheldon White, *Policy Research: Belief and Doubt;* Henry Aaron, *Politics and the Professors: The Great Society in Perspective* (Washington, DC: Brookings, 1978); and Aaron Wildavsky, *Speaking Truth to Power* (Boston: Little Brown, 1979).

[58] John Kingdon, *Agendas, Alternatives and Public Policies* (Boston: Little Brown, 1984), pp. 122–151.

over what was important about existing and possible future mixes of energy technology.[59] Proponents of the soft path contended that the energy problem was one element in a fundamental crisis affecting the future structure and survival of society. Hard path advocates argued that the problem was best understood more narrowly as one of how to develop new energy supplies to meet the increasing demands of growing economies. These kinds of debates are *formative* to the preference policy makers and citizens will have regarding the issue; different ways of interpreting events engage values in different ways, leading to distinct sets of preferable policy options.[60] The creative search for "the issue," much like the incessant process of combining and recombining products into new "goods" in the marketplace, is a defining characteristic of the practice of politics. Policy analysts, who necessarily define problems in order to offer solutions, are per force participants in this process. Thus to the degree that analysts and their analyses affect the way issues are interpreted— as indicated by the enlightenment literature discussed above—they necessarily affect the *goals* to be sought by public policy.[61]

The policy analysis paradigm, in the pure form described in chapter 2, does not supply a comprehensive or unified interpretation of patterns of events. Meaning and value within the paradigm are derived from the preferences of the individuals that make up society. When social perceptions of a pattern of events are incoherent, in flux and undeveloped, the meaning of events and the value of policies bearing on those events will be indeterminate and volatile. When social perceptions of events jell and become coherent, it becomes possible to measure people's willingness-to-pay to alter those events, and to meaningfully evaluate options for such alterations. It is not necessary that there be consensus regarding the desirability or undesirability of the events, only that individuals agree on the underlying dimensions of debate.[62]

---

[59] See John B. Robinson's "Apples and Horned Toads: on the Framework-Determined Nature of the Energy Debate," *Policy Sciences*, vol. 15 (1982), pp. 23–45.

[60] The process of competition to impose structures of meaning on patterns of events with implications for public policy is similar to what William H. Riker has called "heresthetics" in politics. See "The Heresthetics of Constitution-Making: The Presidency in 1787, with Comments on Determinism and Rational Choice," *American Political Science Review*, 78(1) (March 1984), pp. 1–16. This element of policy analysis is explored in greater detail in chapter 4.

[61] Richard Nelson, in *The Moon and The Ghetto*, puts the matter succinctly: "Persuasive analysis can urge and manuever, not merely guide, policy, by pointing to problems and providing interpretations of them. Analysis influences the way the world is seen; it has the power to delude, to misguide, as well as to provide direction to where we truly want to go." P. 15. Also see Aaron Wildavsky's *Speaking Truth to Power,* wherein analysis is described as a process of discovering and matching ends with viable means. For Wildavsky, analysis is *inherently* creative, rather than merely *reflective* of social preferences.

[62] For a related discussion of the requirement that dimensions of value exist in order for political valuation of outcomes through elections, see William H. Riker, *Liberalism Against Populism* (San Francisco, CA: Freeman, 1982), chapter 7.

The value or *placement* on that dimension can then be measured by appropriate willingness-to-pay analysis.[63]

The policy analysis paradigm, then, cannot supply the one best solution before social preferences have jelled and become coherent. Throughout that process, of course, analysis can play a significant role in shaping perceptions of patterns of events, defining "social problems." Nonetheless, in the initial stages of problem definition at least, there is no single optimal solution; the creative process of politics, in which analysis may play an important part, must have intervened first. Concerning these events, then, analysts scrupulously adhering to the policy analysis paradigm are most unlikely to unanimously offer a single best choice to decision makers. Even in a political setting ideally tailored to provision of analytical advice, analysts uniformly employing a fully developed policy analysis paradigm would leave considerable room for alternative interpretations of social problems and, therefore, relevant solutions. Of course, the existence of excess ideological baggage, widely spread among analysts, could be posited in order to predict a uniform, and therefore influential, provision of advice by analysts.[64] In that case, the uniformity would stem from covert consensus on values among analysts, masquerading as value-neutral policy analysis. The point here is that no basis for such uniformity is inherent in the foundations of policy analysis.

This section has surveyed the critiques of policy analysis that are based on the contention that analysts, as bearers of the policy analysis paradigm, will develop unrepresentative influence through the advice they provide policy makers. The dystopian argument holds that analysis will become increasingly influential as demand for advice burgeons, as bureaucratic control becomes more centralized in the hands of the analysts, and as the perfection of analytic techniques lead to uniform analytical advice—the one best solution. The available data indicate that analysis has not yet become *directly* influential in policy formulation, though it may have a more substantial *indirect* bearing on policy development. The promulgation of analysis has not led to centralization of power in the hands of the analysts; in fact, analysis has become more *decentralized* throughout the bureaucracy and the various governments of the United States. Most importantly, the policy analysis paradigm itself cannot provide a uniform best solution to policy problems until a pattern of events

---

[63] Note that a continuum of types of societies is implied here—from a highly consensual society in which common and stable preferences rapidly form, to one of prevalent disensus. The policy paradigm would more frequently be in a position of influence in the former.

[64] That argument is made, for example, by Ida Hoos, *Systems Analysis and Public Policy: A Critique,* and seems to be a crucial element of the argument advanced by Hawkesworth, *Theoretical Issues.*

has been interpreted and somewhat coherent and stable perceptions and social preferences have developed regarding those events.

Can we conclude that the dystopian fears of unrepresentative power by bureaucratic analysts are unfounded? On the basis of the evidence surveyed here, I think not. What has been shown is that analysis has *not yet* become as influential as the dystopians—and many proponents of analysis—have argued it would, and that such influence cannot stem from distillation of a uniform best solution to policy problems through important ranges of the policy process. In large part the difficulty in assessing the dystopian charges—as well as the claims of proponents of the policy analysis paradigm—stems from the fact that analysts and their work are viewed in varying degrees of abstraction, isolated from important structural incentives and realities of the policy environment. It is interesting and revealing that, for every generalization regarding the influence of analysts, there exists a counter generalization based on different presuppositions regarding the analytical environment; those who foresee significant independent influence by analysts imagine a world in which a key set of factors obtain, including analytical certainty, organizational independence of analysts from decision-making clients, and an identifiable and stable distribution of citizen preferences regarding the issue at hand. Those who see analysts as mandarins, on the other hand, presuppose a world in which analysts are unconstrained by analytical or procedural norms in the provision of advice, where analysts are dependent on clients, and where analytical uncertainty reigns supreme. Specific examples can be and are raised that conform with each characterization. Without attention to the systematic ways in which the structural incentives and realities of the policy environment may shift, little headway can be made toward resolving the issues raised by the dystopians.

The problem of unrepresentative influence is but one attack made on the policy analysis paradigm by its critics. Another theme of criticism, relying less on the presupposition of analytical influence, is that the widespread provision of analysis fundamentally distorts the processes by which social preferences are translated into public policy.

_____ 3.2 _____
THE NORMATIVE ASSAULT ON THE POLICY ANALYSIS PARADIGM

Drawing upon its origins in the social sciences and economics in particular, the policy analysis paradigm in pure form would provide only "objective" analysis and advice (that is, for a given policy option, the results of analysis would reflect the maximized sum of objectively measured and aggregated net benefits for the individuals constituting society). Thus, in an important sense, analysis is antipolitical; it is designed to remove social decision making "from the tumult of politics to the domain of putatively scientific, dispassionate inquiry."[65] Policy analysis is to be a vehicle whereby political conflict over public policy is reduced. At least in part, this element of the policy analysis paradigm reflects the stance of the prophets of the "end of ideology," contending that the withering of ideological differences will lead to a commonality of ends, wherein only means will remain in dispute.[66] According to two leading proponents of policy analysis:

> One objective of descriptive analysis is to narrow areas of disagreement in policy disputes. . . . Policy disagreements would lessen—and perhaps vanish—if we could predict with certainty the safety consequences of the breeder reactor, or the cost of annual upkeep of clay [tennis] courts, or whether a special shuttle bus for the elderly would be heavily used.[67]

Analysis can thus reduce political conflict by moving the debate from argument about values—about which "men can only ultimately fight"[68]—to discussion of predictions about means, which can be resolved through analysis.

Critics of policy analysis, however, point out that the policy analysis paradigm itself is a purveyor of a well-developed ideological perspective—that of individualistic utilitarianism. Further, utilitarianism has been under extensive attack within the field of moral philosophy.[69] Perhaps the most serious reservations concerning utilitarianism stem from its lack of distinction between values—push-pin and poetry are accorded equal status. Within the general critique of utilitarianism the great difficulty in handling such concepts

---

[65] Max Nieman, "The Ambiguous Role of Policy Analysis and an Illustrative Look at Housing Policy," (paper presented at the annual meeting of the Western Political Science Association, Sacramento, CA, April 1984).

[66] Daniel Bell, in *The End of Ideology* (New York: Free Press, 1960), makes this argument. Also see the editorial commentary by Bell and Irving Kristol in the first issue of *The Public Interest*, 1(1) (1965), pp. 3–5.

[67] Edith Stokey and Richard Zeckhauser, *A Primer for Policy Analysis* (New York: W.W. Norton, 1978), p. 261. Stokey and Zeckhauser approvingly quote Milton Friedman's *Essays in Positive Economics* (Chicago: Chicago University Press, 1953) that "Differences about policy among disinterested citizens derive predominantly from different predictions about the economic consequences of taking action—differences that can in principle be eliminated by the process of positive economics—rather than from fundamental differences about which men can ultimately only fight." p. 5.

[68] Friedman, *Essays in Positive Economics*, p. 5, op. cit., p. 261.

[69] See Samuel Gorovitz, ed., *Utilitarianism with Critical Essays* (Indianapolis, IN: Bobbs-Merrill, 1977) and J. J. C. Smart and Bernard Williams, eds., *Utilitarianism: For and Against* (Cambridge, MA: Cambridge University Press, 1973).

as rights and obligations, which have traditionally found bases outside the language of preference and utility, has received significant attention; can lying, unjustly punishing the innocent, or even repression of a small minority be justified on the basis that doing so increases *aggregate* well-being?[70] Though recent utilitarian theorists have sought to find a natural basis in enlightened self-interest for rights and obligations (e.g., derived from within Rawls' "veil of ignorance"), utilitarianism remains a problematic basis for prescriptive political theory.[71] This has led one critic of the policy analysis paradigm to exclaim:

> It is amazing that economists can proceed in unanimous endorsement of cost–benefit analysis as if unaware that their conceptual framework is highly controversial in the discipline from which it arose—moral philosophy.[72]

Mainstream critics of utilitarianism are joined in condemnation of the norms implicit in the techniques of the policy analysis paradigm by spokespersons of the political left and right. One fearsome prospect raised by dystopian critics is that the encroachment of ostensibly objective technique on the policy-making process will lead to "reverse adaptation" of individuals and society; technique that previously served the ends of mankind now works to smooth and homogenize human tastes and actions to make them more amenable to the application of technique.[73] The purported consequences of reverse adaptation take extreme form in the writings of the political left,

---

[70] In positive economics, as in moral philosophy, it is sometimes argued that utilitarianism is objective because it is derived from observation; people make choices and (it is assumed) in so doing act to maximize their own utility. Thus "positive" utilitarianism is held to be based on objective facts and verifiable theories. When extended from description to prescription, however, a problem arises: how is maximization of aggregate well-being to be justified as an overall goal of public policy? That, too, must be derived from preferences of individual citizens, unless such a preference is held to be a "natural" human sentiment. See the positive view and the utilitarian argument in J. S. Mill, *Utilitarianism*, in *Utilitarianism, Liberty, and Representative Government* (New York: E. P. Dutton, 1951), pp. 1–60; and William Riker and Peter C. Ordeshook, *An Introduction to Positive Political Theory* (Englewood Cliffs, NJ: Prentice-Hall, 1973), Chapter 2. For a critique of Mill, see William T. Bluhm, *Theories of the Political System* (Englewood Cliffs, NJ: Prentice-Hall, 1973), pp. 445–450.

[71] See John Rawls, *A Theory of Justice* (Cambridge, MA: Harvard University Press, 1971) and Brian Barry, *The Liberal Theory of Justice* (Oxford: Clarendon Press, 1973). More generally, see William T. Bluhm's "Liberalism as the Aggregation of Individual Preferences: Problems of Coherence and Rationality in Social Choice," (presented at a Conference on the Crisis of Liberal Democracy, SUNY—Geneseo, October 1983).

[72] Steven Kelman, "Cost–Benefit Analysis: An Ethical Critique," *Regulation,* 5(1) (January/February, 1981), pp. 33–40; p. 34. For a more general critique of the use of economic theory in public policy analysis, see Steven Rhoad's *The Economist's View of the World* (New York: Cambridge University Press, 1985).

[73] Langdon Winner, *Autonomous Technology: Technics Out-of-Control as a Theme in Political Thought* (Cambridge, MA: MIT Press, 1977), pp. 238–251.

expressed as "suffocation of those needs which demand liberation . . . while it sustains and absolves the destructive and repressive functioning of the affluent society."[74] No less dire results are expected from the right, for whom the application of ever more technique and social planning threatens to submerge the individual into the collective and to erode the foundations of individual liberty.[75]

When brought to bear more specifically on the techniques of the policy analysis paradigm, two major critical themes have focused on the norms implicit in analysis. These themes are intriguingly inconsistent, if not contradictory. Both critiques take exception to the self-proclaimed objective neutrality of policy analysis, finding its origins in the delusions of the "end of ideology" movement in the 1950s and 1960s. One critical theme, drawing heavily from the more general critiques of utilitarianism, holds that the techniques of analysis significantly distort the values and preferences of members of society that they are employed to measure and thus if employed will muddy the waters of representative policy making. Other critics, taking a similar point of departure, argue that the self-consciously value-neutral approach of the techniques of analysis is reflective of an apolitical (or anti-political) stance that, running aground on the resilient shoals of politics, has nullified the potential contributions of analysis. These themes of criticism are examined in turn.

The criticism that the dominant mode of policy analysis distorts public values and preferences takes aim at a number of practical and theoretical issues. One of the most common claims is that analytic techniques, in the zeal to quantify, tend to underemphasize those costs and benefits that are intangible or that are external to market valuation.[76] Though it may eventually prove technically feasible, valuation of non-marketed goods—such as rights or life—has proved difficult and consensus regarding appropriate techniques elusive.[77] Critics of analysis contend that these soft values tend to be ignored, while easily measured values are emphasized; when attempts at valuation *are* made, that valuation may be more akin to "subjective guesses" than objective

---

[74] Herbert Marcuse, *One Dimensional Man.* Hans Dreitzel takes a similar position in "Social Science and the Problem of Rationality: Notes on the Sociology of Technocrats," in *Politics and Society,* 2(2) (Winter 1972), pp. 165–182.

[75] See, for example, Friedrich A. Hayek, *The Road to Serfdom,* and Edward Banfield, "Policy Science as Metaphysical Madness," *Bureaucrats, Policy Analysts, Statesmen: Who Leads?* ed. Robert Goldwin, (Washington, DC: American Enterprise Institute, 1980), pp. 1–19.

[76] See Laurence Tribe, "Trial by Mathematics: Precision and Ritual in the Legal Process," *Harvard Law Review,* vol. 84 (1971), pp. 1361–1365; Laurence Tribe, "Policy Science: Analysis or Ideology?" *Philosophy and Public Affairs,* vol. 2, (Fall 1972), pp. 67–110; Kelman, "Cost–Benefit Analysis," pp. 33–40; and Paris and Reynolds, *Policy Inquiry,* pp. 118–123.

[77] See Richard Zeckhauser, "Procedures for Valuing Lives," *Public Policy,* 23(4), (Fall 1975), pp. 419–464.

science.[78] This view was eloquently expressed by Supreme Court Justice William J. Brennan in dissent to a recent Court decision limiting the exclusion of evidence illegally obtained by police:

> The Court seeks to justify this [limit on the exclusion of evidence] on the ground that the "costs" of adhering to the exclusionary rule exceed the "benefits." But the language of deterrence and cost/benefit analysis, if used indiscriminately, can have a narcotic effect. It creates an illusion of technical precision and ineluctability. . . . When the Court's analysis is examined carefully, however, it is clear that we have not been treated to an honest assessment of the merits of the exclusionary rule, but have instead been drawn into a curious world where "costs" of excluding illegally obtained evidence loom to exaggerated heights and "benefits" of such exclusion are made to disappear with a mere wave of the hand.[79]

Another cause for concern among critics of analysis is grounded in perceived flaws in methods used for the aggregation and comparison of values. As described in chapter 2, ideal analysis would express the value of the costs and benefits of policy options in a common metric, preferably dollars. These valuations are to be accomplished through determination of an individual's willingness-to-pay to obtain (avoid) the benefit (cost). This approach permits the comparison of a wide range of policies over all affected values. The policy option that maximizes aggregate well-being (dollars) is selected, and those who lose would (ideally) be compensated through lump-sum transfers. Critics contend, however, that this approach ignores the *structure* of values; it ignores the possibility that certain values may have, for example, a lexicographical ordering in which some minimum level of good x must be obtained before *any* x will be traded for good y.[80] Put differently, no amount of y can compensate for the loss of x below some threshold. According to Laurence Tribe, in such circumstances

> [T]he very concept of proper distribution (of x and y) must now be defined not with respect to the single homogeneous entity called 'wealth' but with respect to the *enjoyment* of these rights as such.[81]

Where such orderings hold, Tribe argues, the principle of compensation of the losers by the winners fails; discontinuous preference orderings for rights

---

[78] Paris and Reynolds, *Policy Inquiry,* p. 120.

[79] From the case *United States* v. *Leon,* 104 S. Ct. 3430 (1984).

[80] Laurence Tribe compares trades of "breathing opportunities" with "polluting opportunities." See "Policy Science: Analysis or Ideology?", *Public Affairs,* pp. 87–88.

[81] Ibid., p. 88. Emphasis in original. Tribe, in the tradition of Ludwig Wittgenstein, seeks to find "deep structures" in human values, analogous to Wittgenstein's culturally localized "bedrock" in language games, that indicate what kinds of social preference orderings can exist, and the principles considered therein can be related. Pp. 93–94.

cannot be reduced to the same "undifferentiated mass" of total welfare as continuous preference orderings for marketable goods and services.

Taking a somewhat different tack, one particularly compelling critique of benefit–cost analysis points out that, in order for analysis to be applied to a specific policy, the analyst must decide *which preferences count*—that is, which preferences have "standing" in benefit–cost analysis.[82] In the abstract, benefit–cost analysis should count *all* benefits and costs associated with the policy under scrutiny—regardless of who bears those benefits and costs. In point of fact, however, analysts routinely reject many preferences as illegitimate; the lost value to criminals of illegal activity is usually not counted as a cost in analyses of criminal justice policies,[83] nor are the benefits or costs of immigration policies for illegal aliens. Debates over how to count benefits and costs for future generations, inanimate objects (e.g., rivers), nonhumans (e.g., endangered species), fetuses, and others are indicative of the breadth of the standing problem.[84]

For the dominant policy analysis paradigm, the standing issue presents a particularly thorny problem; how are analysts to decide which preferences to include or exclude? Given that *some* preferences are socially (and politically) unacceptable, the analyst must make such a decision, and making such a decision forces the analyst outside of the (relatively) safe domain of efficiency analysis. *Some* criteria of justice or equity must be invoked, at least implicitly. The great danger here is that analysts' criteria of justice will masquerade behind a facade of objectivity and thus be opaque to decision makers, the public, and even analysts themselves.

A special case of the distortion of the structure of values by techniques of the policy analysis paradigm concerns the focus on the end-result of policy (maximizing net social welfare) to the exclusion of focus on the *procedure* by which policy choice is made. That procedure is held to be of intrinsic value in

---

[82] See Duncan MacRae, Jr., and Dale Whittington's "The Issue of Standing in Cost–Benefit Analysis," *Journal of Policy Analysis and Management*, vol. 5, no. 4 (Summer 1986), pp. 665–682; also see their "Assessing Preferences in Cost–Benefit Analysis: Reflections on Rural Water Supply Evaluation in Haiti," *Journal of Policy Analysis and Management*, vol. 7, no. 2, (Winter 1988), pp. 246–263. Peter Brown, in "Ethics and Education for the Public Service in a Liberal State," argues that the issues of standing and legitimacy of preferences are essential points-of-entry for ethics in public policy analysis. *Journal of Policy Analysis and Management*, vol. 6, no. 1 (Fall 1986), pp. 56–68.

[83] A noteworthy exception is David Long, Charles Mallar, and Craig Thornton, "Evaluating the Benefits and Costs of the Job Corps," *Journal of Policy Analysis and Management*, vol. 1, no. 1 (Fall 1981), pp. 55–56.

[84] See David L. Weimer and Aiden R. Vining, *Policy Analysis: Concepts and Practice* (Englewood Cliffs, NJ: Prentice-Hall, 1989), pp. 78–79, for a general discussion of the legitimacy—and the related problem of interdependent utilities—in policy analysis.

democratic societies,[85] independently of the end-result of policy. Policy analysts, the critics argue, typically justify process

> [E]ither in purely formal, positivist terms or in terms of a superior tendency to maximize aggregate satisfaction in the end, rather than in terms intrinsic to the process itself in its constitutive function of defining substantive human roles, rights and relationships and structuring their evolution over time.[86]

Perhaps most notably, the *legitimacy* accorded decisions reached through sanctioned procedures may be largely independent of the substantive content of policy. Cognizant only of end-results, analysts may fail to capture an essential element of value. In this view, the value of a policy choice cannot be ascertained in absence of consideration of the procedure from which it is derived.

Equally troubling to these critics, the very application of techniques of the policy analysis paradigm to values subject to discontinuous preference orders serves to *erode* those values. One critic argues that widely held social rights or decision procedures are withheld from the run of more common questions by excluding them from the benefit–cost calculus.[87] To attempt to impute a dollar value to such "specially valued things" eliminates their special status, thus reducing their value. "Cost benefit analysis thus may be like the thermometer that, when placed in a liquid to be measured, itself changes the liquid's temperature."[88] In this view, analysis not only distorts human values, but destroys them as well.

Critics are concerned that the policy analysis paradigm may erode more than end values, however. An increased reliance on the essentially static and passive measures of individual preferences, as typically conducted for benefit–cost analysis, diminishes or eliminates the role of active debate and expression in a public forum as a means to develop and channel citizen preferences. As noted in chapter 2, the conception of democratic governance implicit in the policy analysis paradigm envisages an existing universe of individual preference functions that may be tapped in order to "discover" optimum policies.[89] The role of the analyst, using shadow prices to inform willingness-to-pay

---

[85] Some theorists disagree: Hayek believes democratic political institutions have value in as much as they contribute to the preservation of liberty. See *The Constitution of Liberty* (Chicago: University of Chicago Press, 1960), pp. 104–106.

[86] Tribe, "Policy Science: Analysis or Ideology?", *Public Affairs,* p. 82.

[87] Kelman, "Cost–Benefit Analysis," *Regulation.* Also see Arthur Okun, *Equality and Efficiency: The Big Tradeoff* (Washington, DC: Brookings, 1975), pp. 6–30.

[88] Kelman, "Cost–Benefit Analysis," *Regulation,* p. 38.

[89] Though the policy paradigm does not preclude public debate prior to measurement of preferences, the techniques developed—particularly market and shadow prices—indicate that such debate is not an integral part of the process.

analysis, is to determine the value of particular options based on the given distribution of tastes. This vision of democracy, with its emphasis on accurate *reflection* of individual tastes in public policies, radically departs from the conception of the *process* of democracy—and participation in particular—as important to the formation of tastes, the legitimization of public choice, and the full development of the political individual.[90] At bottom, the emphasis on process in democracy is based on the contention that the deliberative process is more than a summation of tastes. It is a process by which individuals *arrive* at policy preferences through exposure to the preferences of others and reasoned discourse,[91] or through the competition for votes and necessity for compromise. Preferences are formed, as well as expressed, as they are found through political processes.

The policy analytic techniques employed to measure citizen preferences depart from the process views of democracy in a number of ways. Benefit–cost analysis, for example, commonly employs market prices, or estimated shadow prices, to calculate the value of benefits produced or resources used in public policy. Taking a more direct approach, many major cities now incorporate annual or biennial surveys of citizen opinions on tax and expenditure issues as a routine part of policy development.[92] Thus, indirect measure through price or price estimates, or direct solicitation of preferences through surveys, supplement or replace more traditional processes of politics.

One important criticism takes direct exception to the use of prices—either actual or estimates—as indexes of citizen preferences for public policies. Market prices are the result of a myriad of private, individual choices regarding consumption or provision of the good in question. In using those prices, critics contend, the analyst wrongly presumes that the citizen values goods exchanged in purely private transactions identically with the value of those things in *public* use. Thus, one critic contends, policy analysts "insidiously" assume that ". . . there should be no difference between private behavior and

---

[90] The development of the political individual as a primary end of the process of democratic politics is emphasized in the theory of participatory democracy. See Carole Pateman, *Participation and Democratic Theory* (Cambridge: Cambridge University Press, 1970); and C. George Benello and Dimitrios Roussopoulus, eds., *The Case for Participatory Democracy* (New York: Grossman, 1971).

[91] An important distinction between classical democratic theories and the approach of the policy analysis paradigm is that the former typically are gravely concerned with the origins of citizen preferences, whereas the policy analysis paradigm takes these preferences as "given." Thus there is no place in the policy analysis paradigm (or the economic theories of democracy that it emulates) for the assurance of long-term political stability through *channeling* preferences. For that reason the policy analysis paradigm and all theories of politics that take preferences as given are best understood as *partial* political theories.

[92] See F. William Hess, "Listening to the City: Citizen Surveys," *Urban Affairs Papers*, vol. 2 (Summer 1980), pp. 1–9; Brian Stipak, "Local Government's Use of Citizen Surveys," *Public Administration Review*, vol. 40 (September/October 1980), pp. 521–525.

the behavior we display in public life."[93] Social values that for some reason are not expressed in private behavior are excluded from the calculus of public decision, and therefore the valuations reached through benefit–cost analysis are flawed.[94] More importantly, the use of private preference and behavior reflected in price as a guide for public decision would seem to lock public decision into the pattern set by private behavior; rather than exploring what values *ought* to be served, public policy would be a reflexive mimic of existing private behavior. The formative role of politics as a shaper of public values is thus eroded.

The use of citizen surveys as a device for policy formation is similarly susceptible to attack for its exclusion of the formative qualities of process. Surveys are akin to snapshot photographs; a well-designed survey, asking the right questions, may measure the preferences of the respondents at the time of the survey and—if not methodologically flawed—adequately reflect the likely responses of the broader population.[95] However, surveys are *passive* measures, for which a sample of citizens' answers are solicited to policy questions about which the respondents may or may not have devoted significant thought and reflection. The important presumption underlying the use of surveys in policy formulation is that coherent preferences on policy issues actually exist, preferences that are susceptible to measurement and that are reasonably stable. Critics have argued that these presumptions are in error for a broad array of public issues, including the most important issues.[96] On most complex policy issues, the nature of public opinion may be better described as a "natural force," like ". . . currents of the air or ocean, constantly changing in their contours and directions."[97] Uncertainty, lack of information, the compelling novelty of the survey situation, and question construction and phrasing all serve in many cases to make "public opinion"

---

[93] Kelman, "Cost–Benefit Analysis," *Regulation*, p. 38.

[94] Strictly speaking, this is a mistaken view of benefit–cost analysis. A perfect analysis would capture these excluded social values and would treat them analogously to externalities of market price. While conceptually straightforward, this would prove difficult to accomplish in practice, and therefore the criticism may have more weight in practice than it does in theory.

[95] Surveys are, of course, subject to serious limitations when attempts are made to measure attitudes or preferences that do not have some kind of behavioral counterpart. Questions with a tangible referent (e.g., regarding voter preference, or consumer behavior) can be measured with reliable results. Amorphous questions regarding attitudes or preferences without such a tangible referent are quite slippery and can be more responsive to question wording than to substantive content. See the wide range of responses given by West Germans to questions regarding installation of the Pershing missiles in Everett Ladd, "Question Wording Makes A Difference: German Public Attitudes Toward Deployment," in *Public Opinion*, 6(6) (December/January 1984), pp. 38–39.

[96] See Leo Bogart, "No Opinion, Don't Know, Maybe, No Answer," *Public Opinion Quarterly*, vol. 31, (Fall 1967), pp. 332–45; Christopher Achen, "Mass Political Attitudes and the Survey Response," *American Political Science Review*, 69(3) Fall 1975, pp. 1218–1231; and Henry Farlie, "Galloping Toward Dead Center," *The New Republic*, 178(4) (April 8, 1978), pp. 18–21.

[97] Bogart, "No Opinion," *Public Opinion*, p. 334.

on policy issues unintelligible if not misleading. The point of this line of criticism is that the well-formed public opinion presumed to exist will in many cases be absent; the development of stable and intelligible public preferences occurs through the workings of the political process—the public forum for raising, defining, and debating public issues. Surveys used in absence of this process, or surveys used to *replace* this process, will fail to find—or what is worse, will fabricate—what does not exist.

In summary, both the use of market prices and survey results as the basis for public policy are criticized because they exclude what critics contend is the essential formative role in citizen preference formation performed by the policy process. Exclusion of that step confuses public and private choice, excludes the possibility of reasoned debate over what values *ought* to be inculcated (i.e., what kind of people should we become?), and in many cases inhibits the very formulation of public opinion. In addition, analysts are forced to make decisions on the standing of preferences, requiring choice among criteria of justice—a task for which the analyst is *not* prepared by the dominant policy analysis paradigm. Furthermore, it is charged, the techniques of analysis distort existing preferences, reducing complex relations within and among human values to a structureless mass. Finally, in application of the techniques of analysis, soft or intangible values are ignored or underemphasized when compared to more tangible values. Overall this indictment of the sins of analytical techniques—sins of omission as well as commission—leads critics to believe that we are in danger of *too much* analysis,[98] and that the techniques of analysis must be transformed to overcome "the ideological structure of particular errors that . . . have flowed from the basic axioms of policy analysis and related techniques. . . ."[99] Analysis, therefore, distorts public preferences in formulation and expression, thereby threatening the effective operation of the democratic process.

How have the advocates of the policy analysis paradigm responded to these criticisms? Regarding the overall success of their venture, the analysts have been fairly contrite. Viewing the potential contribution of analysis more favorably than do the critics, the defenders acknowledge that the apolitical stance of the policy analysis paradigm has inhibited the ability of analysis to contend with the processes of real-world politics. Attempts to provide only

---

[98] Kelman, "Cost–Benefit Analysis," *Regulation,* p. 40.

[99] Tribe, "Policy Science: Analysis or Ideology?" *Public Affairs,* p. 106. Tribe suggests several reforms: (1) elimination of the attempt to provide objective analysis in favor of a more impassioned and self-consciously value-laden approach, and (2) the adoption of a ". . . subtler, more holistic and more complex style of problem solving, . . . relying at each stage on the careful articulation of a wide range of interrelated values and constraints through the development of several distinct 'perspectives' on a given problem, each couched in an idiom true to its internal structure rather than translated into some 'common denominator'" (p. 107). Thus Tribe has in mind a radical transformation of policy analysis.

dispassionate advice in the interest of maximizing net utility, ignoring the interests and influence of the various actors in the political process, policy analysts are often relegated to an insignificant role in the political process.[100] The range of specific self-criticisms of this type is considerable, extending from problems with the timing of the provision of advice,[101] to lack of salesmanship of the results of analysis,[102] to misperception of the process of advice-giving itself.[103] The point of these self-criticisms is that by attempting to remain dispassionate and aloof from the policy process, the beneficial contributions of the policy analysis paradigm are muted or lost in the roar of the political fray.

When responding to the more specific charges of the critics of the policy analysis paradigm, however, the analysts take off their gloves, and debate is joined. Though fought over many years and issues, the dynamic of this debate has remained consistent: critics, working from the logical implications of the techniques of the policy analysis paradigm, point out potentially serious deficiencies of those implications when applied to democratic public decision making. Proponents of the policy analysis paradigm have typically responded that the critics have extended the logical implication of policy techniques *too* far, and that these techniques are merely tools to be applied *along with* more traditional moral values and decision rules. In a recent and illustrative debate, for instance, a critic of the techniques of policy analysis charged that the underlying philosophy of benefit—cost analysis—individualistic utilitarianism—would permit what are considered to be morally reprehensible acts in the interest of maximizing utility.[104] A defender of those techniques responded

> [the critic] . . . hints that 'economists' are so morally numb as to believe that a routine cost—benefit analysis could justify killing widows and orphans, or abridging freedom of speech, or outlawing simple evidences of piety or friendship. But there is nothing in the theory or practice of cost—benefit analysis to justify that judgment. Treatises on the subject make clear that certain ethical or political principles may irreversibly dominate the advantages and disadvantages capturable by cost—benefit analysis.[105]

---

[100] Martin Rein and Sheldon White, "Can Policy Research Help Policy?" *The Public Interest*, vol. 49 (Fall 1977), pp. 119–136.

[101] See James S. Coleman, *Policy Research in The Social Sciences* (Morristown, NJ: General Learning Press, 1972).

[102] See Howell S. Baum's "Analysts and Planners Must Think Organizationally," *Policy Analysis*, 6(4) (Fall 1980), pp. 479–494; and Robert Behn's "Policy Analysis and Policy Politics," *Policy Analysis*, 7(2) (Spring 1981), pp. 199–226.

[103] Rein and White, "Policy Research: Belief and Doubt," *The Public Interest*, and Weiss, "Research for Policy's Sake," *Social Sciences*.

[104] Kelman, "Cost—Benefit Analysis," *Regulation*, pp. 33–36.

[105] Robert M. Solow, "Defending Cost—Benefit Analysis," *Regulation*, 5(2) (March/April 1981), p. 41. Solow did not indicate which treatises to which he was referring.

In other words, the economists and policy analysts, like other people, have recourse to "other ethical or political principles" that may overwhelm the result of benefit–cost analysis.[106]

In a further response to their critics, the proponents of the policy analysis paradigm address the relationship between the techniques of analysis and political process. Far from *precluding* such processes, the analysts argue, the use of analytic techniques can serve as but one "loop" in the iterative process of arriving at a decision.[107] Policy goals are specified and provided to analysts, who then determine what policy options best achieve these goals. Options in hand, the analysts submit their results to policy makers, who again assess goals in light of necessary means. Thus analysis plays a constructive and informative role in the policy process.[108]

The broadest rejoinder to the critics of the policy analysis paradigm is that, though there may be limitations or flaws in the techniques of analysis, tough decisions regarding the use of scarce resources must be made, and such techniques as benefit–cost analysis are useful aids to such decisions. As three federal analysts argued in defense of benefit–cost analysis in a recent debate

> [W]e do not dispute that cost–benefit analysis is highly imperfect. We would welcome a better guide to public policy, a guide that would be efficient, morally attractive, and certain to ensure that government follow the dictates of the governed.[109]

But, they add, no such better guide is evident. Says another defender of benefit–cost analysis

> [Benefit–cost analysis] is not the way to perfect truth, but the world is not a perfect place, and I regard it as the height of folly to react to the greater (though still incomplete) rigour which [benefit–cost analysis] requires of us

---

[106] In another response to the same critique of benefit-cost analysis, Robert Nisbit argued that utilitarianism had transcended the crass hedonism of Jeremy Bentham in the writings of J. S. Mill. See "Defending Cost–Benefit Analysis," *Regulation*, 5(2) (March/April 1981), pp. 42–43. Nisbit points out that Mill acknowledged a class of overriding utilities, including liberty, that are to be treated as different in kind as well as degree . Nisbit fails to point out the problematic basis of Mill's overriding utilities, which for Mill arise out of education and experience, and are to be specified by those who have the most of both. See Mill, *Utilitarianism;* and Bluhm, "Individual Preferences," pp. 445–448.

[107] See Allan Williams, "Cost–Benefit Analysis: Bastard Science? And/Or Insidious Poison in the Body Politick?", in *Public Expenditure and Policy Analysis*, eds. Robert Haveman and Julius Margolis, 2nd ed. (Chicago: Rand McNally, 1977), pp. 519–545.

[108] This comes quite close to the role for analysis expressed by Aaron Wildavsky in his book *Speaking Truth to Power*.

[109] See the arguments of Gerard Butler, John Calter, and Pauline Ippolito, "Defending Cost–Benefit Analysis," *Regulation*, 5(2) (March/April 1981), pp. 41–42.

by shrieking "1984" and putting our heads hopefully back into the sand (or the clouds) . . .[110]

The critics of analysis are thus viewed as hypercritical, rejecting the promising techniques of the policy analysis paradigm for fear of overblown imperfections, and having nothing to offer in their stead.

In a nutshell, proponents, critics and defenders all evoke different visions of the role analysis is to play. The proponents have been reformists. As indicated in chapter 2, the partial political theory underlying the policy analysis paradigm suggests sweeping changes in political institutions in order to better map the social welfare function into public policies. At the very least, the techniques of policy analysis are seen as a significant corrective for the practice of politics-as-usual. For their part, the critics of the policy analysis paradigm take the proponents (or perhaps, the more extreme proponents) at face value; what would the world look like, they ask, should the policy analysis paradigm be fully implemented without restraint in public policy making? Their conclusion is that such a world would be dreadful. Defenders, finally, scoff at the critics' concern, knowing full well that analysis and analytical techniques are far from singularly influential in public decisions. They point out that policy analysis competes with other institutions, theories and methods for policy making that—though inferior—predominate now and probably will in the future. The defenders need not take the critics seriously because analysis is seen by the defenders as but one all-too-insignificant piece among many in the Rube Goldberg policy machine; in the defenders' view, the critics' excesses stem from erroneously believing that economists are "morally numb," and from "having their heads in the sand (or clouds)."

The import of this debate is that it reveals an important escape valve for practitioners of policy analysis. As long as analysis is but one voice—more often than not crying in the wilderness—its potential excesses need not be of great concern. Though both critics and defenders can point to instances in the use of analysis that bolster their respective cases,[111] rarely have either given sufficient attention to what general sets of circumstances in the policy environment lead to a greater or lesser role for analysis. Should such circumstances be identified, it would prove possible to apply the critiques of analysis with a sharper analytical scalpel. That effort is made in the chapters of Part II.

---

[110] Allan Williams, "Cost–Benefit Analysis," *Public Expenditure*, p. 543.

[111] More broadly, critics could observe the Reagan Administration's Executive Order 12291, which requires federal agencies to produce benefit–cost analyses for all "major regulations." Defenders, in turn can refer to the vast literature on the limits and failures of analysis to influence policy, as cited above. For a compelling argument for the defenders' case, see the concluding chapters of Greenberger, et al., *Caught Unawares*.

_____ 3.3 _____

STRAINS ON DEMOCRATIC PROCESSES

The critiques of analysis reviewed thus far have been concerned with the effects of analysis on the shape and content of public policies. A quite different set of qualms is raised regarding the effect of the attempt to employ analysis—regardless of whether it is deemed "successful" or substantively influential by its practitioners—on political processes and institutions.

One important concern is that analysis will make entry into the political debate more costly, excluding the lay public and inhibiting reasoned debate among public officials. In very broad terms, the employment of analysis is accused of increasing the perceived complexity of social problems, as well as their potential solutions, all the while clouding the meaning of the debate with technical jargon. This strains institutional processes even if analysis has little substantive influence. According to Edward Banfield:

> If the policy maker himself is impervious to policy analysis, its impact upon *policy* may nevertheless be great. Indeed, the proliferation of policy science is making policy problems more numerous and complex.[112]

Noting the progression of increasingly sophisticated policy studies focused on education since the Supreme Court decision in *Brown* v. *Board of Education,* Banfield contends:

> The quality of the research improved as research went on, but the outcome was usually not greater clarity about what to think or do, but, instead, a greater sense of complexity, a shifting in the forms of the problem, and more 'mystification' in the interpretation of findings. . . . Perhaps we are justified in concluding . . . that it is easily possible to have too much of a good thing: that an analytical society may increase its problems while decreasing its ability to cope with them.[113]

A plethora of newly discovered problems of increased complexity and mystification reduce the competence of lay citizens to understand, let alone participate in, the pressing political debates of the time. Such citizens are gradually excluded from the debate, eclipsed by analytically sophisticated insiders and/or analysts. Moreover, the sense that public institutions generally are competent to grapple with pressing public issues is undermined. Though

---

[112] Edward Banfield, "Policy Science," *Who Leads?,* pp. 13–14.

[113] Ibid., p. 14. In their book, *Usable Knowledge* (New Haven, CT: Yale University Press, 1979), Charles Lindblom and David Cohen agree. They argue that "the usual effect of [policy analysis] is to raise new issues, stimulate new debate, and multiply the complexities of the social problems at hand." (p. 40) Neither Banfield nor Lindblom and Cohen accuse analysis of generating misinformation; apparently they believe the policy problems faced are genuinely complex. The evil of analysis in this view is that it generates even more calls for complex public intervention.

important elements of liberal democracy may be preserved under such circumstances,[114] the reduction of the sphere of participatory democracy encroaches on the possible developmental aspects of politics.[115] In the words of one theorist, the eclipse of public debate by a policy elite of the analytically sophisticated would "deny survival to an entire class of human impulses"— impulses to engage in meaningful participation in decisions that affect one's life.[116] Thus, an unintended side effect of policy analysis may be to erect barriers in the way of important ends of participatory democracy.

In part the apparent complexity of policy problems confronting citizens and representatives may be spurious. Fundamental questions of policy—both empirical and normative—may become submerged under a veil of complex data and equations as models are used to defend implicit ideological perspectives rather than inform the policy debate.[117] Arguments over data and modeling assumptions then replace discussion of the fundamental questions involved, impoverishing the political debate.[118] For example, a lay person or legislator could be excused for believing a debate over the likely supply response of the natural gas industry to a change in price to be largely technical in nature—a "fact" to be determined by experts that, combined with judgment, could facilitate consensus in debate over regulation of natural gas. However, in the 1978 debates over the National Gas Policy Act, that question became the *focus* of debate. Those who advocated unfettered allocation of natural gas via the market system employed studies and experts predicting large increases in gas reserves from small price increases; ample supplies would be assured at only moderately higher prices to consumers. Those advocating continued regulation used analyses showing little if any response of supply to price, leading to large price increases and little additional supply.[119] Those who understand the modeling techniques, then, can wage debate

---

[114] Giovanni Sartori argues that the gradual displacement of citizens by experts in important policy areas is inevitable, but not to be feared "as long as what is essential—and therefore *must* be controlled—is kept within the area of democratic control." Though it is clear that Sartori would include the definition of ultimate goals of public policy among what must be controlled, he offers no guidelines for where the line between ultimate and intermediate goals should be drawn. *Democratic Theory*, pp. 404–410.

[115] See Peter Bachrach, *The Theory of Democratic Elitism: A Critique* (Boston: Little, Brown, 1967), for a discussion of the ill effects of an elite—no matter how knowledgeable and well-intentioned—on participatory democracy.

[116] Henry Kariel, *The Promise of Politics* (Englewood Cliffs, NJ: Prentice-Hall, 1966), p. 85.

[117] For a general discussion of ideological uses of quantitative models, see Martin Greenberger, et al., *Models in the Policy Process* (New York: Russell Sage Foundation, 1976), p. 337.

[118] A detailed example of this process is provided in Michael Malbin, "Congress, Policy Analysis, and Natural Gas Regulation: A Parable About Fig Leaves," in *Bureaucrats, Policy Analysts, Statesmen: Who Leads?*, ed., Robert Goldwin, (Washington, DC: American Enterprise Institute, 1980), pp. 62 87.

[119] Ibid.

over ideological issues under the guise of impartial analysis—distorting and submerging the real issues of importance. The "end of ideology" ethos of analysis may contribute to this tendency by stressing "facts" to the exclusion of "values." In the view of one critic:

> Members of Congress apparently are *ashamed* to discuss public issues without clutching the numbers provided by economists. In a post-Weberian world, where "facts" and "values" are thought to have distinct cognitive foundations, politicians are embarrassed about basing political choices on principles of justice, or "basic values." Or they are ashamed to acknowledge it when they debate the issues in public.[120]

The result—an unintended side effect of analysis—is that policy debate becomes opaque to citizen understanding, weakening an already strained representative link in policy formulation.

Critics contend that the strain imposed on political institutions by the employment of policy analysis extends still further, threatening the very organizational processes by which information is gathered and processed for policy decision making. A number of scholars have taken exception to the goal of comprehensive rationality imbedded in the policy analysis paradigm, arguing that it would overwhelm the data-gathering and decision-making capabilities of public officials.[121] In this view, actual public decision making is rarely, if ever, comprehensive and fully integrated across policy areas; rather, policy is made in incremental steps and minute departures from prior policies, and issue areas tend to be segmented. This process allows decision makers to concentrate on familiar and better known experience (e.g., last year's budget), reduces the number of options requiring consideration, and dramatically reduces the complexity of the decision. Within this process, contention among political values and compromise among many competing interests are central factors.[122]

Attempts to impose the comprehensive rationality of the policy analysis paradigm clash radically with the incremental process of policy making. Under the former, demands on the cognitive processes of decision makers would be overwhelming; in strict accordance with the norms of the policy

---

[120] Ibid., p. 85.

[121] The chief proponents of this view have been Aaron Wildavsky and Charles Lindblom. See Wildavsky's "The Political Economy of Efficiency: Cost–Benefit Analysis, Systems Analysis, and Program Budgeting," in *Public Administration Review,* 26(4) (December 1966), pp. 292–310; and more generally *The Politics of the Budgetary Process* 3rd ed. (Boston: Little, Brown, 1979). See Lindblom's "The Science of Muddling Through," *Public Administration Review,* 19(2) (Spring 1959), pp. 79–88; and (with David Baybrooke) *A Strategy of Decision* (New York: Free Press, 1963).

[122] The most well-developed description of this process is in Wildavsky's *The Politics of the Budgetary Process,* chapters 2 and 3. Also see Lindblom's *The Policy-Making Process,* (Englewood Cliffs, NJ: Prentice-Hall, 1968).

analysis paradigm, all conceivable goals and options for achieving those goals would be assayed, keeping the *relative* worth of all goals sought simultaneously and explicitly in mind. Reliance on prior-years' activities as a base from which to proceed in calculations would be forbidden; the costs and benefits of each policy would need to be reviewed "from the ground up" in each budgetary cycle. Thus Wildavsky says of PPBS, "Failure is built into its very nature because it requires ability to perform cognitive operations that are beyond present human (or mechanical) capacities."[123]

Successful implementation of the comprehensive rationality of the policy analysis paradigm would require a radical transformation of the current political process—a transformation that critics find to be both undesirable and (given the current distribution of power) unlikely.[124] Because political institutions will not and (according to these critics) *should* not be adapted to comprehensive analysis, attempts to impose such analysis serve primarily to increase the load on decision makers and bureaucrats with no discernible improvement in policy decisions.[125] Reams of data are produced, reports generated, hearings held, and countless hours spent in a fruitless and "irrational" bid for comprehensive rationality.

Attempts to implant the policy analysis paradigm in the policy making process may increase the strain on decision makers and institutions in yet another way. As noted earlier, Banfield has argued that the use of policy analysis may actually contribute to the increase in the number and complexity of policy problems placed on the political agenda,[126] increasing the flood of issues policy makers must address. Attempts by legislators to contend with the rising issue load have been responsible in part for the often minute separation and specialization of legislative functions through the committee and subcommittee system.[127] Within that specialized system, legislators have sought to manage the work load through reliance on committee and personal staff experts to sift and distill relevant information. Rather than easing the load on individual legislators, the reliance on expert staff has *further* expanded the work load, reducing legislators' time for reflection and delibera-

---

[123] Wildavsky, *Politics of the Budgetary Process*, p. 199.

[124] In agreement with the dystopian critics discussed earlier in this chapter, Wildavsky argues that full implementation of the policy paradigm would require an extensive centralization and concentration of governmental power in the executive. See ibid., pp. 188–191.

[125] Ibid., pp. 207–221.

[126] Banfield, "Policy Science," *Who Leads*, p. 14. Also see Lindblom and Cohen, *Usable Knowledge*, pp. 40–54.

[127] For a discussion of this process, see Steven Hazberle, "The Institutionalization of the Subcommittee in the U.S. House of Representatives," *Journal of Politics*, 40(4) (November 1978), pp. 1054–1065; and Norman Ornstein, "Causes and Consequences of Congressional Change: Subcommittee Reform in the House of Representatives, 1970–1973," in *Congress in Change: Evolution and Reform*, ed. Norman Ornstein, (New York: Praeger, 1975), pp. 88–114.

tion. The reason, according to Michael Malbin, is that staffers tend to have their own agendas. By virtue of the expertise and contacts acquired, staff positions tend to be stepping stones to more rewarding careers. In order to rise to prominence within their particular policy subcommunity, expert staffers must offer up issues for consideration, criticism, or legislative proposal.[128] The result is a plethora of issues, hearings, and amendments for the already busy legislator to consider. As put by Malbin:

> [I]nstead of freeing the members to concentrate, the staffs contribute to the frenetic pace of congressional life that pulls members in different directions, reduces the time available for joint deliberation, and makes concentration all but impossible. . . . The situation feeds on itself. The members need staff because they have so little time to concentrate, but the new work created by the staff takes even more of the members' time, indirectly elevating the power of the Washington issue networks in which the staff play so prominent a role.[129]

Thus analysis is implicated in a process of institutional overload within policy-making institutions—particularly Congress. The use of analysis per se adds to the number and complexity of perceived policy problems and the cognitive load that decision makers are expected to carry. The increased load leads decision makers to hire more expert staff, which in turn further exacerbates the work load problem. It is not hard to imagine such a system, caught in a self-reinforcing cycle, collapsing from the weight of superfluous analysis.

A less apocalyptic and more reasonable concern is that the use of analysis and additions to expert staff tend to rigidify and increase the importance of issue networks, or policy subsystems, that permeate the policy process. Recent study of the American political process has indicated that analysts and experts on given policy issue-areas coalesce into loose "webs of influence" that work to "influence, provoke and guide the exercise of power."[130] Such policy subsystems are highly informal, the members of which are defined by their shared knowledge of specific policy areas. Working from private as well as public positions, members of the subsystem know one another, speak the same language, and—while often not agreeing on the optimal policy—have a shared understanding of the important concepts and features of the policy issue. The boundaries of the subcommunities may shift as perceptions of underlying policy issues change, as issues previously thought distinct are

---

[128] Michael Malbin, *Unelected Representatives: Congressional Staff and the Future of Representative Government* (New York: Basic Books, 1980), pp. 163–165.

[129] Ibid., pp. 243–244.

[130] Hugh Heclo, "Issue Networks in the Executive Establishment," in *The New American Political System*, ed. Anthony King (Washington, DC: American Enterprise Institute, 1978), pp. 87–124; p. 103.

merged, or as specialized subissues split and develop subcommunities in their own right.

Within policy subsystems, the increasingly technical nature of policy debates, and of the language and techniques used in these debates, would tend to reduce eligible and contributing participants to the sophisticated few. These higher barriers to entry may serve to limit still further the infusion of varying viewpoints in the already winnowed perspectives of the policy subsystem. To the extent that such policy subsystems play a significant role in the development and implementation of policies, as suggested by recent research,[131] a narrowing and rigidifying tendency of the policy analysis paradigm would undermine an important source of pluralism in American government.

Not surprisingly, the defenders of analysis have replied vigorously to many of these criticisms. Analysis, it is contended, will *not* lead to a proliferation of policy initiatives because analysis relies on the findings of social science:

> As a profoundly conservative force, [applied social science] can debunk claims that problems exist, and it can show the inadequacy of current governmental efforts. If we take science seriously when it decides that problems exist, and if we use it to help us learn something about the impact of past and present policies, it can become a force for shrinking the government's agenda and redirecting its efforts rather than for expanding the governmental quagmire.[132]

In response to the criticism that the application of analytical technique will overload the rational capacities of decision makers and processing capabilities of institutions, the defenders of analysis argue that the critics have again taken too literal an interpretation of the techniques of analysis. Rather than *replacing* current incremental decision procedures, analysts seek only to add a modicum of rational deliberation about means to ends (and, they ask, who can object to that?). In the view of one champion of analysis, the role of technical analysis can be confined to one "part of the loop" of decision making: finding optimal means to obtain *given* ends.[133] Rather than replacing judgment and statesmanship, analysis is merely to help "structure" and inform perceptions of the problem, and provide a more systematic considera-

---

[131] See Heclo, ibid. Also see Gary Wamsley, "Policy Subsystems as a Unit of Analysis in Implementation Studies," (paper presented at Erasmus University, Rotterdam, June 1983); and Paul Sabatier and Hank Jenkins-Smith, eds. "Policy Change and Policy-Oriented Learning: Exploring an Advocacy Coalition Framework," *Policy Sciences*, vol. 21, nos. 2–3 (1988).

[132] Mark Moore, "Statesmanship in a World of Particular Substantive Choices," in *Who Leads* pp. 33–34. Moore adds: "If [analysts] could be bound to higher professional standards, and if public officials were independently capable of evaluating their arguments, their tendency to 'find' frivolous problems could be stopped," (p. 33). Moore does not elaborate what professional standards he has in mind.

[133] Williams, "Cost–Benefit Analysis," *Public Expenditure*.

tion of alternatives on which judgment can act.[134] The dynamics of debate between critics and defenders of analysis involved here is much like that over potential distortions of costs and benefits: critics focus on and attack the implicit role of analysis as found in the dominant techniques of analysis, while defenders depict a more modest role of analysis as but one (all too slight) force among many.

Agreeing that the introduction of formal analysis has the potential to impoverish or mask policy debate, the defenders argue that the analyst–advisor must become something of a generalist, one who "understands the nature of all the disciplines relevant to his problems, so that without necessarily being familiar with or even understanding their more intricate and esoteric parts, he can marshall them intelligently."[135] Thus a class of analysts who bridge the political and social–scientific worlds are necessary to screen and translate the information produced by their more arcane brethren for use by their necessarily pragmatic clients. Even with such analytical middlemen, political decision makers will need to become conversant with the techniques and knowledge of the analysts and "independently capable of evaluating their arguments."[136] Only then will decision makers be able to intelligently assess the merits of debate cast in the language of policy analysis.

The defenders of analysis acknowledge that the use of technical analysis may effectively preclude intelligent contribution by the lay public to policy debate. Working from the perspective that analysis is a salutary corrective to the ills of government-as-usual, the defenders see this as a significant difficulty: because elected decision makers are ultimately responsible only to the electorate, an electorate that does not understand and utilize analysis in the public interest will not compel politicians to act on the findings of the analysts. Only by convincing the electorate will the results of analysis take on ultimate political force. As described in a recent retrospective survey of the energy policy studies of the 1970s:

> Politicians are born of the people, put in office by the people, and committed to work for the people. As the public becomes better and more responsibly informed in the lessons of policy analysis, politicians will too. That is the sure way for public analysis [i.e., analysis in the public interest] to make contact.[137]

---

[134] Moore, "Substantive Choices," *Who Leads*, pp. 26–28.

[135] Williams, "Cost–Benefit Analysis," *Public Expenditure*, p. 536. Moore makes a similar argument in "Substantive Choices," *Who Leads*, pp. 35–36.

[136] Moore, ibid., p. 33.

[137] Greenberger, et al., *Caught Unawares*, p. 303. Also see Robert Haveman, "Policy Analysis and the Congress: An Economist's View," in *Policy Analysis*, 2(2) (Spring 1976), pp. 248–250. According to Haveman, public awareness of the results of analysis will help ameliorate the "perverse incentive structures" currently in place in Congress.

Thus, for the defenders of analysis, excluding the lay public from debate is an urgent problem not because it stunts the development of participatory man (though that may be of secondary concern), but because it lessens the political influence of analysis.[138]

_____ 3.4 _____
CRITICAL THEMES AND DEMOCRATIC NORMS

As noted in the introduction to this chapter, the critiques of the policy analysis paradigm originate from across the range of political perspectives and find many targets in the techniques and perceived practices of analysis. The primary thrusts of these critiques have been that (1) analysis will gain significant unrepresentative power within the political process, (2) the techniques of analysis would distort the expressed preferences of citizens by reducing them to the categories of costs and benefits, and (3) the employment of analysis in politics has added new and ominous strains to an already burdened set of political institutions and processes. It remains to bring more coherence to the political arguments underlying these criticisms, and to suggest an alternative approach to the problem of analysis as an ingredient of the political process.

In my view the existence of predominant themes of criticism of the policy analysis paradigm occurs because of a shared resonance of those critiques; these criticisms appeal to widely held beliefs in American (and perhaps Western) societies. This shared resonance stems from the appeal of the critical themes to aspects of democratic theory—some of which are in conflict with one another—all of which are common currency in American political thought. These aspects of political theory provide coherent form to the criticisms of the policy analysis paradigm.

As described in chapter 2, the policy analysis paradigm implies at least a partial political theory.[139] The policy analysis paradigm provides a coherent theory of the origin of value, a set of norms to guide public policy making, and preferred institutional forms for democratic governance. "Good" and "value" in society are rooted solely in individual preference; to limit accept-

---

[138] Note that the debate has come full circle: critics who fear that influential analysis will distort public costs and benefits may be mollified by observations that analysis has little direct affect on policy, only to take renewed umbrage that the indirect effect of analysis is to preclude public understanding and participation in policy debates. Defenders of analysis agree, and they argue that public knowledge and acceptance of the results of analysis will _increase_ the influence of analysis. Now the critics are once again in the position of dreading the direct affects of analysis on policy.

[139] References for the propositions stated here are provided in the more detailed arguments made earlier in chapter 2.

able preferences or to find "good" elsewhere is to introduce arbitrariness and "dictatorship" into public decision making. Government policies should be designed to accurately reflect the aggregated preferences of the individual members of society in policy outcomes; good policy results will maximize net social utility. Political institutions should be so designed as to provide optimum incentive for decision makers to implement such policies. The rules for "democratic fairness" proposed by Kenneth Arrow reflect this view well; included are requirements that individuals be able to entertain any logically possible combination of preferences (the "condition of freedom") and that an increase in relative preference for a policy option by any individual improves the chances for adoption of that option.[140] In line with these formal requirements, the policy analysis paradigm accepts the sovereignty of individual preferences and seeks maximum net social welfare. Moreover, the policy analysis paradigm holds promise for correction of some of the flaws in formal democracy, as described by Arrow and others. While one-man-one-vote systems of public choice cannot rule out the possibility of intransitive (and therefore manipulable) collective choice,[141] the use of market prices and simulated market prices can.[142] The emphasis of the policy analysis paradigm is thus on better mapping of aggregated individual preferences into public policies. As long as formal requirements of nondictatorship are fulfilled, the policy analysis paradigm is not concerned that fulfillment of this purpose may lead to concentrations of political power through such reforms as centralization of authority in the executive.

The liberal democratic bases of the critique.   Much of the critique of the policy analysis paradigm can be linked to the long-standing fear by liberal democratic theorists of *concentration* of power. For these theorists, well represented among the American Founding Fathers, concern with preservation of individual liberties ranked at least as high in priority as did accurate mapping of aggregations of individual preferences into public policy.[143] As stated by Giovanni Sartori:

---

[140] See Kenneth Arrow, *Social Choice and Individual Value,* 2nd ed. (New Haven, CT: Yale University Press, 1963). For an introductory description, see William Riker and Peter Ordeshook, op. cit., pp.78–115.

[141] See Riker and Ordeshook, *Positive Political Theory,* pp. 84–94. Also see Riker, *Liberalism Against Populism,* op. cit., chapter 5.

[142] That is, assuming the current distribution of wealth is acceptable or that appropriate weights for persons of different income scales can be derived from individual preferences. See discussion of this point in chapter 2.

[143] See *The Federalist No. 10,* wherein James Madison laments that ". . . measures are too often decided, not according to the rules of justice and the rights of the minority party, but by the superior force of an interested and overbearing majority." Alexander Hamilton, John Jay, and James Madison, *The Federalist Papers* (New York: New American Library, 1961), p. 77. Madison then argues for the necessity of playing many "factions" against one another to prevent the dominance of the state by any faction—be it minority *or* majority.

[T]he very *raison d'etre* of democracy lies in this fact: that it provides the solution to the *problem of the persons* to whom power is to be entrusted. But democracy succeeds, on the whole, in exorcising arbitrary and personal power precisely because it is a mechanism purposely created to this end. . . . It is effective to the extent that it serves this purpose.[144]

The concern over who controls power may seriously inhibit the goal of accurate mapping of aggregated individual preferences into policy:

If we manage to control power, this is largely because democracy works, in practice, as a device for slowing down, filtering, and decanting the processes of power. From the standpoint of the speed at which it works, democracy entails a rather slow and halting process of decision-making; and from the standpoint of its scope of action, democracy implies the restriction of the range of decisions to a somewhat limited area. We cannot avoid paying a price and accepting certain limitations if we want to tame power. The price is a kind of temporizing inertia, often a lack of resolution, and, what is more, a remarkable waste of effort.[145]

Thus, in contrast with the optimism of the policy analysis paradigm, liberal democratic theorists have balanced against the role of democracy as a carrier of the aggregate wills of the people the role of democracy as a counter balance and refractor of power.

The tendency toward centralization of power and authority imbedded in much of the policy analysis paradigm provides a lightning rod for criticism from the liberal democratic perspective. Previously, lightning struck in the battles over whether administration and politics could be thought of as distinct.[146] More recently, the battle has raged over institutionalization of PPBS, ZBB, and other reforms designed to institutionalize policy analysis.[147] What underlies

---

[144] Sartori, *Democratic Theory*, p. 402 (emphasis in original).

[145] Ibid. Contrast Sartori's argument with the pitch for efficiency and a greater weighting toward responsiveness to public preferences made by James Fesler. In Fesler's view, the problem of efficiency versus controlling power "would be eased if we could assume that maximization of control is a desirable objective. In fact the costs of pursuit of such an objective would be intolerable. Why is this so? Because an abundance of negative control creates a pervasive climate of mistrust, which can demoralize those upon whom we depend for achievement of public programs. Because controls external to administration may displace or undermine internal administrative controls. Because controls multiply requirements for review of proposed decisions, increase red tape and delay action; controls, therefore, *may dull administration's responsiveness to its public*" (emphasis mine). *Public Administration* (Englewood Cliffs, NJ: Prentice-Hall, 1980), p. 312.

[146] Woodrow Wilson, in "The Study of Administration," *Political Science Quarterly* (June 1887), pp. 197–222, argues for the separation, while Paul Appleby, *Policy and Administration*, (University, AL: University of Alabama Press, 1949) makes a convincing and currently accepted case for the lack of such separation. Also see Frederick Mosher, *Democracy and the Public Service* (New York: Oxford Press, 1968), pp. 78–95.

[147] See above in this chapter for sources. A succinct critique of systems analysis on grounds that it violates democratic principle is Ida Hoos's "Systems Techniques for Managing Society, A Critique" in *Public Administration Review*, vol. 33, (March/April 1973), pp. 157–164. Hoos argues that perfect solutions perfectly managed are antithetical to democracy.

and unifies these arguments is a genuine tension between the prospective role of government as a maximizer of aggregate utility on the one hand, and as guarantor of individual liberties on the other. The tension has surfaced continually in this century as the prevailing political climate has increasingly been characterized by the optimistic view of democracy as the device to translate aggregated individual preferences into public policy and has encroached on the institutionalized limits on governmental efficacy erected by the liberal democratic framers of the Constitution.[148]

The participatory democratic bases of the critique.   An alternative strain of democratic theory, emphasizing the role of participation, takes aim at elements of the policy analysis paradigm that erode the paths to citizen growth and fulfillment through active participation in policy making. For participatory democrats, both liberal democracy and the policy analysis paradigm are faulted for their one dimensional concern with the outputs of democratic processes to the exclusion of the fruits that may originate directly from the *act* of participation.[149] Individuals gain immeasurably from the process of participation, feeling their way from vague predisposition to reasoned viewpoint through debate and thereby gaining the type of human fulfillment that can only be derived from taking an active part in governing the public forces and institutions that so thoroughly affect our lives.[150] In this view, democratic processes are fundamentally educational.

One objection to the policy analysis paradigm rooted in participatory democratic theory is that the techniques of the policy analysis paradigm *presuppose* the existence of a stable and connected set of preferences concerning the policy questions at hand and holds that these preexisting preferences should guide public policy. According to the participatory democrat, though particular individual preferences may predate the participatory policy process, it is only through direct contact and deliberation with others holding a range of viewpoints in the process of reaching collective decisions that individuals truly discover what they would prefer.[151] Furthermore, even if fully developed preferences *did* exist on some question of policy, individual fulfillment would be undermined if experts were to collect preferences from the (passive) individuals of society, aggregate them, and spew back an optimal public policy. Even if the policy expert were able to determine, through

---

[148] See Emmette Redford's *Democracy in the Administrative State* (New York: Oxford University Press, 1969) and Mosher, *Democracy and Public Service,* for treatment of the broader conflict over "administrative efficiency" and democracy. Also see Douglas Yates' *Bureaucratic Democracy,* (Cambridge, MA: Harvard University Press, 1982).

[149] See Bachrach, *Theory of Democratic Elitism.*

[150] See Pateman, *Participation and Democratic Theory,* and Benello and Roussopoulos, *Participatory Democracy.*

[151] See Pateman, *Participation and Democratic Theory.*

analytical techniques, what is best for others, the sense that *the experts* wield the tools that determine choice will undermine popular participation. As stated by one critic:

> These personages [experts, businessmen, philanthropists] may well know what is best for others. But the better they know, that is, the more objective and helpful they are, the more they jeopardize popular participation. . . . Those whose civic center—or library, museum or city hall—it is must help to create it, even if the policy process thereby becomes untidy and the final result more cluttered and less manageable than professional planners would hope. Economic losses may be political gains.[152]

From the participatory democratic viewpoint, then, the achievement of individual development and fulfillment are seen to run irretrievably counter to the thrust of the policy analysis paradigm as a maximizer of preexisting preferences.

The defenders of the policy analysis paradigm have rebutted the critiques of both the liberal and participatory approaches in several ways, but the predominant method has been to argue that—far from reigning supreme— the techniques and advice of analysis are but one all-too-weak voice in the cacophony of the policy process. The defenders scoff at the notion that optimizing techniques will ever replace logrolling or compromise among interests. In this way many defenders of analysis depart significantly from the vision implicit in the foundations of the policy analysis paradigm and the writings of many of its proponents. For the defenders of analysis the problem is one of imbalance: the concerns for "filtering, decanting and slowing" the exercise of power and for popular participation have great cost in the form of inefficiency (in the special sense of the policy analysis paradigm), hindering translation of preferences into policy. In the defenders' view, those costs are at present too large and must be ameliorated through judicious inculcation of the rationality of the policy analysis paradigm into the political process.

_____ 3.5 _____
SUMMARY

I have argued that elements of the policy analysis paradigm exist in genuine tension with conflicting institutions and principles of democracy. As detailed in this chapter, much of the debate over the threat and promise of policy analysis has revolved around whether the proposals for implementation of the policy analysis paradigm have succeeded in altering the more overtly political patterns of policy making, and if so, what effects those alterations have had.

---

[152] Kariel, *Promise of Politics*, p.67.

Critics and defenders can find ample evidence to support their respective arguments; as described throughout this chapter, all sides to the debate have had recourse to theoretical and empirical evidence condemning or absolving analysis. For each of the major themes addressed, critics argue that the reforms of the policy analysis paradigm would undermine important components of democracy, while defenders point to examples of the subjugation of analysis by politics. The result is considerable ambiguity and confusion: which is correct, and when? What is missing is an explicit recognition and assessment of what is almost always buried deeply in the arguments of both sides: both seem to have a particular kind of environment within the policy process in mind as they make their assessments of the implications of the policy analysis paradigm.

Proponents and critics of the policy analysis paradigm have tended to view the world in which analysis is practiced as a homogeneous place in which factors affecting the relative influence of analysis, the likelihood that analysis can replace more traditional politics, and the likely institutional alterations due to analysis will be constant. That is why generalizations drawn from specific instances of attempts to apply analysis, and why attempts to measure "influence," typically make no distinctions among kinds of policy environments. The implication is that the elements of the policy environment are unchanging or unimportant.

This, I believe, has been a *fundamental roadblock* to progress in thinking about the potential and actual roles of analysis, and to assessment of the strains and similarities between policy analysis and the various types of democratic norms. Serious appraisal requires first, it be recognized that the conduct of analysis will be through individual analysts working within organizational contexts of the political process. Part of what will characterize the role of analysis will be systematic inducements and constraints for particular roles of analysis that a given organizational context provides. Second, the nature of the policy issue under study will have important implications for the role of analysis. Third, the appropriate conceptualization of analysis itself—the focus of inquiry, the means of structuring and comparing values—takes different form in different contexts in the policy environment.

Part Two of this study describes and demonstrates the significance of the systematic effects of organizational setting, the fora in which policies are debated, and the nature of the policy issue itself on the roles played by policy analysts. Once dissected, it will be possible to discuss in more concrete terms how closely the practice of analysis in a particular arena, forum, and issue area parallels the threats and promises depicted by the critics and proponents of the policy analysis paradigm.

PART TWO

A CONCEPTUAL
MODEL OF
POLICY ANALYSIS

CHAPTER 4

Analysis in Practice: Contexts and Roles

It has been recognized for some time that analysis is often not applied as prescribed by the policy analysis paradigm. Despite injunctions to provide only objective, neutral advice, analysts and their analyses often figure prominently in major political battles—often taking positions on opposing sides. Furthermore, many practitioners have been concerned that analysis plays an all too insignificant role in shaping public policy.[1] The result has been an extension of the list of functions of analysis to include explicitly political uses,[2]

---

[1] See chapter 3, section 3.2.

[2] One particularly insightful listing of the functions of analysis is contained in James Marver, *Consultants Can Help: The Use of Outside Experts in the U.S. Office of Child Development* (Lexington, MA: Lexington Books, 1979). For an acerbic (and somewhat overdone) critique of the political uses of analysis, see I. Horowitz, "Social Science Mandarins: Policymaking as a Political Formula," *Policy Sciences*, vol. 1 (1970), pp. 339–360.

and repeated calls for analysts to play a more vigorous role in advocating efficiency in public policy.[3]

Recognition that analysis in practice departs from the policy analysis paradigm permits focus on more relevant influences that shape the practice of policy analysis in bureaucratic settings. How might the process of analysis be more usefully characterized? What factors in the analysts' organizational setting, and in the activity of analysis itself, shape the political practice of analysis?

This chapter is focused on these questions. First, a conceptual view of the *process* of analysis is presented, in which analysis is seen as a collective activity within *policy subsystems*. Factors that constrain and channel analytical activity can then be described. Second, analysis is viewed from the perspective of the individual analyst, with attention to the characteristics of analysis and the organizational environment that bear on the provision of analysis. From this vantage point, the roles prescribed for policy analysts from the literature in the field can be assessed and evaluated. In both cases, the intent is to provide a more realistic depiction of the processes of analysis, and of the role of the individual analyst, from which to confront the praise and criticism of policy analysis raised in preceding chapters.

_____ 4.1 _____
CHARACTERIZING ANALYSIS

What are the processes by which policy analysis—the application of policy-relevant theory and data to policy issues—is solicited, supplied, and responded to within policy subsystems?[4] When analysis is provided to advise or influence the choices of decision makers, the analyst generally attempts to craft a set of (often quantitative) statements about a policy issue that: (1) specify relationships between manipulable policy variables and resultant policy "outcomes," (2) indicate the relevant "dimensions of value" along which the policy outcomes can be ranked, and (3) provide some criterion for selection of a

---

[3] See C. K. Leman, and R. H. Nelson, "Ten Commandments for Policy Economists," *Journal of Policy Analysis and Management,* 1(1) (Fall 1981), pp. 97–117, and J. M. B. Fraatz, "Policy Analysts as Advocates," *Journal of Policy Analysis and Management,* 1(2) (Winter 1982), pp. 273–276.

[4] The depiction of the role of analysis developed here varies from Carol Weiss's conception of the "enlightenment function" in important ways. According to Weiss, the results of analysis have a gradual, cumulative effect on the conventions, beliefs, and priorities of decision makers. See Carol Weiss's "Research for Policy's Sake: The Enlightenment Function of Social Research," *Policy Analysis,* 3(4) (Fall 1977), pp. 531–545. I will argue that this aggregated view of the role of analysis is understated in important ways because it gives insufficient attention to the policy context in which analysis is provided. Disaggregation of the policy context, as developed in this chapter, allows a much more specific means to assess the probable role of policy analysis.

preferred policy option. In the ideal formulation of the policy analysis paradigm, outcomes would be aggregated and weighed on a single dimension, measuring net social benefits, and the criterion of choice would call for selection of the policy option that generates the largest net benefits.[5] However, even under the best of circumstances, it typically proves difficult to collapse the disparate outcomes of policy options onto a single dimension because important outcomes are frequently incommensurables, such as equity, "national security," and economic efficiency.[6]

Another aspect of the multidimensionality of the policy space concerns the question of "standing" raised in chapter 2; the matter of *whose* benefits and costs should be considered is often subject to considerable disagreement.[7] Analysts can accommodate that disagreement by treating benefits and costs to various classes of individuals as distinct dimensions of value, thereby allowing analysts and their clients to weight the several dimensions differently. This has been the pattern in analyses that consider the effects of policies that fall outside a country's borders (e.g., the effects of acid rain on Canadians versus Americans) or across distinct age groups (the benefits and costs of Social Security programs on the elderly versus the young). The process of analysis therefore involves specification of an array of salient dimensions of value, and proposed weights, reflecting the expected effects of policies on various groups of individuals.

Finally, even when it is feasible to reduce all outcomes to net social benefits, the pace of the policy process seldom permits sufficient time for the necessary data collection and analysis. For these reasons, analyses tend to present *multiple dimensions* of value, making application of straightforward decision rules—like maximization of net social benefits—difficult, if not impossible, to apply.

This being the case, what kind of information can analysis contribute to political actors in the policy subsystem? Analysis offers what might be called an "analytical policy space," built upon multiple dimensions of value, that provides a conceptual framework from which to compare the merits of policies across various incommensurable classes of outcomes. While most

[5] See, for example, E. J. Mishan, *Cost Benefit Analysis*, 3rd ed. (Boston: George, Allen, Unwin, 1982), and Edith Stokey and Richard Zeckhauser, *A Primer for Policy Analysis* (New York: W. W. Norton, 1978).

[6] See Otto Eckstein, "A Survey of Public Expenditure Criteria," in, *Public Finances: Needs, Sources, and Utilization,* Universities-National Bureau for Economic Research, (Princeton, NJ: Princeton University Press, 1961), pp. 439–504.

[7] See Duncan MacRae, Jr., and Dale Whittington's "The Issue of Standing in Cost–Benefit Analysis," *Journal of Policy Analysis and Management,* 5(4) (Summer 1986), pp. 665–682; also see their "Assessing Preferences in Cost–Benefit Analysis: Reflections on Rural Water Supply Evaluation in Haiti," *Journal of Policy Analysis and Management,* 7(2) (Winter 1988), pp. 246–263.

political actors are equipped with at least a rudimentary conception of this policy space, analysis is frequently called upon to flesh out that conception, point out possible pitfalls, and clarify connections between the means at decision makers' disposal and the ends of public policy.[8] Perhaps more frequently, various subsystem participants holding differing conceptions of the policy space (later described as policy "belief systems") attempt to convince decision makers of the appropriateness of their particular understanding and policy preference.[9] Over time, experience in the implementation of policies on a given issue generates new data, allowing for debate and (sometimes) learning about dimensions of value and revised or (sometimes) improved understanding of connections between means and ends. In this usage, then, the provision of analysis is integral to the process of change in policy beliefs and learning by subsystem actors, providing a cognitive basis from which policy choices can be made.

When advocacy intensifies in the policy subsystem, analysis almost inevitably becomes a political resource in the struggle to adopt and implement preferred policy options.[10] Among adversarial providers of analysis, the primary struggle is over *manipulation of the shape and content of the policy space* in ways designed to improve the chances for adoption of the analyst's preferred policy choice. Manipulation of this kind is an attempt to tailor the policy space—to delete or add dimensions of value, to alter the weighting of dimensions, and to shift placement of expected outcomes of specific policy options on the dimensions—in order to make the preferred policy choice as attractive as possible to key decision makers. Strategies toward this end characterize the provision of analysis by adversarial subsystem actors.

Those in a position to demand analysis of policy issues are also able to employ it as a political resource; political actors sometimes may adopt or promote analyses that provide congenial conclusions, while refuting, ignoring, or suppressing analysis that comes up with the "wrong answer."[11] The call for new research can be used by political actors to delay what appears to be a painful choice—as in the acid rain controversy—or as a retrograde tactic

---

[8] See Alice Rivlin, *Systematic Thinking for Social Action*, (Washington, DC: Brookings Institute, 1971); Stokey and Zeckhauser, *A Primer* and Mishan, *Cost Benefit*.

[9] See the excellent description of this process in John Kingdon, *Agendas, Alternatives and Public Policies* (Boston: Little, Brown, 1984), pp. 131–134.

[10] See the "rules of thumb" for analytical disputes among policy advisors in Howard Margolis, *Technical Advice on Policy Issues*, (Newbury Park, CA: Sage, 1973), pp. 33–34. Also see Christopher Leman and Robert Nelson, "Ten Commandments," and J. M. B. Fraatz, "Policy Analysts."

[11] See, for example, Mark Rushefsky, "The Misuse of Science in Governmental Decision Making," *Science, Technology, and Human Values*, 9(3) (Summer 1984), pp. 47–59. Also see Horowitz, "Social Science Mandarins."

to undermine and reverse the advance of an undesirable policy initiative.[12] Thus analysis provides a tool with which to engage in political struggle as well as a cognitive basis for policy choice and implementation.

Though the distinction between the provision of analysis as a cognitive basis for policy action and as a political resource can be made with some conceptual precision, these uses are probably rarely separable in practice.[13] The differing policy preferences that often lead to the use of analysis as a political resource may themselves derive from differing "belief systems" and perceptions of the policy space.[14] Convinced of the correctness of a particular understanding of the policy problem and the effects of relevant options on important values, an analyst would be remiss if he or she made no attempt to present a compelling case to decision makers.[15] Thus there need not be an attempt to "bias" analysis or to mislead consumers of analysis in the attempt to manipulate the policy space as described above. Even when analysts knowingly bias analysis in favor of one or another option, they may do so under the presumption that their own contribution is but part of a larger adversarial or pluralistic process.[16] In that view, failure to engage in partisan analysis would amount to an abandonment of the field to other players, and would leave important issues and values unaddressed.[17] For these reasons, the provision and use of analysis as a cognitive basis for choice and as a political resource cannot be considered separately.

It is not news that the provision and use of policy analysis within policy subsystems often involves competing claims and advocacy.[18] My concern is with the *limits* and *channels* within the political process that tend systematically to foster or inhibit such practices and with the general features of the policy context that may enhance or diminish the importance of analysis as a

---

[12] This use of analysis is called a "retrograde tactic" in Hank Jenkins-Smith and David Weimer, "Analysis as Retrograde Action: The Case of Strategic Petroleum Reserves," *Public Administration Review,* 45(4) (July/August 1985), pp. 485–494.

[13] For a particularly insightful view of the interplay between ideology, interest, and knowledge, see Carol Weiss, "Ideology, Interests, and Information: The Basis of Policy Positions," in *Ethics, The Social Sciences, and Policy Analysis,* eds. D. Callahan and B. Jennings (NY: Plenum, 1983), pp. 213–245.

[14] See John Robinson, "Apples and Horned Toads: On the Framework-Determined Nature of the Energy Debate," in *Policy Sciences,* vol. 15, (1982), pp. 23–45.

[15] Robert Behn, "Policy Analysis and Policy Politics," *Policy Analysis,* 7(2) (Spring 1981), pp. 199–226.

[16] See Margolis, *Technical Advice on Policy Issues,* and Arnold Meltsner, *Policy Analysts in the Bureaucracy,* (Berkeley, CA: University of California Press, 1976), pp. 150–152.

[17] See K. A. Archibald's "Three Views of the Experts' Role in Policymaking: Systems Analysis, Incrementalism, and the Clinical Approach," *Policy Sciences,* vol. 1 (Spring 1970), pp. 73–86. Also see John L. Foster, "An Advocate Role Model for Policy Analysis," *Policy Studies Journal,* 8(6) (Summer 1980), pp. 958–964.

[18] Indeed, some observers see advocacy as the norm, as do Horowitz, "Social Science Mandarins"; Margolis, op. cit.; and Foster, "Advocate Role Model."

source of policy development and of policy-relevant learning among policy elites. To that end, subsequent sections of this chapter provide a more detailed depiction of policy subsystems and what are, in my view, the primary factors that affect the provision and use of analysis in the policy process.

—————— 4.2 ——————
ANALYSIS IN POLICY SUBSYSTEMS

Policy analysis, as practiced in governmental bureaucracies, is characterized by specialization.[19] Because of the complexity and breadth of modern policies, few analysts can develop sufficient expertise to provide analysis in more than one or two policy issue–areas. Thus analysts, as well as other political elites, tend to become specialists concerning one or more policy problems or issue–areas.

As policy-area specialists, analysts become members of the relevant "issue network"—or *policy subsystem*—made up of those actors in legislative committees; interest groups; executive agencies; academia; the press; and elsewhere who play important roles in the identification of "problems;" the development, dissemination, and evaluation of policy options; and the implementation of final policies.[20] What binds these disparate actors together is their concern and focus on a common policy problem. In stable subsystems, the interaction on the issue is sufficiently frequent to permit the more consistently active members to know one another by reputation and policy viewpoint.

Within subsystems, members respond to a variety of external factors including broad cultural and constitutional constraints (for example, what is culturally acceptable and legal), the enduring features of the policy problem (for example, the geopolitical distribution of natural resources), electoral changes, and policy decisions and spillover effects from other subsystems (for example, the effect of oil price decontrol on prospects for natural gas deregulation). What is important for this discussion is the apparent leeway, within

---

[19] For a useful discussion of long-term policy change with a focus on subsystems, see the articles in the symposium edited by Paul Sabatier and Hank Jenkins-Smith, "Policy Change and Policy-Oriented Learning: Exploring an Advocacy Coalition Framework," *Policy Sciences*, vol. 21, nos. 2–3, (1988). The following paragraphs draw on the articles in that symposium, particularly Sabatier's "An Advocacy Coalition Framework of Policy Change and the Role of Policy-Oriented Learning Therein," pp. 129–168, and Jenkins-Smith's "Analytical Debates and Policy Learning: Analysis and Change in the Federal Bureaucracy," pp. 169–211.

[20] Kingdon, *Agendas, Alternatives;* and Sabatier and Jenkins-Smith, "Policy Change." Also see Hugh Heclo, "Issue Networks in the Executive Establishment," in *The New American Political System,* ed. Anthony King (Washington, DC: American Enterprise Institute, 1978), pp. 87–124. Also see Heclo's excellent study, *Social Policy in Britain and Sweden* (New Haven, CT: Yale University Press, 1974).

these constraints, for maneuvering to shape policy by subsystem participants.[21] Review of the studies of policy change within subsystems over time
suggests that there normally exists substantial room for discretion by subsystem actors, within which those actors can attempt to mobilize resources to
affect the course of policy development.[22]

Although most models of bureaucratic politics highlight the clash of
political interests and the exercise of influence,[23] the mobilization of "information" and analysis also plays a significant role in shaping public policy.[24]
In practice, while analysis may typically have little direct effect on policy,
policy analysis *interacts with* "interests" and "ideologies" that *do* fundamentally shape policy. Sometimes the interaction is *instrumental,* as in clarification
of cause-and-effect relations that bear on achievement of ideological commitments;[25] sometimes analysis interacts through *mediation* when ideology
conflicts with interest.[26] On still other occasions, analysis serves to modify
preexisting information or beliefs. Thus analysis, as employed within subsystems, can have a substantial indirect and interactive effect on policy development and change.

What the foregoing suggests is that analysis is important primarily for its
effect on the beliefs, or belief systems, of political elites within policy subsystems. Belief systems, as held by these relatively sophisticated policy elites,
incorporate the key values, interests, and sets of causal assumptions applied
to policy issues by individual subsystem actors.[27] The belief structures them-

---

[21] Kingdon (*Agendas, Alternatives*) argues that specialists and analysts who are members of policy subsystems have greater independent influence with regard to the *generation and critique* of policy alternatives than they have with *rise* of issues and problems to the forefront of the policy agenda itself.

[22] See Heclo, *Social Policy;* Crista Altenstetter and R. Bjorkman, "A Longitudinal Study of Health Care Policy in Several American States," (paper presented at the Annual Meeting of the American Political Science Association, Chicago, September 1976); and Martha Derthick, *Policymaking for Social Security* (Washington, DC: Brookings Institute, 1979). Also see Kingdon, *Agenda, Alternatives.*

[23] See James Q. Wilson, ed., *Politics of Regulation* (New York: Basic Books, 1980), especially chapter 10; A. Lee Fritschler, *Smoking and Politics,* 3rd ed. (Englewood Cliffs, NJ: Prentice-Hall, 1983); and Erwin Krasnow and Lawrence Longley, *The Politics of Broadcast Regulation* (New York: St. Martins, 1978).

[24] Weiss, "Ideology, Interests, and Information," pp. 228–239.

[25] See Martin Rein and Sheldon White, "Policy Research: Belief and Doubt," *Policy Analysis,* 3(2) (Spring 1977), pp. 239–271, for a description of the erosion of ideological commitment through analysis.

[26] Weiss, "Ideology, Interests, and Information," pp. 237–239.

[27] Sabatier, "Advocacy Coalition"; Robert Axelrod, ed., *Structure of Decision: The Cognitive Maps of Political Elites* (Princeton, NJ: Princeton University Press, 1976). Adopting a different language, the belief system might be divided into an individual's "objective function" and perceived causal relations. These tend not to be independent, however, and both are subject to change through introduction of new information, so (following Sabatier) I describe them here under the common heading of belief systems.

selves can be understood as a set of dimensions of value believed to be related in important ways to the policy issue at hand (for example, human health, economic efficiency, environmental quality, employment levels, and regional equity as related to acid rain policy) and a set of causal relations believed to underlie the problem (for example, the relation between coal-fired industrial and utility emissions and the incidence of acid rain).[28] The belief system is connected to policy via the linkage between a set of manipulable policy variables and policy outcomes (for example, regulation and/or tax incentives to encourage installation of scrubbers, which reduce sulfur dioxide emissions, and thereby lessen acid rain). Within this belief system the subsystem actor is able to link policy options with subjectively probable outcomes and to attach relative valuation to those outcomes.[29]

The causal relations and value implications imbedded in the belief system can usefully be divided into two parts: a "core," consisting of the primary interests and fundamental values that underlie general policy objectives, and a "periphery," including secondary and instrumental values and causal relations.[30] By this is meant that, for a holder of a policy belief system, some subset of values and related causal assumptions will provide a fundamental basis for understanding a policy issue–area, imputing meaning to it, and formulating a general policy prescription.[31] This is the core of the belief system, and change in these values (or their weights) and causal assumptions would alter the holder's basic perception of, and policy prescription for, the issue. For example, in the analytic debates over Alaskan oil export policy—to be examined at greater length in the following chapter—proponents of a continued ban on exports consistently laid heavy emphasis on the need for a robust domestic

---

[28] See Jenkins-Smith, "Analytical Debates."

[29] This view of belief systems presumes significant cognitive consistency on the part of subsystem actors. It is important to note, however, that these actors are *policy elites*, among whom it is presumed that there is some selection bias toward those with such cognitive consistency. See Abraham Tesser, "Self Generated Attitude Change," *Advances in Experimental Psychology*, no. 11 (1978), pp. 289–338, and Axelrod, *Structure of Decision*. Even theorists who find fault with the demanding assumptions of "rational choice" models of behavior see room for such consistency. See Herbert Simon, *Models of Thought* (New Haven, CT: Yale University Press, 1979).

[30] Sabatier ("Advocacy Coalition") introduced the concepts of core and periphery to policy beliefs systems within subsystems. For more general discussions of the concepts of core and periphery in belief systems, see Imre Lakotos, "History of Science and its Rational Reconstruction," in *Boston Studies in the Philosophy of Science*, no. 8 (1971), pp. 42–134; Giandomenico Majone, "Policies as Theories," in *Omega*, no. 8 (1980), pp. 151–162.

[31] Sabatier ("Advocacy Coalition") develops an alternative and more elaborate structure of belief systems that puts greater emphasis on fundamental ontological axioms regarding the nature of man, society, and distributive justice as constituent elements of the core, and less emphasis on political and economic self-interest. Often—though certainly not always—interest *underlies* profession of these ostensibly more fundamental beliefs. It is my guess that, for many participants of analytical debates, elements attributed by Sabatier to the belief system core are susceptible to shift s as perceived interests shift. For that reason I would opt for a more flexible definition of the belief system core, as described above.

merchant tanker fleet to maintain national security, contending that removal of the export ban would decimate the existing domestic fleet. Over the course of the debate it became clear that preservation of the domestic tanker fleet per se was an important aim of these participants. These values and causal linkage formed the core of their belief system. What were, for these participants, peripheral elements—the values of efficiency and energy security, and causal effects on such factors as domestic-energy production rates—were core issues to others in the debate. The strategies in the provision and use of analysis employed by all sides reflected—indeed, were tailored to—the belief systems of the actors and the perceived belief systems of others.

Belief systems need not be (and generally are not) fixed or fully developed; beliefs—particularly those of the periphery—may be tentative and subject to revision on the basis of feedback and experimentation.[32] On the other hand, beliefs are (usually) not held as the end product of dispassionate scientific and philosophical inquiry; once beliefs concerning values or causal relations have been accepted and become salient to the core of the belief system, there is often strong resistance to change even in the face of extensive evidence for such change.[33] As I will argue in later pages, the often intractable nature of the analytical questions involved and the frequently permissive nature of the fora in which analytical debates are waged make resistance to modification of beliefs all the more plausible and defensible.[34]

The degree of consensus among subsystem actors regarding core elements of belief systems is an important factor bearing on the nature of conflict within subsystems and on the manner in which policy analysis is provided and used. Were all subsystem actors to hold unique and conflicting belief systems—a case of extreme fragmentation—analysis of belief systems would be of little use in providing general explanation of subsystem politics.[35] Fortunately, such extreme fragmentation is probably rare. While individual belief systems regarding a policy area can and do vary considerably, existence of a common

---

[32] Analysts and theorists have long argued that the primary role of policy research is to provide such experimental feedback. See, for example, John Dewey, *The Public and Its Problems* (Chicago: Swallow Press, 1927), wherein Dewey writes: ". . . policies and proposals for social action [should] be treated as working hypotheses, not as programs to be rigidly adhered to and executed. They will be experimental in the sense that they will be entertained subject to constant and well-equipped observation of the consequences they entail when acted upon, and subject to ready and flexible revision in light of observed consequences." Pp. 202–203. More recently, Garry Brewer has argued that the appropriate use of models in the policy process would be as ongoing experiments, in *Politicians, Bureaucrats, and the Consultant* (New York: Basic Books, 1973), pp. 233–235.

[33] See, for example, Irving Janis, *Groupthink* (Boston: Houghton Mifflin, 1983).

[34] In particular, see chapter 6.

[35] In fact, one scholar argues that democratic politics generally is rendered unintelligible in a setting in which there is no agreement over the dimensions of value underlying political conflict. See William H. Riker, *Liberalism Versus Populism* (San Francisco: Freeman, 1982), chapter 5.

political culture, relatively frequent interaction among subsystem members, and common interest among subsets of the members build bridges toward common belief systems.

Within more recently developed and less-established subsystems, members can be expected to evidence greater fragmentation among (and less coherence within) belief systems. As subsystems become more established, and as members engage in repeated interaction and become aware of the range of affected interests, subsystem actors will tend toward a common belief system or—what is more likely—cluster into (often competing) coalitions characterized by shared belief systems.[36] When subsystem actors work for organizations that have adopted a position in the policy debate, the actor frequently adopts a belief system consistent with the agency position. Selection bias in hiring analysts serves to strengthen such consistencies. Where such organizations are involved to a significant degree in the policy debate, they provide a base for coalescence around a particular belief system.

One of the most important factors contributing to relative homogeneity of belief systems within policy subsystems appears to be the relative concentration of focus and specialization among members on common issues, and the frequency of interaction among subsystem members. One acute observer provides illustrative examples of a highly homogeneous subsystem—public health—in contrast to the highly fragmented transportation subsystem.[37] The common focus on specific health-related issues encouraged considerable commonality of concern, interaction, and belief in the former case, while the division of the transportation subcommunity into distinct areas (e.g., railroads and highways) discouraged such coalescence.

Finally, the pattern of interaction within subsystems, often based on the budget cycle, the requirement of statutory renewal of programs, or the vagaries of reelection provides an overriding stimulus to subsystem activity and coalescence. The existence of a recurring and common political forum on the policy issue, to which subsystem members contribute action and/or advice, comes closest to being a sufficient (though perhaps not necessary) condition for subsystem members to coalesce around a small number of belief systems.

4.3
POLICY ANALYSIS AND SUBSYSTEM CONFLICT

The use of analysis in policy debate within subsystems centers on a variety of cognitive and behavioral processes whereby individuals learn—and seek to

---

[36] See Aaron Wildavsky's "The Analysis of Issue Contexts in the Study of Decision-Making," *The Journal of Politics,* vol. 24 (1962), pp. 717–732; and Kingdon, *Agendas, Alternatives.*

[37] Ibid., pp. 124–125.

communicate to others—means to realize or defend the core precepts of their belief system. Sabatier has developed a useful point of departure for examination of these processes in his model of "strategic interaction" within policy subsystems.[38] Included are: (1) improving one's understanding of the variables defined as important by one's belief system (or, secondarily, by competing belief systems), (2) refining one's understanding of logical and causal relationships internal to a belief system—typically with a focus on the search for improved mechanisms to attain core values, (3) identifying and responding to constraints external to one's belief system—such as changes in levels of political support, the activities of others, or the emergence of anomalous new data—through modification of (first) peripheral and (if necessary) core precepts of the belief system, and (4) responding to exogenous opportunities (that is, creatively responding to new opportunities in a manner consistent with one's belief system). Thus *policy-oriented learning* is the process of attempting to better understand and achieve core policy objectives until confronted by new constraints or opportunities, at which point one attempts to adjust to the new situation in a manner that is consistent with the core. Although events external to the subsystem (for example, economic, social, or political change) or opponent's activities may force the reexamination of belief systems, the resistance to alteration of elements of the core means that learning occurs most readily in the peripheral aspects of a belief system.

One of the basic processes in policy evolution involves the development of, and interaction among, different advocacy coalitions. One very general depiction of this process is as follows: a few people perceive a problem or source of dissatisfaction (for example, dying northeastern forests and lakes) and search for information. They identify one or more causes—such as the burning of high-sulfur coal—and then propose one or more policies to deal with the specific causes. Thus a policy belief system is developed and employed in the policy process. Each policy alternative, such as compulsory installation of scrubbers in industrial and utility plants, implies a set of costs or benefits to various actors. Those who feel themselves aggrieved by the proposed policy have a number of options. They can:

1. challenge the data concerning the seriousness of the problem (are the lakes and forests *really* dying?);
2. challenge the causal model (is coal burning *really* the culprit?);
3. challenge whether this is the best policy for dealing with a cause by pointing to its costs to themselves and others (high utility rates, loss of jobs in the industrial Midwest) and/or by mobilizing political opposition to the proposal.

---

[38] Sabatier, "Advocacy Coalition."

POLICY ANALYSIS IN THE PROCESS OF SUBSYSTEM CONFLICT *

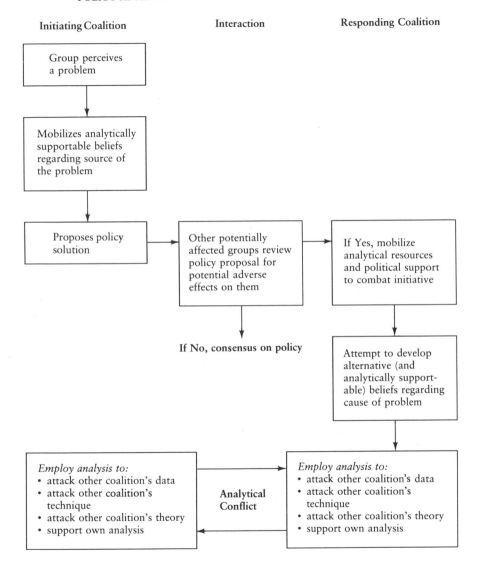

FIGURE 4-1

*Paul Sabatier presents a more elaborate depiction of this process in "Advocacy Coalition,"
Policy Sciences, vol. 21, nos. 2–3 (1988), pp. 129–168. Adopted by permission.

Thus the aggrieved actors construct an alternative, conflicting belief system
and, with it, weigh in against the initiative of the first group. The original
group normally responds to these challenges, thereby initiating the process
outlined in figure 4-1. Frequently more than two groups are involved, either

stemming from a diversity of interests within the policy subsystem or from one or more groups having been drawn into the process from connected and overlapping policy subsystems. In this process each group attempts to (1) convince key policy decision makers that its belief system is the appropriate one, leading to the preferred policy choice, or failing that, (2) to restructure the policy space as perceived by key decision makers in order to achieve a policy outcome approximating as closely as possible their own position.

Drawing upon the concepts of belief systems, policy subsystems, and the model of interactive learning described above, a set of hypotheses are proposed linking central factors of the policy debate to the ways in which analysis is used and to the likelihood of policy learning and (therefore) change. These hypotheses are described at length below, and are applied to a set of case studies presented in later chapters.[39]

Levels of conflict.   The likelihood that provision and use of analysis will result in significant modification of existing policy belief systems with policy implications is a function of the level of subsystem conflict attending a particular issue. Levels of conflict, as defined here, reflect the degree of incompatibility of belief systems of competing subsystem coalitions.

The more directly the core precepts of each competing coalition are supported or threatened by the analytical issue, the higher the level of conflict attending that issue. In general, the level of conflict has two offsetting effects on the provision of, and receptivity to, policy analysis by subsystem participants. First, the higher the level of conflict (i.e., the more directly the core is threatened), the greater the incentives of both subsystem coalitions to commit resources to provide and use analysis to defend the core. Second, as conflict rises, and both coalitions have more at stake, the receptivity of subsystem participants to analytical findings that *threaten* their existing belief systems will decline.

Intense conflict results from struggle over initiatives, and the claims used to support and oppose such initiatives, that impinge upon the core of the opposing belief systems; success for one coalition would entail losses on core dimensions of value and/or repudiation of core beliefs regarding causal relations for their opponents. It is in cases of intense conflict—with core values and precepts at stake—that the use of analysis is most likely to be employed primarily as a political resource; strident claims that the defended belief system is appropriate, and that the opposing one is fundamentally flawed, are the norm. All sides have great incentives to make their "best case," and to give as little ground as possible. Learning and belief system modification by subsystem members is particularly difficult in this situation because the stakes

---

[39] These ideas were applied in a slightly different way in Jenkins-Smith, "Analytical Debates."

are high and the core threatened. This is apparently what one congressman had in mind who, when asked whether he weighed scientific advice in arriving at policy positions, responded: "We don't. That's ridiculous. You have a general posture, you use the scientist's evidence as ammunition. The idea that a guy starts with a clean slate and weighs the evidence is absurd."[40]

When the cores of competing coalitions are less directly threatened by the analytical issue, the level of conflict is moderated. When core values and precepts draw support from a large number of interrelated beliefs about the world, a successful assault on one of those beliefs may not seriously jeopardize the core itself. In such situations, neither coalition sees the outcome of the debate as *decisive* for the core, but a favorable outcome *would* provide marginal support for that core. Thus, while both coalitions are stimulated to provide information and analysis supporting their respective belief systems, neither has excessively high stakes in the outcome. In conflict situations of this kind, subsystem members will evidence significant (but not unlimited) flexibility in questioning and modifying their own belief systems. Compromise, and partial acceptance of the opponents' claims—and thereby the admission of a modified understanding of the policy issue—is an acceptable result to both sides. Note, however, that the less support for the core that is available from other indirect or direct sources, the more important the remaining support becomes. In that way, what was previously a matter of only moderate conflict can be escalated to intense conflict if other support has been successfully assaulted. The reverse is also true; what were highly tendentious issues in the past, permitting little learning among subsystem members, can become less crucial to the core through the cumulation of broader support from other sources, thus permitting relaxation of the rigid defensive posture accompanying vital defense of the core.

At the further extreme, an element of the policy debate may be peripheral for both subsystem coalitions. This occurs when, for example, the implementation of a policy position is expected by both sides to have some set of repercussions that—in the view of the participants—are insignificant or offset one another. In this case neither side has much to gain by rigidly adhering to a set of beliefs on the matter, but—more importantly—neither side has much reason to introduce information or analysis on the question. The net effect is that the matter receives little attention or only (at best) superficial analysis because the engines of interest in the policy debate are focused elsewhere. It is interesting to note that economic efficiency, as a policy value, has long held this status, and that such luminaries as Charles Schultze have attempted to lift it from this status by the injection of "partisan efficiency advocates"—for

---

[40] John Kingdon, *Congressmen's Voting Decisions* (New York: Harper and Row, 1973), p. 223.

whom economic efficiency is prominently a part of the core—throughout the policy subsystems of government.[41]

To summarize, prospects for adjustment of belief systems in light of new information and analysis are highest when neither coalition perceives the core of its belief system to be at stake; the vigor with which members engage in the production of information and analysis rises as the importance of the implications of the matter for the core is increased. Thus, at high levels of conflict, much analysis is produced, and the uses to which it is put will be largely "political," such as delay and justification. Moderate levels of conflict provide the set of incentives most conducive to the provision and use of analysis to inform public decisions as prescribed by the policy analysis paradigm; moderate incentives exist to provide analysis, and some willingness to change belief systems exists. Under low-level conflict, analysis is typically not provided, or it is partial or haphazard at best.

Constraints on subsystem conflict.   Subsystem coalitions are not wholly unconstrained in their provision of, and response to, analytical claims in support of their belief systems. Occasionally, even when the core is at stake, analysts for competing coalitions will acknowledge the veracity of threatening claims made by their opponents. Put differently, the range of intensities of conflict within which analysis can be employed to modify belief systems and policy positions varies. What accounts for this variability?

Several key elements of the subsystem environment, and characteristics of the policy issue itself, appear to critically affect the manner in which analysts promote, refute, or adjust to potentially threatening analytical claims. The most important of such factors appear to be (1) the *analytical tractability* of the issue under study, and (2) the *nature of the forum* in which the debate is conducted. In both cases, the constraints affecting the latitude for analytically plausible responses and strategies by the participant to the threat are materially affected. These factors are discussed in turn.

Analytical tractability.   Policy analysis, like science, is a social activity. It is grounded in the process of finding agreement among practitioners regarding what count as valid bases for claims made regarding policy-relevant facts and values.[42] While the process in policy analysis is necessarily more tentative, less

---

[41] Charles Schultze, *The Politics and Economics of Public Spending* (Washington, DC: Brookings Institution, 1968).

[42] For a description of this activity within the social sciences, see, Arnold Brecht, *Political Theory: The Foundations of Twentieth Century Political Thought* (Princeton, NJ: Princeton University Press, 1959), p. 114.

precise, and more eclectic than is true of the sciences,[43] policy analysis has nonetheless developed a substantial body of concepts, methods, and guidelines (often borrowed from the social sciences) that constitute broadly accepted means to analyze policy issues and provide advice.[44] Within given policy subfields, analysts typically come to recognize and employ common sources of data, concepts, and theories regarding the subject at hand.[45] These commonalities provide the epistemological basis for convincing subsystem participants of the veracity of policy-relevant assertions; when the techniques of analysis, theory, and data regarding an issue are well developed and widely agreed upon, the validity of such assertions can be assessed with respect to a common standard. Also of importance is the existence of an agreed-upon value or goal with which to compare options. Determining the least-cost route for a sanitation vehicle or the optimal location for a fire station within an urban area, would readily permit such an assessment.[46] On these issues, the range of professionally acceptable analytical disagreement is fairly narrow. Such issues are analytically tractable.

But often the issue at hand is less subject to commonly acceptable analytical theories, concepts, and sources of data. This is particularly likely when the focus of analysis is on complex phenomena, when important relationships span several policy issue–areas, and when the issue concerns multiple policy objectives that may conflict. On such issues, analysis is subject to a great deal of uncertainty, and not surprisingly, different analysts are prone to provide estimates and analytical conclusions quite at variance with one another. On such issues, sufficient uncertainty exists to permit wide substantive disagreement without placing any of the protagonists beyond the pale of analytical plausibility. In general, the less well developed an area of inquiry, the more elusive the necessary data, and (above all) the weaker the *agreement on theory and data,* the greater the level of analytical intractability. Such intractability, in turn, admits a greater degree of analytically plausible "difference of opinion" among analysts.

In the extreme, the complexity and uncertainty of some policy issues are sufficient to admit wholly divergent belief systems, dissimilar enough that

---

[43] See chapter 2 for a description of the nature of policy analysis.

[44] Often these concepts, methods, and guidelines are likened to the analyst's "toolkit." See, for example, Edith Stokey and Richard Zeckhauser, *A Primer,* chapters one through three; David Nachmias, *Public Policy Evaluation: Approaches and Methods* (New York: St. Martins Press, 1979); and Carol Weiss, *Evaluation Research: Methods of Assessing Program Effectiveness* (Englewood Cliffs, NJ: Prentice-Hall, 1972).

[45] Kingdon, "Agendas, Alternatives," p. 84.

[46] For a celebrated case of the success of policy analysis regarding the processing of fire alarm calls in New York City, see Martin Greenberger, et al., *Models in the Policy Process* (New York: Russell Sage Foundation, 1976), chapter 8. In that instance, though the policy environment evidenced quite a bit of conflict, the tractability of the issue permitted clear-cut demonstration of the veracity of the analytical claims. After several tries, the policy recommendation was adopted.

common bases for evaluating the validity of policy-relevant assertions are entirely lacking. On such issues, analytical debates take on the following characteristics:

> Underlying the factual issues apparently in dispute are the differences at the "framework" level, that is, differences in basic presuppositions and in patterns of thinking employed. In the main these differences manifest themselves in differences concerning the nature of present social reality, the focus of interest of analysis and policy, and the interpretation and use of data. *None* of these differences . . . can be unambiguously resolved since the *criteria* in terms of which such a resolution should be made are *themselves* in dispute.[47]

On issues characterized by such fundamental differences in basic belief analysts cannot resolve competing analytical claims by recourse to a common body of analytic knowledge and technique. In effect, there is no overlap—no common ground—across belief systems from which to develop consensual resolution of competing analytical claims. Resolution of the policy debate in such situations typically awaits change imposed on belief systems from outside the subsystem, such as turnover in subsystem participants through large-scale electoral change.

In general, then, the greater the analytical tractability with respect to a policy issue, the wider the range of subsystem conflict that could accommodate the use of analysis to modify competing belief systems. Conversely, intractable issues permit a wide range of plausible analytical positions, allowing subsystem participants with conflicting belief systems to promote and defend their conflicting analytical claims with relative impunity. Thus intractability serves to *decrease* the range of conflict within which belief system adjustment and policy learning take place.

The nature of the analytical forum.   Because analysis is a social process in which subsystem participants endeavor to find agreement about policy-relevant facts and values, important characteristics of that process are in part a function of the *number and kinds of people* involved in the process. The forum can range from one in which all interested parties can take part—an open forum—to one in which admission is strictly controlled through some kind of screening—a closed forum. The importance of the degree of openness of the forum is twofold: first, certain types of screening for admission to the debate may assure that those who do participate can speak a common analytic language and can find common bases for verification of analytical claims.

---

[47] John Robinson, "Apples and Horned Toads," p. 24. Emphasis added. Also see David Webber, "Obstacles to the Utilization of Systematic Policy Analysis: Conflicting World Views and Competing Disciplinary Matrices," in *Knowledge: Creation, Diffusion, Utilization,* 4(4) (June 1983), pp. 534–560.

Second, screening may limit the number of—and conflict among—belief systems represented in the forum.

Open fora are those in which all mobilized participants within the subsystem are able to actively engage in the debate. The usual locus of such fora is the Congress, in which floor debates and committee hearings provide ample opportunity for all sides to be heard. In open fora, with the very broad range of backgrounds and levels of technical sophistication of the participants, room exists for a very wide range of beliefs. Furthermore the common training, experience, and professional peer-group pressure that might serve to constrain analytical claims are lacking. In such fora, analysis can be expected to back many sides of the debate, and generally will not provide a basis for consensus in resolving competing analytical claims. As one observer remarked about the open Congressional forum:

> The dominant mode of analysis on Capitol Hill, the pressure-group model, is uncongenial to policy analysis based on other models. . . . Policy analysis is seen as merely the continuation of pressure politics by other means, another weapon to be used to support predetermined positions. What counts is . . . what side it supports.[48]

Not all fora admit such a plurality and range of beliefs and assumptions, however. By design, some fora effectively screen participants in a manner designed to foster commonality of language, assumptions, and belief systems. Of such kind are *professionalized fora*, which admit participants on the basis of professional training and technical competence. Such fora are typically created to conduct analysis in specialized areas believed to fall within the peculiar competence of the professional group involved. Examples range from the staffs of administrative and independent regulatory groups within government[49] to such private organizations as the Brookings Institute, the American Enterprise Institute, and the Energy Modeling Forum.[50]

---

[48] David Seidman, "The Politics of Policy Analysis: Protection or Overprotection in Drug Regulation?" *Regulation,* 1(1) (July/August 1977), pp. 22–37.

[49] Recent literature on the use of analysis in regulatory decision making has suggested that the European style of regulatory debate and decision may be better likened to the professionalized fora than are arenas provided by U.S. regulatory agencies. See Ronald Brickman, "Science and the Politics of Toxic Chemical Regulation: U.S. and European Contrasts," in *Science, Technology, and Human Values,* vol. 9, issue 1 (Winter 1984), no. 46, pp. 107–111. Also see Harvy Brooks, "The Resolution of Technically Intensive Public Policy Disputes," *Science, Technology, and Human Values,* vol. 9, issue 1, (Winter 1984), no. 46, pp. 39–50, and Nicholas Ashford, "Advisory Committees in OSHA and EPA: Their Use in Regulatory Decisionmaking," in, *Science, Technology, and Human Values,* vol. 9, issue 1, (Winter 1984), no. 46, pp. 72–82.

[50] A professionalized forum that is a mixture of the public and private types mentioned here is the technical trade group mobilized within an industry to advise governmental agencies. Within the energy area, the National Petroleum Council is such a group. For an intriguing example from the telecommunications industry and the FCC, see Richard Barke's "Technological Change and Regulatory Adjustment: The FCC and Technical Standard Setting," (paper delivered at the meetings of the Association for Public Policy and Management, New Orleans, October 1984).

Within such fora, analysts are much more likely to find shared bases for verification or rejection of analytical claims than is true of an open forum. Education within a professional field serves in part to narrow the range of acceptable beliefs and to provide a common pool of knowledge and technique with which to assess analytical claims.[51] Economists, engineers, operations researchers, policy analysts, and other professionals who regularly contribute to analysis strive for such a restricted set of beliefs, and for development of a common pool of knowledge and procedures, as a matter of course.[52] Those who propose creation of an authoritative "science court" to adjudicate among competing policy-relevant scientific claims seek to formally employ these consensus-engendering aspects of the professional scientific fields. To the extent that an analytical forum is restricted to members of such a profession, then, one could anticipate that the range of analytical disagreement would be narrowed, and that the frequency with which competing analytical claims could be (at least tentatively) resolved would increase.[53]

While little empirical research has been done comparing the resolution of policy analytic conflict between open and professionalized fora, recent and ongoing work in this area suggests that within some professionalized fora, even highly contentious issues, on which a great deal is at stake for competing parties, can be resolved by consensus.[54] Whether consensus is made possible because verification of factual assertions is made easier, or because certain claims are excluded by dint of professional blinders, remains an open and important question.

Often the screening of participants in analytical fora takes place on bases other than technical and professional proficiency. With some frequency, admission is controlled by one or more (usually high-level) officials for one or more of several reasons: (1) because information bearing on national security

---

[51] Thomas Kuhn argues that the training of scientists, employing standardized texts and common experimental reinforcement, serves to induct new generations of scientists into common, existing paradigms of scientific thought. The paradigm then serves to orient research, indicate what counts as valid data, how to construct and carry out tests, and the like. See his "Postscript—1969," in *The Structure of Scientific Revolutions*, 2nd ed. (Chicago: University of Chicago Press, 1970), pp. 174–210, especially 176–191. In less elaborate form, a similar phenomenon takes place in the training of policy analysts, economists, operations researchers, and others who regularly engage in the analysis of public policy.

[52] The "case method" approach of teaching policy analysis employed at the Kennedy School of Government, Harvard University, is an explicit attempt to build up such a common pool of knowledge and experience for policy analysts.

[53] This should not be taken to mean that professionalized fora foster agreement across professional groups—only within them. For an interesting cross-sectional view of the beliefs of scientists, economists, and administrators regarding health and safety regulation, see Robert Crandall and Lester Lave, eds., *The Scientific Basis of Health and Safety Regulation* (Washington, DC: Brookings Institute, 1981).

[54] See Barke, "Technological Change." Similar research has been proposed by John Weyant, to focus on the process of policy debate within the highly professionalized Energy Modeling Forum at Stanford University.

is involved, (2) because the issue is politically sensitive and the involved decision makers wish to explore the issue without the glare of public scrutiny, and (3) to limit "spurious" conflict within the forum by excluding members of known (and disapproved) predispositions.[55] Screening for such reasons results in *closed fora.*

Occasionally the creation of a closed forum can result in seriously biased and misleading analysis. When decision makers are committed to a particular policy option, and want analysis to serve mainly as justification for that course of action, compliant analysis can be obtained by screening participants according to policy viewpoint. Such strategies were employed with some frequency within the Environmental Protection Agency (EPA) under Director Ann Gorsuch Burford.[56] The EPA reportedly employed "secret science courts" that excluded participation by a large fraction of the policy subsystem—including "not only the traditional public interest groups, but the entire scientific and public health community as well."[57] The resulting analysis did provide the desired conclusions, but only at the cost of alienation of much of the policy subsystem.[58]

The conduct of analysis within closed fora is and will doubtless remain an important and attractive option for decision makers. However, because analysis is by definition an activity reliant on informed consensus within subsystems, the use of closed fora will inevitably involve certain tensions. A successfully closed forum becomes, in a sense, its own analytic microcosm; its work cannot be critically debated and verified or rejected by the excluded members of the subsystem. In that case, the effect is to limit the information provided to decision makers and may even inhibit consensus that would develop in a broader, open forum.

In sum, the characteristics of the forum in which analysis is employed, like the tractability of the issue itself, can materially affect the ways in which analysis is used. In open fora, greater latitude exists for expression of conflicting analytical claims. In these cases, analysis is likely to be employed by all sides in the debate, and rarely will analytical conflict be resolved. Restricted fora may enhance prospects for consensus by ensuring that participants have shared bases for verifying analytical claims (professional fora), or

---

[55] One proponent of the use of closed fora argues that, given that experts disagree, the decision maker should select expert advisors based on their acceptance of a common paradigm in order to avoid "disfunctional disagreement." See D. C. Phillips, "When Evaluators Disagree: Perplexities and Perspectives," *Policy Sciences,* vol. 8 (1977), pp. 147–159.

[56] Rushefsky, "Misuse of Science," pp. 47–59. For a more general indictment, see Horowitz, "Social Science Mandarins."

[57] Rushefsky, "Misuse of Science," p. 51.

[58] Documents pertaining to the restricted forum and the suppression of undesirable conclusions by EPA officials were subsequently obtained by reporters. (Ibid.) Exposure of these transgressions contributed to the eventual resignations of EPA Director Gorsuch and many other high-level EPA officials.

by screening participants on the basis of policy viewpoint. At the same time, restricted fora may bias the core values and beliefs introduced into the analysis. These characteristics, and their implications for the role of policy analysis in policy making, are summarized in table 4-1.

TABLE 4-1

Effects of conflict, analytical tractability, and analytical forum
on the role of policy analysis in policy debates

Level of conflict	Analytical tractability	Analytical forum
Low: Only peripheral beliefs and policy positions involved. Subsystem coalitions are willing to consider belief change, but have very little incentive to invest analytical resources. Learning via analysis is therefore unlikely.	*Low:* Little agreement on theory or data, leading to a *broad range* of plausible analytical positions. Analysis can be mobilized to support a wide array of policy positions with relative impunity.	*Open:* All active subsystem participants admitted to the debate; results in a wide range of professional backgrounds and a *lack of common bases for assessment of analytical claims.* Reduces the role of analysis in shaping or constraining policy debate.
Medium: A mix of policy core and peripheral beliefs and policy positions involved. Coalitions willing to alter some beliefs and policy positions on the basis of analytical results. Best prospects for learning through policy analysis.		*Professionalized:* Participants admitted on basis of professional/ technical competence, and thus *share common bases for assessing analytical claims.* Enhances role of analysis in contraining the scope of plausible claims made in policy debate.
High: Core and policy core beliefs involved. Coalitions are very willing to commit analytical resources but are unlikely to alter beliefs or policy positions on the basis of analytical results. Analysis serves primarily as analytical ammunition in policy debates.	*High:* Substantial agreement on data and theory, leading to a *narrow range* of plausible analytical claims. Increases the political costs of maintaining an implausible policy position, even in the face of high levels of conflict.	*Closed:* Admission to forum is based on screening by political elites. Effect is dependent on the type of screening. Useful in that it permits analyses of unpopular policy options, but may limit the scope of debate and bias analysis for political purposes.

_____ **4.4** _____

PRESCRIPTION OF PROFESSIONAL ROLES

To this point this discussion has been focused on the *processes* of analysis in policy subsystems, with only indirect reference to the professional activity of individual analysts.[59] The major characteristics of the mobilization and use of analysis described thus far—conflict among belief systems, recalcitrance of the beliefs of subsystem participants, and the constraints imposed by fora and analytical tractability—all have direct and often decisive effects on the choices and resultant behavior of analysts. My intent in this section is to apply these factors more directly to the roles played by the analyst as particular policy issues are analyzed. This shall be done by first developing a more concrete depiction of the key factors of the policy context as they bear on individual analysts and, second, by describing the primary professional roles that have been proposed for analysts who work in that context.

With the shift in focus from the process of analytical debate within subsystems to the activities of individual analysts, concern also shifts from primary focus on conflict among competing belief systems to advocacy in the interest of particular policy positions. As described above, particular policy preferences are typically drawn from a broader underlying belief system, and debates over specific policy issues often represent battles within a larger war among competing belief systems.[60] However, there are instances—to be described below—when an analyst's advocacy of a policy viewpoint is somewhat removed from larger battles over belief systems. Therefore the following sections will refer primarily to analysis as used to assess, defend, or critique particular policy positions, rather than belief systems.

The remainder of this chapter will focus on a general set of questions: What are the primary roles prescribed for the practice of analysis? Under what sets of conditions in the policy context are these roles likely to be successfully employed? Finally, in what ways do these roles reinforce or undermine the praise and criticisms of analysis raised in prior chapters?

The literature of the field offers three predominant models of the role of policy analysts. I call these models the *objective technician*, the *issue advocate*, and the *client's advocate*. These models—or styles of analysis—prescribe the analyst's obligations to his client, the values to be pursued, and the role to be played in the policy-making process. In seeking to define the analyst's role, the critical question is whether the analyst's obligations in each of these roles

---

[59] The following sections draw heavily on Hank Jenkins-Smith, "Professional Roles for Policy Analysts: A Critical Assessment," *Journal of Policy Analysis and Management*, 2(1) (Fall 1982), pp. 88–100. Reprinted by permission of John Wiley & Sons, Inc.

[60] See Joseph Falkson, "Minor Skirmish in a Monumental Struggle: HEW's Analysis of Mental Health Services," *Policy Analysis*, 2(1) (Winter 1976), pp. 93–119.

are congruent with the pressures and incentives in the analyst's environment. Careful study of the prominent factors shaping the analyst's environment indicates that each of the three styles of analysis may harmonize well with some elements of the analyst's environment but may conflict with others. Such conflict will result in significant tensions, or ethical dilemmas, for the analyst. Furthermore, the existence and severity of such tensions will indicate the likely *success* of these styles of analysis—how widely they are employed and with what degree of conformity among analysts.

The Policy Context

In providing advice for a client, the analyst must work within a political context. No analyst is immune to the stresses and strains of that context, such as perceived threats to career advancement or pressures from colleagues,[61] but such stresses will vary according to several factors. The key factors are the client-analyst relationship and the "policy arena" with which the analyst is concerned.

Client-analyst relationship.   One important factor is the degree to which incentives are present for the analyst to treat his analysis and advice as tools to serve the interest of the client. I call this the level of "organizational allegiance" to which the analyst is subject. Three characteristics of the organizational setting have a primary bearing on the level of organizational allegiance. First, and most obvious, are the analyst's conditions of employment. Organizational allegiance is fostered when the client has significant influence over the analyst's career. This means, for example, that analysts protected by civil service are likely to have lower levels of organizational allegiance than analysts hired to work on the personal staffs of members of Congress. By the same token, analysts that are easily employable elsewhere will have lower levels of organizational allegiance than those without easy alternatives. The organizational allegiance of the analyst who operates as an independent consultant may be curbed by the fact that his relation with the client is clearly limited and transitory. Allegiance will be increased, however, to the extent that the analyst is dependent on the client for future contracts.[62]

A second important characteristic is the analyst's proximity to the client. Relations between the analyst and client will differ in terms of the number of

---

[61] See, for example, Aaron Wildavsky, "The Self-Evaluating Organization," *Public Administration Review,* 32(5) (Sept./Oct.), 1973, pp. 509–520. The more general question of actors in bureaucratic institutions is discussed in William Niskanen, "Bureaucrats and Politicians," *Journal of Law and Economics,* 18(3) (December 1975), pp. 617–643; and Anthony Downs' *Inside Bureaucracy* (Boston: Little, Brown, 1967).

[62] For an excellent discussion of the role of consultants in policy analysis, see Marver, *Consultants Can Help.*

intervening bureaucratic layers between them; the secretary of an administrative department will typically have to pass analytical requests through many layers of underlings before they reach the analyst. That is an instance of great organizational distance. On other occasions, the analyst works in close proximity to the client—perhaps as a "special assistant" within the secretary's office. In general, the ability of the client to gain adequate feedback on the behavior of his analysts can be expected to increase as the organizational distance between them is reduced. Proximity promotes feedback; feedback as a rule increases organizational allegiance by sharpening rewards and punishments.[63]

The policy arena.   Other important factors that shape the policy environment are the characteristics of the policy issue and the politics that surround it. From the perspective of the analyst, three factors are critical: (1) the degree to which the client is committed to a particular policy position, (2) the level of analytical tractability of the issue, and (3) the predisposition of analysts to view other analysts as playing the role of advocate.

First, a client who is highly committed to a policy position on a given issue is likely to be immune to persuasive analysis. Members of Congress tend to support pork-barrel legislation favoring their districts even though the programs involved can be shown to be highly inefficient; congressional support for the various federal water projects and the Clinch River Breeder Reactor are notorious cases in point. In executive agencies, clients may be committed on anything from policy objectives to questions of jurisdictional turf. Clients who are highly committed to a policy choice on an issue are more likely to want ammunition to defend their point than they are to want balanced and neutral advice.[64]

---

[63] Herbert Kaufman, *Administrative Feedback: Monitoring Subordinate's Behavior* (Washington, DC: Brookings Institute, 1973), p. 5.

[64] There will be occasions when even a client committed to a particular policy outcome will prefer balanced advice rather than analytical ammunition. When an issue is new, or recently transformed and in the early stages of the policy process, the belief systems of policy elites concerning the issue typically remain ill-defined, and stable coalitions in favor of particular positions have yet to develop. The newness of the issue and the uncertainty it engenders provide even a committed client with incentives to acquire balanced analysis that attempts to look at the issue in a dispassionate manner. Possible political drawbacks to the position taken by the decision maker may be exposed, such as the discovery of previously unknown vested interests, as well as unexpected general "costs" attributable to the position. On the other hand, when belief systems are well developed, with most active policy elites adopting one of a few opposing views of the problem, the committed client is less likely to want balanced analysis. Indeed, balanced analysis of a controversial issue could prove a threat if it were to undermine his or her position and be leaked to the press. The "issue context" is thus important in shaping the decision maker's preferences for analysis. Aaron Wildavsky has outlined a typology of issue contexts that is useful for understanding the patterns of use of analysis. See "The Analysis of Issue Contexts in the Study of Decision-Making,".

A second characteristic of the policy arena that has an important bearing on the role the analyst plays concerns the analytical tractability of the policy problem as described earlier. One of the more effective restraints against blatant abuse of policy analyis is that the analyst's product is often subject to scrutiny by other analysts. Deviation from accepted analytical norms can be the cause for significant professional embarrassment and the loss of credibility.[65] But often the line between neutral and biased analysis is far from clear. When the issue is analytically intractable—and the problem involves parameters or relations about which very little is known—the analyst can reasonably make any of a range of analytically plausible assumptions about those parameters or relations. Where the issue is more tractable, the range of plausible results is narrowed; here the analyst finds it more difficult to shade the analysis to support a preconceived policy position for fear that colleagues will condemn the analysis as "cooked."[66]

The problems created by analytically intractable issues are compounded by the specialized, insular nature of the bureaucracy. By virtue of the accretion of specialized expertise in various agencies, analysts from those agencies hold, in effect, "turf rights" with respect to particular analytical questions. Two examples of such control over elements of analysis that are important to the case studies presented in later chapters are the suzerainty of the tax analysts in the Treasury Department over estimates of the effect of various policies on federal tax receipts, and the control of the Maritime Administration over estimates of present and future oil tanker shipping charges. When combined with an advocacy role, analysts in such favored positions are given wider latitude—at least in the short run—to manipulate the dimensions of value and causal relations underlying analysis. Over time, of course, if any agency vested with such turf rights appears to have consistently given greater weight to its advocacy role than to the provision of balanced analysis, the agency's credibility may be undermined, and other less-biased sources of advice may be sought. Thus advocates must employ their control over turf with care; they must weigh the urgency of the present analytical battle against the potential loss of credibility required to wage future analytical battles.

The latitude permitted by analytically intractable issues is in part determined by the technical capabilities of those who judge the analysis. In an open forum, when analysts in many quarters are involved, analysts will be constrained primarily by the tractability of the issue. But frequently the fora are closed: in the context of the repetitive cycle of analyses characteristic of federal agencies, in which deliberations are often buried deeply within the bureau-

---

[65] Michael Malbin, *Unelected Representatives: Congressional Staff and the Future of Representative Government* (New York: Basic Books, 1980), pp. 204–236.

[66] For another discussion of the role of uncertainty in constraining analysis, see Guy Benveniste's *The Politics of Expertise* (Berkeley, CA: The Glendessary Press, 1972), p. 45.

cracy and typically out of view of those who might critically judge analytical merit, the immediate influence of analysis on policy is wholly dependent on its appeal to the decision-making client. Thus, when the client lacks "analytical sophistication" and is therefore unable to arbitrate among opposing advocate analysts on grounds of analytical quality, the scope for attempts to manipulate the policy space is broadened, and the use of nonanalytical forms of persuasion becomes increasingly important. Particularly, rhetorical tactics tend to play an important role; greater emphasis is placed on "packaging," appeal to political symbols, and attempts to undercut the credibility of opposing analyses.

In addition to factors that indicate the limits within which attempts to manipulate the policy space may take place, an additional feature of the bureaucratic policy environment affects the *predisposition* of analysts to actually engage in such activities. Many analyses in the federal bureaucracy are joint exercises (though not necessarily conducted in an open forum), involving analysts from several departments or from several offices within a department. Furthermore, it is only natural that analysts often have differing views about what constitutes "balanced" advice. For that reason analysts working on the same issue are often confronted with what *appear* to be biased analyses originating from other quarters. In such a setting, even an analyst who would prefer to provide his client with balanced advice may feel compelled to try to shade the analysis in order to increase the attractiveness of those options undervalued by other analysts. To provide neutral advice while other participants shade the analysis in favor of a particular option is to give away the game; clients taking the "weight of the evidence" will get a skewed picture. Particularly when the issue is sufficiently intractable to make repudiation of biased analyses difficult, the inclination will be to counter bias with bias. Attempts to skew the analysis in one direction can be offset by attempts to skew it in the opposite direction, hopefully resulting in a balanced *composite* analysis. Thus the joint nature of bureaucratic analysis, combined with the heterogeneous views of analysts themselves in issue—areas frequently characterized by uncertainty, provides inducements for even the most fairminded and "objective" analysts to engage in advocacy.

The interaction.   The context of the policy analyst is shaped in large part by the manner in which the client-analyst relationship and the policy arena fit together. Contexts range from those in which the analyst faces strong incentives to provide a committed client with analytical ammunition to those in which the client is uncommitted and desires neutral advice. Even when the client remains uncommitted, however, the perception of advocacy on the part of other analysts may provide incentives to engage in advocacy analysis. Furthermore, depending on the level of analytical tractability, the analyst's ability to shade analysis to provide ammunition, or to provide unambiguous and neutral advice, will vary. Because the nature of the policy question itself is critical in determining the analyst's environment, the environment will change as the analyst shifts focus from one policy question to another; it is likely to differ, as well, as the issue moves through the policy-making process, from the development stage to the adoption stage and finally to the implementation stage.[67]

Roles in Policy Analysis

I have argued that the role that the analyst assumes is intimately related to the context in which he or she operates. This relationship is not unique to policy analysts. Even within a well-established profession, such as the law, the contexts in which the advisor operates are quite diverse. Professional norms reflect that diversity. For example, the code of ethics of the American Bar Association takes special cognizance of the multiple roles attorneys play; lawyers have somewhat different obligations to their clients, the courts, their colleagues, and the public.[68] In medicine the primary roles of the physician have centered around the doctor-patient relationship and relationships within the medical profession.[69] Likewise, a professional role for policy analysts will necessarily take shape around the various institutional actors, functions, and circumstances confronting its practitioners.

If the primary functions of policy analysts are to analyze and evaluate policies in order to advise policy makers, there seem to be crucial relationships that a professional code for policy analysts must address. One way of identifying and pursuing those relationships is to look at each of the three predominant models of analysts' roles and to explore the implications of each, with a series of questions in mind: analysts' value structure implied by the model, the role for analysts that the model implies, analysts' obligations to their clients; and whose interests analysts serve, if not those of their clients (that is, who is the analysts' beneficiary?).

The objective technician.   Perhaps the most widely held—and certainly the most widely criticized—style of analysis for policy analysts is what I call the

---

[67] Aaron Wildavsky's *The Politics of the Budgetary Process*, 3rd ed. (Boston: Little, Brown, 1979) and Eugene Bardach's *The Implementation Game* (Cambridge: MIT, 1977) address parts of this issue.

[68] See John F. Sutton, Jr., "The American Bar Association Code of Professional Responsibility: An Introduction," *Texas Law Review*, 48(2) January 1970, pp. 255–266.

[69] The increasing focus on the rising cost of health care, and on the physician's role in medical expenditures has added an important new role to those of the physician; now the doctor is asked to limit medical expenditures for the good of society as a whole. This new role and the potential conflict it engenders with the ethical demands of the doctor-patient relationship has led to significant debate in medical ethics. See, for example, Robert M. Veatch, *Professional Ethics: New Principles for Physicians?*, (Hastings-on-Hudson, NY: Hastings Center, 1980).

objective technician.[70] More than any other, this style is closely tailored to fit the dominant policy analysis paradigm. One observer describes the technician as follows:

> The technician is an academic researcher—an intellectual—in bureaucratic residence. No admirer of bureaucratic folkways, he weaves around himself a protective cocoon of computers, models, and statistical regressions. He knows about politics, but not much. Politics is somebody else's business.[71]

The technician's job is "to point to the best program rather than the most popular one."[72]

In keeping with the policy analysis paradigm, the objective technician sees no inconsistency between his objective stance and his prescription of a "best program." "Best" means maximizing net social benefits. Objectivity is not threatened because—according to the policy analysis paradigm—net benefits provide a single unidimensional measure of efficiency and an unambiguous decision rule.[73] Distributional questions create more difficulty because there are many competing criteria of equity among which to choose. The typical means by which technicians cope with distributional problems is to apply a criterion for adoption of a program that economists refer to as the Kaldor-Hicks variant of Paretian optimality: if the net benefits of the program can be distributed so that at least some people would be made better-off and none made worse-off, the program should be instituted.

Setting aside for now the theoretical and normative problems implicit in this role (see chapters 2 and 3), practicing analysts are rarely in a position to pursue very far their search for the most efficient program. The pace of the policy process puts constraints on the time and resources an analyst may commit to a policy problem.[74] Because time and resources are limited, the technician is driven to concentrate on programs that enjoy broad consensus and political support.[75] Furthermore, as a practical matter, on issues that are

---

[70] "Technician" is borrowed in part from Arnold Meltsner's *Policy Analysts,* on which I draw heavily in the pages that follow. I have added "objective" to reflect the analyst's view that he works only with neutral facts and unbiased analytical techniques.

[71] Ibid., p. 18.

[72] Ibid., p. 22.

[73] Of course, in practice there are great problems in the calculation of net benefits. See Aaron Wildavsky's "The Political Economy of Efficiency: Cost–Benefit Analysis, Systems Analysis, and Program Budgeting," in *Public Administration Review,* 26(4) (December 1966), pp. 292–310; and Julius Margolis, "Shadow Prices for Incorrect or Nonexistent Market Values," in *Public Expenditures and Policy Analysis* 2nd ed., eds. Robert Haveman and Julius Margolis (Chicago: Rand McNally, 1977), pp. 204–220; and chapter 3 of this volume.

[74] James S. Coleman, *Policy Research in the Social Sciences* (Morristown, NJ: General Learning Press, 1972), p. 4.

[75] Meltsner, *Policy Analysts,* pp. 100–102.

analytically intractable, the technician may not be able to unambiguously specify net social benefits, let alone the distributional problems involved.

Objective technicians' desire to remain aloof from politics is key to understanding how their style of analysis links them to the political system and their clients. Among objective technicians working in the federal bureaucracy, the opportunity to do research in a policy-making environment is the central motivation for their work.[76] Once in the policy-making environment, such analysts want to be insulated from the internal games of influence and policy disputes among governmental bureaus and agencies. They want to be set free to develop "the best program" in the hope of having it selected on the basis of its objective merits.[77]

Objective technicians may well be free to practice their preferred approach in contexts in which their clients have no desire for ammunition as protagonists, or in which their clients do not have the power to compel analysts to deliver support for preconceived policy positions. The ideal context for such an analyst will thus be one with a low level of organizational allegiance and an uncommitted client. However, where the client is committed, and the analyst faces considerable organizational allegiance to the client, strong incentives to support the client's position will be present. It is in such areas that the bureaucratic analyst is likely to confront ethical dilemmas that pit concerns to maintain "objective" standards against the incentives to support a given position.[78]

A similar tension exists for objective technicians who work in private firms that contract with the government to do policy analysis. The dilemma has been described in the following terms:

> Evaluation Incorporated (a hypothetical contracting firm that specializes in evaluation) has managers who are concerned with survival. It has members who must be induced to remain. It has clients who must be served . . . When demand for services is high, it will be able to insist on the evaluative ethic.

---

[76] Ibid., p. 18.

[77] According to Meltsner, another prominent goal of technicians is simply to know they have conducted "good research." Ibid., pp. 27–30. Alternatively, Howell S. Baum suggests that this reward for having done good research is the analyst's response to frustrations at not having the autonomy and power needed to "solve problems." See Baum's "Analysts and Planners Must Think Organizationally," *Policy Analysis*, (6)4 (Fall 1980), pp. 479–494.

[78] An example of a dilemma that pits objectivity against organizational incentives can be seen in the cases of Drs. Albert Sabin and Russell Alexander, described in Richard Neustadt and Harvey Fineberg, *The Swine Flu Affair* (Washington, DC: Dept. of Health, Education and Welfare, 1978). These analysts were caught between their doubts concerning the utility and safety of the proposed swine flu immunizations and their colleagues' pressures to close ranks in favor of the program. Both chose to make their doubts public, and suffered for it. As Neustadt and Fineberg put it, the reactions of Alexander and Sabin's colleagues ". . . remind us of [the Nixon] White House reactions against favored columnists who come up with what staffers take as slurs upon the President . . . They are scornful of Sabin yet. Alexander they merely cold shouldered." Pp. 46–47.

But when demands are low, Evaluation, Incorporated, must trim its sails. It has a payroll to meet. . . .[79]

Objective technicians in private firms, therefore, face frequent demands for organizational allegiance because of the organization's need for future contracts from government agencies. For some specialized analysts, being "blacklisted" by one agency for being "difficult" can lead to generalized blacklisting by other agencies.[80] Objective technicians therefore gain little support from the environment in which they are characteristically obliged to function.

Of late, many scholars and practitioners of policy analysis have criticized the objective technician model for a variety of reasons. Some have held that the attempt to provide neutral and objective advice has led analysis to have little persuasiveness in shaping public policy.[81] Other observers have pointed out that apparently "value-free" analytical techniques widely used in policy analysis are subject to many implicit though unobvious biases, and therefore the technician's aim to be objective is difficult if not impossible to achieve.[82] Finally, it has long been contended that actors in bureaucratic organizations are primarily responsive to institutional incentives and constraints,[83] making it unlikely that analysts could remain detached while advising from within political institutions.[84] As a result of these criticisms, a great deal of literature has emerged that calls for styles of analysis that embrace advocacy, rather than neutrality.[85]

---

[79] Aaron Wildavsky, "The Self-Evaluating Organization," p. 515.

[80] Benveniste, *Politics of Expertise*, p. 44. James Coleman contends that private firms contracting to do research for government will typically be more independent—and therefore less biased—than research departments within government. See *Policy Research*, p. 21. Ida Hoos takes the opposing and provocative position that consultant analysts bring in their own technocratic biases because they are not held politically accountable for their recommendations. See her *Systems Analysis and Public Policy: A Critique*, (Berkeley, CA: University of California Press, 1972), pp. 243–245.

[81] See Martin Rein and Sheldon White's "Can Policy Research Help Policy?", *The Public Interest*, vol. 49, (Fall 1977), pp. 119–136; and Michael Goldstein et. al., "The Nonutilization of Evaluation Research," *Pacific Sociological Review*, 21(1) (January 1978), pp. 21–44.

[82] See chapter 3. In particular see Laurence H. Tribe, "Policy Science: Analysis or Ideology?", *Philosophy and Public Affairs*, vol. 22 (Fall 1972), pp. 52–109; and Henry Rowan, "The Role of Cost–Benefit Analysis in Policymaking," in *Public Expenditures and Policy Analysis,* 2nd ed. Eds. Robert H. Haveman and Julius Margolis (Chicago: Rand McNally, 1977), pp. 546–555.

[83] See Anthony Downs, "Inside Bureaucracy," and William Niskanen, "Bureaucrats and Politicians."

[84] For a particularly critical view see Horowitz, "Social Science Mandarins."

[85] For two recent examples, see Leman and Nelson, "Ten Commandments," and Fraatz, "Policy Analysts."

The issue advocate.   The issue advocate is a political actor, an analyst who acts in accordance with a preexisting belief system, pursuing specific substantive values and goals in the policy problems analyzed and advice given. These values may take a wide range of forms: the analyst, for instance, may be an advocate for reform of social programs in the interest of efficiency or equality, or for fiscal restraint on the part of government, or perhaps even for such abstract values as the freedom and dignity of man.[86] Analysts as advocates differ from technicians in that they see their role as one of active participation in the political process; they are involved in influencing the final form of public policy. At heart, this style of analysis may be based on some sort of a pluralist conception of policy making, in which many competing actors may have a part.[87] Alternatively, it may be based on an adversarial perception of the political process, in which various policy options have their day in court to be supported by their advocates and opposed by their detractors. In either case, an open forum for analytic debate is presupposed, in which (presumably) all significant policy viewpoints are represented.

One discussion of the viewpoint of the issue advocate is based on Charles Lindblom's conception of policy analysis as "muddling through" or as "disjointed incrementalism." From this viewpoint, the analyst

> [f]eels he can afford to make mistakes because policymaking is serial and fragmented . . . The incrementalist feels that he can ignore consequences at will because if those ignored should prove damaging to certain groups such groups will press for new analyses and new decisions . . . he depends on politics in a plural society to provide, eventually, whatever degree of closure is feasible in an obstreperous world.[88]

Analysts championing a particular cause or social interest may fit this conception best, as would the federal analysts cited by Meltsner who saw themselves as advocates for the poor.[89]

While rejecting the detached and neutral role of the technician in the political process, many issue advocates still adhere to the injunction of the policy analysis paradigm that the public interest is best served through maximizing net social welfare, or the more practical goal of promoting economically efficient programs.

Once the analyst has decided what constitutes the "best program," he or she becomes an advocate for that program. This requires the advocate to map

---

[86] Harold Lasswell espouses the values of the freedom and dignity of man as the underpinning of the "policy science" profession in "The Policy Orientation," in *The Policy Sciences*, eds. Max Lerner and Harold Lasswell (Stanford, CA: Stanford University Press, 1951) pp. 1–15.

[87] See Archibald, "Three Views," p. 76.

[88] Ibid., p. 76.

[89] Meltsner, *Analysts in the Bureaucracy,* pp. 102–103.

out and implement a strategy for gaining acceptance of the preferred policy choice.[90] Such strategies range from devising ways to be more persuasive with clients, to actually targeting and mobilizing coalitions that will support the policy.[91] As long as the analyst remains convinced that his or her option is the best available, that goal dominates over the interests of the analyst's client. Service of the client's interests is incidental to—or perhaps instrumental in—pursuit of that preferred option. Issue advocates want to persuade clients of the appropriateness of their plans; but failing that, the analyst ". . . does not let his immediate client constrain him. If one client will not listen, others will."[92]

The advocate's objective of having his preferred policy enacted over those that may be preferred by his client is of great significance in defining his position in the policy environment. In all client–analyst relationships, the client by definition holds the power to use the analyst's advice to affect policy.[93] Advocates therefore will have to rely on the fortuitous circumstance of having an uncommitted or like-minded client if the advocates' preferred policy is to be adopted. Because advocates are seeking opportunities for shaping policy in specific directions, they confront a question that Albert O. Hirschman has so cogently addressed in his *Exit, Voice, and Loyalty*.[94] The analyst has a choice between working within the organization to achieve his purpose or leaving the organization to work from the outside. Given the widespread existence of misdirected or inefficient public policies, it is not surprising that the possibilities of using voice or exit as tools of influence are extensively explored by the issue advocates. The advocate's objective is to promote "better" policies even if they conflict with the client's interests. Thus the issue advocate desires enough autonomy from the client to be free to exercise voice. This leads one advocate to argue that ". . . autonomy has value insofar as it permits policy analysts and planners to interject reasonable analyses and recommendations into decisionmaking. If policy analysts and

[90] Robert Behn captures the advocate's obligations nicely: ". . . if honest, neutral analysis reveals that one or several alternatives are preferable . . . the policy analyst has a clear obligation to maximize the chances for their adoption." He calls this a "political responsibility of the analyst." In "Policy Analysis," p. 221.

[91] Meltsner's entrepreneur—the analyst who is both technically and politically competent—is a "pragmatist, educator, manipulator, coalition builder" who "engages with relish in his political and organizational environment." *Policy Analysts,* pp. 36–37. Robert Behn calls for analysts to ". . . identify those paying net costs, arouse their displeasure, motivate them to action, and provide them with a vehicle for opposition" in the interest of enacting efficient programs. "Policy Analysis," p. 217.

[92] Meltsner, *Policy Analysts,* p. 37.

[93] Ibid., pp. 199–294.

[94] Albert Hirschman, *Exit, Voice, and Loyalty* (Cambridge: Harvard University Press, 1970).

planners do not possess autonomy, they should consider why they do not and how they might acquire it."[95]

The use of voice may be particularly important for issue advocates who work within the dominant policy analysis paradigm. Efficiency, as defined within that paradigm, has no natural lobby because the net costs of inefficient programs are usually widely dispersed. One writer suggests that, when dealing with inefficient programs toward which clients are indifferent, analysts should persuade through harnessing self-interest in order to create conditions favorable to the adoption of more efficient policies.[96] Analysts thus become "partisan efficiency advocates."

When voice fails to convince clients to support analysts' policy choice, issue advocates may be forced to turn to exit as their only means of influence. They may seek other, more receptive, clients in the bureaucracy or they may leave the bureaucracy in order to be able to promote their policies from outside.[97] For the issue advocate, keeping one's bags packed may be an ethical imperative. Other types of analysts will face the choice between exit and voice, but perhaps not as unambiguously. Because other analysts are either not political activists, or because they are content to pursue values framed by others, they will not be likely to feel as strongly the strain to practice exit or voice.

The issue advocate therefore is likely to be particularly unhappy when faced with high levels of organizational allegiance and a client committed to a policy choice with which the analyst disagrees. Not only would such an environment inhibit the advocate's ability to exercise voice, but—as mentioned earlier—one of the factors contributing to strong organizational allegiance is a lack of attractive alternatives to the analyst's present position, which may make exit a costly option for the analyst. An issue advocate could work well with a committed client only if the analyst agreed with the client's policy position. Otherwise, the analyst would prefer an uncommitted client who may be persuaded to adopt the analyst's policy preference.

The degree of analytical tractability surrounding the policy issue will also be important for the issue advocate—though the effects of intractability differ depending on what the analyst is advocating. An issue advocate serving the interests of a particular class or group through promotion of a predetermined policy option may prefer a degree of intractability that permits the shading of the analysis in favor of the preferred outcome without undermining the

---

[95] Baum, "Analysts and Planners," p. 480. For a particularly useful discussion of the options available to advocate analysts, see David L. Weimer and Aidan R. Vining, *Policy Analysis: Concepts and Practice* (Englewood Cliffs, NJ: Prentice-Hall, 1989), chapter 2.

[96] Behn, "Policy Analysis," p. 217.

[97] See Meltsner's discussion of his "entrepreneur" analyst's use of exit to gain influence over policy formulation on pp. 38–39, *Policy Analysts*. Also see the discussion of exit, voice, and "disloyalty" in Weimer and Vining, *Concepts and Practice*.

analytical plausibility of the analysis. Efficiency advocates, on the other hand, will prefer more tractable issues; sufficient conceptual clarity, data, and (above all) agreement on validity of analytical claims to make a strong case for the efficient program will be desired. The high levels of uncertainty accompanying intractable issues may force the efficiency advocate to admit that there is some probability, however small, that the proposed policy or reform will result in net social costs rather than benefits. This admission will undermine the efficiency advocate's arguments, and his opponents are likely to make the most of it.

The client's advocate.   The client's advocate, like the issue advocate, is an active player in the political process. However, the client's advocate does not act in response to substantive values or goals. Rather, this analyst sees his or her primary tasks as providing ". . . the best possible case for a client's policy recommendation or continuing program . . ."[98] Again the underlying conception seems to be one of a pluralist decision-making process.[99] The analyst is in effect hired by the client to further the client's interests, acting within the restrictions set by procedural norms. The policy-making process is a struggle between clients with competing policy positions; the advice of the analyst provides the client with a strategy and with ammunition for the struggle.

Some scholars have held that the model of the client's advocate is the rule in government bureaucracies.[100] The analyst, according to this view, is called on only after policies have been decided, and then only to justify the policies; the cloak of value-free science is used to legitimate the decisions of the policy makers.[101]

Despite views of this sort, under some conditions the client's advocate does have the potential to improve both the content and effectiveness of policy analysis. Where rival advocates dominate the process, each representing an alternative belief system and promoting conflicting policy options, they bring all the virtues and limitations of the adversary proceeding. Collectively, the different advocates may offer a complete analysis, each contributing a particular portion.[102] On the other hand, the different portions contributed to the analysis may not add up to a complete picture. It may be that important constituencies are unrepresented in the policy subsystem, or that a closed

---

[98] Foster, "Advocate Role Model," pp. 958–964.

[99] There is only a partial analogy between the adversarial legal process and the client's advocate style of analysis. Though this analyst serves the interests of his client, the client as a decision maker does not take the case before a person or body analogous to an impartial judge.

[100] Meltsner, *Policy Analysts*, p. 168.

[101] Horowitz, "Social Science Mandarins," pp. 339–360. Guy Benveniste, in *The Politics of Expertise*, pp. 40–48, also makes note of the "legitimation function" of policy analysis, though he lists it as a "secondary function" of planning.

[102] Meltsner, *Policy Analysts*, p. 151.

forum excludes some view from expression. In these cases, the availability of only partial analysis will skew the available information regarding the policy issue. Furthermore, it is important that all relevant views have sufficient incentive to *mobilize* analysis. For these reasons the client's advocate will serve best in a policy arena characterized by high-level conflict in a wide-open forum.

In addition, the client's advocate will be most at home working on the more intractable policy issues. The resulting uncertainty will permit the analyst to shade analysis in the client's favor without moving beyond the pale of analytical plausibility.[103]

A final point that scholars make regarding the style of client's advocate is that in some policy environments it brings into the open, and makes use of, the high levels of organizational allegiance that exist between policy analysts and their clients. Given a policy environment characterized by highly intractable policy issues and a committed client, an attempt by the policy analyst to maintain the image of an objective, value-free scientist may actually undermine the credibility of policy analysis.[104]

Because the issue advocate is primarily concerned with making a good case for the client's policy position, the immediate beneficiary of this style will necessarily be the client. However, if analysts openly advocating their client's positions can improve the policy-making process by harnessing the virtues of the adversarial process, as is sometimes asserted, then the analyst may have two beneficiaries: the client and the system at large.

In sum, the client's advocate seems particularly well adapted to an environment in which there is a high level of organizational allegiance involving intractable analytical issues and high levels of subsystem conflict. The principle tensions to be expected in such a setting derive from the abuse of analytical expertise in "making a case" for the client's policy position. Furthermore, the appropriateness of this style of analysis presupposes a generalized conflict within subsystems in which all relevant policy viewpoints are represented. Clearly, conditions appropriate to client's advocates may prove hostile to activity of objective technicians and partisan efficiency advocates.

Styles of analysis in context.   In the foregoing sections I have argued that elements of the policy context in which analysis is practiced systematically inhibit or encourage the practice of the various styles of analysis. What is more, the *appropriateness* of each of the styles is fundamentally dependent on

---

[103] John L. Foster argues that a client's advocate model would work only in a policy environment in which (1) there is a "reasonably clear client commitment to a program or policy option," and (2) there is a "relatively high uncertainty about the impact of the program on other parties, or society in general." In "Advocate Role Model," p. 960. In terms of the policy framework developed here, this is congruent with a policy context with a committed client and an issue involving a high level of analytical intractability.

[104] Ibid., p. 961, and Horowitz, "Social Science Mandarins," pp. 339–341.

the context in which it is practiced. Tentative conclusions regarding the mix of environmental factors conducive and appropriate to the practice of each have been provided above and are summarized in table 4-2. Of particular importance is the conclusion that the more hospitable and appropriate set of conditions for one style of analysis usually prove hostile and detrimental to the practice of another style. Furthermore, the simultaneous practice of the various styles of analysis within any given policy issue–area may serve to undermine the appropriateness of *all* styles. Advocates undermine the credibility of objective technicians, while objective technicians may fail to provide the necessary *complementary* analysis to "correct for" the potential biases of the advocates. Clearly, then, critique of policy analysis—either from the standpoint of the practice of a particular style of analysis or the broader normative questions raised in chapter 3—must take cognizance of the variability of the conditions of the policy context.

TABLE 4-2

Policy context and styles of policy analysis

Style of policy analysis	Typically preferred level of tractability of policy issue	Level of sub-system conflict and client com-mittment on policy issue	Type of analytical forum	Level of organizational allegiance
Objective technician	High	Low conflict; uncommitted client	Professionalized or closed forum	Low
Issue advocate	Low— unless an-alyst is partisan efficiency advocate	High conflict; uncommitted (or like-minded) client	Open forum— though partisan efficiency advocates may prefer a professionalized forum	Low
Clients' advocate	Low	High conflict; committed client	Open forum	High

———— 4.5 ————

SUMMARY

This chapter has developed a conceptual model of the process of analysis within subsystems, and has provided an overview of the primary styles of analysis prescribed for practicing analysts. I have argued that, considered as a process, the primary dynamic of analysis is driven by the level of conflict within policy subsystems. The level of conflict, stemming from the clash of opposing belief systems, seems to explain a large part of both willingness to commit analytical resources and readiness to consider change in preexisting belief systems. At low levels of conflict (low either because the issue is peripheral to all concerned or because those for whom the issue is of core concern are excluded from the forum) little analytical attention will be paid to the issue. At high levels of conflict, extensive analytical resources are committed to the issue, but—because the matter concerns issues and beliefs at the core of competing subsystem coalitions—few participants are willing to adjust existing belief systems in light of new analytical findings. In such instances, analysis tends to be more a tool of legitimization and criticism than of learning and policy adaptation. When conflict is more moderate, the issue can be expected to receive somewhat less analytical attention, but—because belief system cores are not directly at stake—participants are more willing to adjust beliefs in light of analytical results. Thus it is in cases of moderate conflict that analysis can be expected to play the largest contributive role in the policy debate. Finally, given any level of conflict, the prospects for independent contribution by analysis to policy formulation are expanded or restricted by the degree of analytical tractability of the issue under debate, and by the openness of the analytical forum in which the policy debate is conducted.

For the individual policy analyst, elements of the process of analysis are perceived as characteristics of the policy context. Most important of such characteristics are the degree of the client's commitment to predetermined policy positions, the level of organizational allegiance, the analytical tractability of the policy issue under scrutiny, and the nature of the analytical forum in which the issue is debated. Three predominant styles of analysis have been prescribed for analysts—here called the objective technician, the issue advocate, and the client's advocate. I have argued that none of these styles is likely to be practicable nor appropriate over the full range of policy environments, and that each "fits" nicely within a particular range of conditions.

How well does this conceptual depiction of the process and practice of analysis square with actual practice? The following chapters provide at least a partial answer; case studies of the use of analysis in four policy debates are reviewed in detail. The first, presented in chapter 5, recounts in depth the use of analysis in the debate over U.S. oil export policy conducted within the Reagan Administration in 1981. This case portrays the *process* of analysis in the bureaucratic setting, with particular attention to (1) the roles played by individual analysts, and to (2) the responsiveness of the analytical strategies employed to factors in the policy context. The subsequent chapter examines a cross section of analytical debates—again relating to energy policy—with emphasis on the adaptation of the process and role of analysis to a range of differing policy contexts.

One preliminary point: all of the cases to be used here concern energy policy. Why? In the selection of cases it was necessary to balance the need to provide a range of types of policy environments and issue characteristics against the pragmatic need to keep the range of issues sufficiently narrow to permit mastery and description of the often highly detailed technical issues involved. Ideally, the range of characteristics of environs and issues reviewed would extend from the tightly controlled budgetary process within the Department of Defense under McNamara,[105] in which analysis frequently considered fairly tractable issues of the cost-effectiveness of various weapons systems, to the much less tractable and often faction-riddled issues of social health and welfare policy.[106] However, to have adequately explored instances of analysis over this range of issues, in the level of detail that is necessary to illustrate and assess the argument of this book, would have greatly extended an already overlong volume. More importantly, the natural resource issues— and energy policy in particular—seem to occupy an important midpoint in this range of policy issues. The techniques for study of resource issues are fairly well developed, allowing at least a fair degree of tractability on many issues. At the same time, resource policy issues have developed significant policy subsystems, frequently attended by a number of well-developed advocacy coalitions.[107] Finally, energy policy issues in particular have been extensively analyzed within a wide range of policy contexts since the 1973–1974 oil supply crisis, providing ample opportunity for study of the process of analysis.[108] For these reasons, then, a set of cases in policy analysis of energy issues was selected to cover a sufficiently wide range of types of analytical problems, and of policy environs, to illustrate the practice of analysis generally. Nevertheless, the concepts and framework developed here *are* intended to be generalizable across the gamut of policy issue–areas; I therefore urge the

---

[105] See Alan Schick, "A Death in the Bureaucracy: The Demise of Federal PPB," in *Public Expenditure and Policy Analysis*, 2nd ed., eds. Robert H. Haveman and Julius Margolis (Chicago: Rand McNally, 1977), pp. 556–576; also see Alain Enthoven and Wayne K. Smith, *How Much is Enough?* (New York: Harper and Row, 1971).

[106] See Henry Aaron, *Politics and the Professors: The Great Society in Perspective* (Washington, DC: Brookings Institute, 1978) and Joseph Falkson, "Minor Skirmish in a Monumental Struggle: HEW's Analysis of Mental Health Services," *Policy Analysis*, 2(1) (Winter 1976), pp. 93–119.

[107] See John Robinson, "Apples and Horned Toads," and Christopher Leman, "Political Dilemmas in Evaluating and Budgeting Soil Conservation Programs: The RCA Process," in *Soil Conservation: Policies, Institutions, and Incentives*, eds. Harold Halcrow, Earl Heady, and Melvin Cotner (Ankeny, IA: Soil Conservation Society of America, 1982), pp. 47–88.

[108] See Martin Greenberger, et al., *Caught Unawares: The Energy Decade in Retrospect* (Cambridge, MA: Ballinger, 1983), chapter 3, for an overview of many of the important energy analyses conducted through the 1970s.

reader to apply the framework to other cases of policy analysis, and to put my claims of generalizability to the test.[109]

---

[109] This has been attempted, though primarily to resource policy issues, in Sabatier and Jenkins-Smith, "Policy Change." Current research is underway to apply the framework to nonresource issues, such as airline deregulation and technical standard setting. See Martha Derthick and Paul Quirk, *The Politics of Deregulation* (Washington, DC: Brookings Institute, 1984), and Richard Barke, "Technological Change."

CHAPTER 5

Adversarial
Analysis of U.S.
Oil Export Policy

Study of the relationships between the policy context and the process of policy analysis in bureaucratic settings has suffered in part because the necessary data has been obscure or unavailable. Much of the process of analysis at the federal level is buried deeply within the departments of the administrative branch, becoming visible only upon the infrequent disclosure of sensational political infighting or violation of analytical norms. The detail of the process of analysis—the roles played by the various analysts, the strategies adopted, and the adaptation to policy context—are still less frequently reported. The case presented in this chapter is an attempt to ameliorate this lack of data: it provides an in-depth illustration of the development and use of policy analysis in a recent review of U.S. policy regarding export of Alaskan crude oil.

This case study is particularly useful because of the *level of detail* available. Not only were the competing analytical claims observable, but the roles adopted by the various analysts and the analytical strategies employed were discernible as well. As a result, the case well illustrates the playing out of the analytical process and the adaptation of the participants to the policy context.

As described in the preceding chapter, policy analysts provide decision makers with an analytical policy space, based on multiple dimensions of value, that constitutes a conceptual framework from which to compare various policy options across incommensurable classes of outcomes. In this instance, the analysis was characterized by intense conflict, and in the process various analytical strategies were employed in attempts to wrest the shape and content of the policy space in a direction that improved the chances for adoption of the advocates' preferred policies.

The dynamic of this debate well illustrates the predisposition to generalized advocacy in the bureaucratic setting, despite an initial predisposition toward the role of objective technician on the part of some participants. Of particular interest is the *adaptation* of analytical strategy to the changing characteristics of the policy context; the analytical tractability of the issue under study proved to be central to these strategies. In broadest terms, the case demonstrates the dramatic departures of the practice of policy analysis in bureaucratic settings from the prescriptions of the policy analysis paradigm outlined in chapter 2.

Presentation of an extensive analytical debate of this sort requires that background and basic analytical terms of the debate be described in some detail. Though that discussion is necessarily somewhat arcane, where possible the more technical elements have been relegated to the footnotes. Readers desiring only an overview of the case and the conclusions drawn from it are referred to sections 5.3 and 5.5.

————— 5.1 —————

BACKGROUND ON THE ALASKAN OIL EXPORT ISSUE

Huge reserves of oil were discovered in the Prudhoe Bay region of northern Alaska in January of 1968. The field was estimated to contain 10 billion barrels of recoverable oil, a significant boost for domestic reserves in the face of declining domestic production and rapidly increasing foreign oil imports. The chief hurdle in bringing Alaskan oil to market was in choosing a route for transporting it to refiners—a hurdle that escalated into a major political battle. Several options were proposed, the chief alternatives being a pipeline to supply tankers to run from Prudhoe Bay to Valdez, Alaska, and a pipeline to cross Canada to Keg River, Alberta, where it would join pipelines to both eastern and western states. The Prudhoe to Valdez trans-Alaska route was the early favorite.

The early political battles over whether to build the trans-Alaska pipeline were dominated by environmental and wildlife groups, which succeeded in blocking construction first on the grounds that provisions of the National Environmental Policy Act had not been met,[1] and later on a provision of the Mineral Leasing Act of 1920 that limited the width of pipeline rights-of-way across federal lands to fifty feet. Environmentalists were joined in opposition to the trans-Alaska pipeline by congressmen from the "frostbelt" states who feared that oil companies would use the trans-Alaska pipeline to deliver oil to Japan, rather than their own oil-poor states. These congressmen wanted to hold out for the trans-Canadian route.[2]

Supporters of the trans-Alaskan route argued that the paramount consideration should be to bring the new domestic oil to market as soon as possible, and that the trans-Alaskan route would accomplish this. This argument took on urgent economic and national security overtones when war erupted between the Arabs and Israelis in 1973, leading to the Arab oil embargo and the tripling of world oil prices. In order to entice frostbelt congressmen away from the coalition with environmentalists, proponents of the trans-Alaskan route offered to amend legislation designed to clear away court challenges to construction of the pipeline to include provisions limiting export of Alaskan oil.[3] The result was passed as the 1973 Trans-Alaska Pipeline Authorization Act (TAP), which held, in part, that export of Alaskan crude was to be permitted only if the president found that (1) exports would not decrease the amount of oil available domestically, and (2) exports were in the "national interest." The Congress could override the president's finding by concurrent resolution within sixty days.

With passage of the TAP Act, work on what was to become the largest construction project undertaken in U.S. history commenced. Four years and monumental cost overruns later, the line was completed, and North Slope oil began to flow to Valdez in mid-1977. In 1979 approximately 1.2 million barrels per day (mmb/d) of Alaskan crude were shipped out of Valdez, of

---

[1] "National Environmental Policy Act," Public Law 91–190, December 22, 1970, 83 Stat. 852. The provisions were requirements to file environmental impact statements for construction projects on federal lands.

[2] Considerable sentiment against the major oil companies also seemed to play a part in opposition to the trans-Alaska pipeline (TAP). Sen. Walter Mondale (D–Minn.) in arguing against construction of the Trans-Alaska pipeline on the Senate floor, said:

> I believe Congressional approval of the committee bill [TAP] would say to the oil industry and to any governmental agency that if you violate the law often enough, long enough, and set up enough obstacles in the way of rational judgment, sooner or later you will have your way. . . .

See the description of Congressional battles over the Trans-Alaska pipeline in the *Congressional Quarterly Almanac*: 92nd Congress, 1973, (Washington, DC: Congressional Quarterly, 1973), pp. 596–614.

[3] Senator Jackson (D–Wash.) made the amendment in the Senate, and Representative Saylor (R–Penn.) offered a similar amendment in the House. Ibid., p. 602.

which .8 mmb/d went to the U.S. West Coast (West Coast) while .4 mmb/d were shipped through the Panama Canal to the U.S. Gulf and East coasts (Gulf Coast, East Coast). Another .1 mmb/d were shipped directly to the Virgin Islands and Hawaii. By 1980 the Department of Energy (DOE) estimated that Alaskan oil production had reached 1.5 mmb/d, of which .9 mmb/d were shipped to the West Coast, .5 mmb/d via Panama to the Gulf Coast, and the remainder to Hawaii and the Virgin Islands.[4]

The ban on exports of Alaskan crude effectively restricted all ocean transport of the oil to U.S. flag tankers.[5] The Merchant Marine Act (Jones Act) of 1920 holds that all shipping between U.S. ports must be carried on unsubsidized U.S. flag tankers.[6] U.S. flag tankers cannot compete on an equal footing with foreign flag ships; because of higher labor and construction costs, U.S. flag-tanker rates are roughly twice as high as foreign tanker rates on comparable routes.

The addition of the Alaskan crude trade to the demand for U.S. flag tankers was a monumental boost for an industry that had been in decline since the Vietnam War. By 1975, the number of U.S. tankers had fallen to only 30 percent of the level of the late 1960s, and the outlook for tanker construction was equally desolate. Within the context of this decline, the prospect of a monopoly on the Alaskan crude trade looked attractive indeed to the U.S. maritime industry. In 1972, Secretary of Commerce Stans told an appreciative National Maritime Council (an industry trade group) that the Trans-Alaska Pipeline "offers perhaps the greatest single opportunity for new cargos and jobs that the American fleet has ever had."[7] Events since then have borne out Stans' prediction; by 1981 fully 62 percent of the unsubsidized U.S. tanker fleet was engaged in the Alaskan crude trade, involving as many as 75 tankers. Thus, for the U.S. maritime industry, the ban on exports of Alaskan crude had proven to be a considerable prize.

Since 1977 the ban on exports of Alaskan oil has repeatedly come under congressional and executive scrutiny. In 1977 President Carter asked Congress to ease restrictions on oil exports, only to be rebuffed by even more

---

[4] Department of Energy, *Exports/Exchanges of Alaskan Oil* (unpublished memorandum, June 30, 1981), p. 3.

[5] The exception was crude oil shipped to U.S. refineries in the Caribbean, which was permitted to use foreign flag shipping. Maritime interests have repeatedly sought to close this "loophole" both in the courts and in Congress.

[6] The "Merchant Marine Act of 1920" (June 5, 1920, Ch. 250, 41 Stat. 988) limits trade between U.S. ports to U.S. flag tankers without operating subsidies (frequently called "Jones Act" ships). U.S. tankers with operating subsidies are limited to operation in the international trades unless they receive special waivers from the Federal Maritime Commission.

[7] *Congressional Quarterly Almanac*: 96th Congress, 1977, (Washington, DC: Congressional Quarterly, 1977), p. 566.

stringent prohibitions in the 1977 Export Administration Act.[8] In 1979 the Congress again reconsidered the ban, this time tightening it such that in order to permit exports the president must show that:

1. exports will not diminish the total quantity of oil in the United States;
2. an exchange of Alaskan for foreign crude would mean reduced acquisition costs for refiners, three-fourths of which would be passed on to consumers;
3. any export contract could be terminated if oil supplies to the United States were threatened or diminished; and
4. the exports were clearly necessary to protect the "national interest."[9]

The Congress would need to *approve* the President's report by concurrent resolution within sixty days, meaning that either House could block export by simply not voting its approval. Shortly after the Reagan Administration took office in 1981, the ban came up for reconsideration once again, this time within the executive branch. This reconsideration, and the roles played by policy analysts who participated in it, provides the focus for this chapter's examination of the use of analysis in public decision making.

————— 5.2 —————

BASIC ANALYTICAL CONSIDERATIONS

The analysis of the Alaskan oil export ban was conducted with the use of a simple simulation model of oil export flows and wellhead profits. Differing sets of assumptions about the appropriate "inputs" to the model were proffered and defended by the competing analysts involved in the debate. In order to give the reader the necessary information to follow the debate and the analytical strategies used, the following sections describe, in nontechnical language, the basic analytical terms and assumptions employed in the analysis of the oil export ban. Using those terms and assumptions, the factors that would affect production and distribution of Alaskan oil *in absence of* the export ban are described, followed by a description of the *differences* in production and distribution attributable to the existence of the ban.

Several preliminary points merit emphasis. The following is *not* an endeavor to provide a "true" or objective analytical framework for analysis of the ban on oil exports. It is intended to depict the actual analytical approach

---

[8] "Export Administration Act," Public Law 95–52, June 22, 1977, 91 Stat. 235. The most important restriction of the Act was a provision allowing either House of Congress to veto a presidential finding that exports should be permitted.

[9] Ibid., section 7-d.

taken in the 1981 cabinet council review of the issue.[10] Further, it attempts to convey the sources of uncertainty in analysis that become the vehicles for advocacy in contentious analytical debates. More detailed inquiry into the analysis of oil exports than is required for these purposes is therefore reserved for the footnotes.

Production and distribution of Alaskan oil without the ban.   In a market unhampered by restrictions on exports, producers of Alaskan crude would be expected to sell their oil to the buyer who offers the largest wellhead price (price at destination less shipping costs). In the oil market of the early 1980s, non-OPEC oil producers were assumed to be "price-takers"; that is, they would sell oil at the price set by the OPEC producers. In general, the price of high-quality Persian Gulf (PG) crude was taken to be the "marker crude" that established the benchmark for pricing other crudes.[11] The price of Alaskan crude in any given market would thus be the price of PG crude, adjusted for the quality differences between Alaskan and PG crudes,[12] *plus* the cost of transporting PG crude to that market.[13] The wellhead price, or "netback," for Alaskan crude would, in turn, be the quality-adjusted PG crude price, plus the PG-to-market transportation costs, *minus* the Alaska-to-market shipping costs.[14] The estimated netback for Alaskan crude was thus dependent on assumptions about the cost of shipping oil on both domestic and foreign routes.

---

[10] For a quite different approach to analysis of this issue, see Terrence Higgins and Hank Jenkins-Smith, "Analysis of the Economic Effects of the Alaskan Oil Export Ban," *Journal of Operations Research,* 33(6) (November–December 1985), pp. 1173–1202.

[11] In economic terms, PG crude was considered to be the "marginal" supply of oil in most markets. Even where PG oil was not imported, its price was assumed to serve as a threatened marginal supply because buyers could turn to it should other sellers attempt to raise their prices above the quality-adjusted price of PG oil. For an economic description of the world oil market employing a model of the OPEC cartel as the dominant producer surrounded by a "competitive fringe" of small producers, see Stephen W. Salant, "Exhaustible Resources and Industrial Structure: A Nash-Cournot Approach to the World Oil Market," *Journal of Political Economy,* 84(5) (1976), pp. 1079–1093.

[12] The quality adjustment of price is the additional cost required, including such operations as catalytic cracking and hydrotreating, to achieve the same mix of petroleum products per barrel from Alaskan oil as could be attained from the higher quality PG crudes.

[13] Mathematically this can be expressed as:

$$PG(q) + T(pg \rightarrow m) = P$$

where $PG(q)$ is the quality-adjusted world oil price, $T(pg \rightarrow m)$ is the cost of shipping crude from the Persian Gulf to the destination market, and P is the world price in the destination market.

[14] This can be represented as:

$$PG(q) + T(pg \rightarrow m) - T(v \rightarrow m) = N(v)$$

where $T(v \rightarrow m)$ is the cost of shipping crude from Valdez, Alaska, to the destination market and $N(v)$ is the netback at Valdez.

TABLE 5-1
Calculation of Alaskan oil netbacks for three markets
(amounts in dollars per barrel)

Shipping rates			
Destination	Origin		Calculation of netbacks
	PG	Valdez	
U.S. West Coast	$1.30p/b	$1.50p/b	PGq + 1.30 − 1.50 = PGq − 0.20
Far East	$0.90p/b	$0.50p/b	PGq + 0.90 − 0.50 = PGq + 0.40
U.S. Gulf Coast	$1.60p/b	$4.00p/b	PGq + 1.60 − 4.00 = PGq − 2.40

In order to receive the highest netback possible, Alaskan producers would sell their crude in the market for which transportation costs from Valdez hold the largest comparative advantage (or least comparative disadvantage) with respect to transportation costs from the PG.[15] This can be illustrated by example. The three markets for Alaskan crude most frequently mentioned in the analytical debates were the West Coast, the Far East, and the Gulf Coast. Using, for illustrative purposes, shipping rates roughly at the mean of those used in the 1981 analyses, netbacks for the three alternative markets would be calculated as shown in table 5-1.

If the shipping estimates in table 5-1 were correct, Alaskan oil sold in the Far East would receive a netback of about $0.60 per barrel higher than it would on the U.S. West Coast, and $2.80 per barrel more than it would in the Gulf Coast. Hypothetically, Alaskan producers would sell as much crude as possible in the Far East—effectively replacing (or "backing out") imports of comparable quality from that market. If more Alaskan crude were available than was demanded at profit-maximizing prices in the Far East, producers would turn to the West Coast as the most attractive alternative market. Thus, assuming sufficient demand could be found, Alaskan producers would ship their crude to markets in the Far East and on the West Coast.

One caveat to this "price driven" view of Alaskan crude distribution needs mention here. The Alaskan oil fields were seen as a *secure source* of crude of predictable quality. The security of the fields increased the likelihood that long-term contracts would be fulfilled even in the event of a major oil supply disruption. In addition, the predictable quality allowed for "fine tuning" of refining processes to obtain the most profitable mix of product output per barrel of crude.[16] Some analysts argued that, as a result of these attributes, Alaskan oil producers who owned domestic refineries would re-

---

[15] Mathematically, Alaskan oil producers would want to maximize: $T(pg \rightarrow m) - T(v \rightarrow m)$.

[16] "North Slope Oil: A Bargain for Lower 48 Refiners," *Oil & Gas Journal*, 78(16) (April 21, 1980), p. 28.

frain from exports to the Far East in favor of deliveries to their own refineries.[17] If this held true, more Alaskan oil would be shipped to domestic refineries and less to the Far East.

In addition to indicating the likely markets for Alaskan oil, estimates of oil shipping charges were central to projecting revenues to be generated by sales of Alaskan crude. A *decrease* in oil shipping costs from the PG to market, or an *increase* in oil shipment costs from Valdez to market, would reduce netbacks for sales of Alaskan oil. For example, if 500,000 barrels of Alaskan crude sold in the Far East were shifted to the West Coast, using the shipping rates shown in table 5-1, netbacks would fall by $0.60 per barrel.[18] The hypothetical reduction in Alaskan oil revenues over a period of one year from such a shift would be:

$$\$0.60 \text{ p/b} \times 500,000 \text{ barrels} \times 365 \text{ days} = \$109,500,000 \text{ per year.}$$

Using the shipping rates estimates from table 5-1, oil producers in an open market would maximize their revenues by selling Alaskan oil in the Far East and on the West Coast. These revenues, however, would be divided among the producing firms, the federal government, and the state of Alaska. As of 1981, the breakdown of producer and government revenues from each dollar of increased netback on Alaskan crude sold was estimated to be as shown in table 5-2.

By this estimate, the federal government would receive approximately 60 percent of each added dollar of netbacks, producers slightly over 8 percent, and the state of Alaska and royalty recipients the remainder.[19]

Increased producer profits would increase the attractiveness of investment in Alaskan oil exploration and production. Economic theory holds that

---

[17] The premium, in this case, must be equal to or greater than the difference between the netbacks for selling Alaskan oil in the Far East and the Gulf Coast. Mathematically:

$$Pr = \{(T(v \rightarrow fe) - T(pg \rightarrow fe)) - (T(v \rightarrow g) - T(pg \rightarrow g))\}$$

where Pr is the premium, $T(v \rightarrow fe)$ is the cost of shipping crude from Valdez to the Far East, $T(pg \rightarrow fe)$ is the cost of shipping crude from the Persian Gulf to the Far East, $T(v \rightarrow g)$ is the cost of shipping crude from Valdez to the Gulf Coast, and $T(pg \rightarrow g)$ is the cost of shipping crude from the Persian Gulf to the Gulf Coast.

In its developed form, the premium argument states that, due to the security of Alaskan oil supplies refiners are willing to pay a premium above the market value of less secure imported crudes. Presumably *all* refiners would see the security of supply as an advantage and bid up the price accordingly. Because the producer therefore gains the security value of the crude *whether or not* it is refined in his own refinery, it is reasonable to assume that the crude would still be sold in the market that provides the highest wellhead price. For a thorough analysis of the economic effects of uncertain supplies of imported oil, see Douglas Bohi and David Montgomery, *Oil Prices, Energy Security, and Import Policy* (Washington, DC: Resources for the Future, 1982).

[18] Using the shipping rates in table 5-1, the calculation is:

$$\text{Netback change} = (\$0.90 - \$0.50) - (\$1.30 - \$1.50) = \$0.60.$$

[19] "Windfall Profits Tax Act," Public Law 96–233, April 2, 1980, 94 Stat. 230. Not all Alaskan oil production was subject to the Windfall Profits Tax. Oil produced north of the Arctic Circle, and outside the Prudhoe Bay region, was exempted from the tax.

TABLE 5-2

Estimated revenue breakdown for sale of
$1.00 of Alaskan oil

Royalties (State and Private)	$0.1250
Alaskan Severance Tax	$0.1313
Windfall Profit Tax	$0.5206
State Income Tax	$0.0699
US Corporate Income Tax	$0.0705
Producer's Profits	$0.0827
TOTAL	$1.0000

SOURCE: "Alaskan Oil Earning Tidy Profit," *Petroleum Intelligence Weekly,* 20(11) (March 16, 1981), pp. 3–4.

the high returns available on investment in Alaskan oil would attract capital that otherwise would have been drawn to enterprises offering a smaller return. A larger investment in oil exploration and development in Alaska would, in turn, increase the level of oil production in that region. Because the availability of investment capital is limited, added investment in Alaskan oil would occur at the expense of investment in other, less profitable industries. The result would nevertheless be an increase in GNP, with a concomitant increase in overall economic efficiency.[20] These diffuse but very real benefits, however, proved very difficult to quantify.

The projected distribution of Alaskan crude and the magnitude of the resultant netbacks were driven by the estimates of the tanker shipping rates entered into the simulation model. This dependency upon estimated shipping rates would not have been a problem if there were a reliable and agreed-upon reference for present and future rates. There was no such reference, however.[21] Present-period rates proved very difficult to pin down. Actual rates were set

---

[20] Arthur Okun, in *Equality and Efficiency: The Big Tradeoff* (Washington, DC: Brookings Institute, 1975) has described the efficiency of market operations as follows:

> Through the market, greed is harnessed to serve social purposes in an impersonal and seemingly automatic way. A competitive market transmits signals to producers that reflect the values of consumers. If the manufacture and distribution of a new product is profitable, the benefits it provides to buyers necessarily exceed the costs of production. And these costs in turn measure the value of the other outputs that are sacrificed by using labor and capital to make the new product. Thus, profitability channels resources into more productive uses and pulls them away from less productive ones. The producer has the incentive to make what consumers want and to make it in the least costly way. (p. 50.)

[21] Several industry groups publish shipping rate schedules, such as WORLDSCALE, published by the International Tanker Nominal Freight Scale Association. These schedules, however, are

in negotiated proprietary contracts (often between departments of the same firm) and in the tanker "spot market." Contract shipping rates may have reflected the accounting practices of the firm rather than market shipping rates,[22] and furthermore were often not publicized by shippers.[23] Spot market shipping prices, on the other hand, represented marginal rather than average shipping rates and tended to fluctuate daily. Thus, the actual shipping rates paid to move oil to market were very difficult to specify with certainty. Estimates of future shipping rates were even more problematical, as they were based on projections of the future supply and demand for shipping. In practice, estimates of current rates were based on figures provided by "knowledgcable persons" in the industry and trade journals. Future rates were projected either by adjusting current (estimated) rates for (estimates of) inflation in future years, or by projection of "break-even" costs for shippers in future periods. Thus, tanker shipping rates and all the estimates that depended on those rates were subject to very high levels of analytical uncertainty.

Effects of the ban on Alaskan oil exports.   In compliance with the restriction of sales of Alaskan crude to domestic markets, Alaskan crude had been shipped to U.S.-owned refineries on the Gulf and West coasts, Hawaii, Puerto Rico, and the Virgin Islands. With the exception of shipments to Puerto Rico and the Virgin Islands (about 11 percent of Alaskan production in 1980), ocean transport of the oil had been made an effective monopoly of the domestic Jones Act tanker fleet.[24] These tankers charged considerably higher prices than did foreign flag tankers on comparable routes.

With the export ban in effect, approximately 500,000 barrels per day of Alaskan crude were shipped to the Gulf Coast in 1981. Transport on this route consisted of large tanker shipment to Panama, trans-shipment through the Panama Canal by light draft tanker or pipeline, and subsequent shipment to the Gulf or East coasts. The cost of shipment on this route, on U.S. flag tankers, and with pipeline shipment across Panama, was estimated to be between $4

---

used by the shipping industry as a reference against which rates are set when contracts are negotiated. Thus, while rates are set at some percentage of WORLDSCALE, the WORLDSCALE rate itself does not set the shipping rate charged.

[22] Oil companies that owned their own tankers had considerable tax incentives to inflate the tanker rates charged for transport of their Alaskan crudes. Wellhead profits were taxed at a much higher rate than tanker profits, due to the Windfall Profits Tax. Therefore integrated oil companies could reduce their overall tax burdens by switching profits from the wellhead to their shipping operations by charging themselves higher-than-justified rates for transport on their own tankers.

[23] Rates are occasionally published, though in a sporadic and piecemeal fashion, in oil industry publications such as the *Petroleum Intelligence Weekly*.

[24] Alaskan oil shipped to U.S. refineries in the Caribbean was exempted from the Jones Act restriction.

and $5 per barrel.[25] Noting again the effect of shipping rates on Alaskan oil netbacks (see table 5-1), netbacks would be considerably smaller for sales on the Gulf Coast rather than in the Far East. The exact difference in netbacks depended on the estimates of shipping rates used. At least part of the difference in netbacks would be translated into gains for the domestic maritime industry. In effect, the incentives to invest in Alaskan oil exploration and production were reduced (as profits were reduced), and at the same time incentives to invest in the domestic shipping industry were dramatically increased. No attempt was made to quantify the aggregate economic losses or gains that resulted from the ban, though economic efficiency losses were cited as one of the costs of the ban.

In addition to higher costs of transportation, it was argued that the ban induced Alaskan producers to "discount" the price of oil sold on the West Coast. The logic of the discount argument was as follows: more Alaskan crude was produced than was demanded on the West Coast at the world price.[26] Because of the export ban, the only alternative market for Alaskan crude was the Gulf Coast, which because of very high transport costs, provided much lower netbacks than did the West Coast (see table 5-1). Alaskan producers could increase their sales to the West Coast by decreasing (discounting) the price of Alaskan oil relative to the world oil price, and thereby gain larger netbacks than would have been obtained by selling on the Gulf Coast. In order to continue to sell on the West Coast, competition would force other Alaskan oil producers to discount the price of Alaskan crude as well. In the extreme, it was assumed that competition among the Alaskan producers would force the price of Alaskan crude sold on the West Coast to drop to the point that netbacks for oil sold on the West and Gulf coasts were equal. (Using the example shown in table 5-1, Alaskan oil prices on the West Coast would drop by $2.20 per barrel below the world price in that case.)

In part, the effect of the West Coast discount was seen as a benefit to West Coast refiners and consumers because the discount subsidized West Coast petroleum consumption. However, the discount also served to further reduce Alaskan oil netbacks, shrinking producer profits and significantly reducing state and federal revenues.

At the time of the 1981 review of the oil export ban, it was unclear whether (or how much) the price of Alaskan crude sold on the West Coast was discounted, or more importantly, whether it would continue to be discounted in the future. Economic theory holds that, in a competitive market,

---

[25] The Northville pipeline across Panama was expected to be operational by late 1982. Transport by pipeline, rather than the Panama Canal was expected to reduce costs of shipment from Valdez to the Gulf Coast by about $1.00 per barrel.

[26] In 1981, when this round of the Alaskan oil export ban analysis was underway, the term "world price" of oil generally referred to the price of Saudi Arabian light crude plus the cost of transport from the Persian Gulf.

producers will sell oil in each market such that the netbacks from oil sold in each are identical. (Otherwise there would be an incentive to shift sales from markets with lower netbacks to those with higher netbacks.) Such was the argument for the existence of the West Coast discount. It was difficult, however, to determine whether the Alaskan oil producers—primarily Sohio, Exxon, and ARCO—were competitive in their West Coast sales. If they were able to exercise "market power," the Alaskan producers would be able to discriminate among different buyers, keeping prices at world levels in all markets. This would allow producers to avoid the revenue loss due to discounting prices on the West Coast. This theoretical uncertainty was enhanced, rather than diminished, by the available empirical evidence. The fact that a considerable, though declining, amount (around 200,000 barrels per day) of expensive Indonesian crude was still imported to the West Coast was taken by some analysts to mean that Alaskan crude was only partially discounted, if at all.[27] In addition, evidence on delivered oil prices was mixed: through the spring of 1981 available data showed West Coast discounts ranging in size from near zero to over $2 per barrel. No trend toward higher or lower price discounting was discernible.[28] Thus, on both theoretical and empirical grounds the argument over the existence, size, and likely duration of the West Coast discount was subject to considerable analytical uncertainty.

If Alaskan crude was discounted on the West Coast, the discounted price of Alaskan crude may have forced the quality-adjusted price of crudes produced in California (CA crudes) to drop as well to compete for sales.[29] This would lower netbacks to California producers, federal revenues, and California state revenues. In addition, the reduced profitability of California crude sales would reduce investment in exploration and production for California oil. Analytically, the competitiveness of Alaskan and California crudes was quite well established. The somewhat lighter Alaskan crudes could replace California crudes in refining and were, on average, more valuable because they required less-expensive refining to produce the mix of products demanded on the West Coast. For that reason, the quality-adjusted California crude price tended to be significantly below that of Alaskan crudes on the West Coast. Thus, if the price of Alaskan crudes was suppressed because of a discount, California crude prices would have dropped as well, or they would

---

[27] Alternatively, the quality differential between the domestic crudes and the lighter, sweeter Indonesian imports may have been sufficiently large to make Indonesian crudes competitive *even though* Alaskan oil was discounted.

[28] See Mark Trexler, *Export Restrictions on Domestic Oil: A California Perspective* (Sacramento, CA: California Energy Commission, November 1982), p. 100.

[29] Crude produced in California is, on average, very heavy and high in sulfur content, making it more expensive to refine than Alaskan oils. However, with such refining operations as catalytic cracking and hydro-treating, refiners can substitute California crudes for lighter, less sulfurous oils and produce an identical mix of petroleum products.

have been replaced by Alaskan crudes. The key *analytical* uncertainty, therefore, was whether Alaskan crudes were discounted.

Effects of lifting the ban.   The primary effects of lifting the ban, based on the analytical assumptions outlined above, would have been the export of some fraction of Alaskan production, and the cessation of most—if not all—Alaskan oil shipments to the Gulf Coast. Because a reliable and valid analytical technique for estimating the quantities of Alaskan crude that would be exported in absence of the ban was not readily available, it was assumed that only the crude that formerly had been shipped to the Gulf Coast would be exported. In 1981, that amount was approximately 500,000 barrels per day.

Had the export ban been lifted, it was assumed that 500,000 barrels per day of Alaskan crude would have been shipped to the Far East, rather than the Gulf Coast, causing netbacks to rise. Using the illustration provided in table 5-1, netbacks would increase by $2.80 per barrel. The yearly increase in revenues from such an increase would have been substantial—over $456 million. In addition, if it were assumed that there was a West Coast discount, the value of Alaskan crude shipped to the West Coast would rise because Alaskan producers would no longer need to reduce prices to avoid the costly shipment to the Gulf Coast. Also, the elimination of the West Coast discount would increase the price of oil produced in California. In each case, increased netbacks would result in increased tax revenues to the federal and state governments, and increased profits to producers (see table 5-2). Increased profits on California and Alaskan oil production would draw new investment and, over time, increase oil production in those regions.

Analysis of the effects of lifting the ban was complicated by the fact that the ban had been in existence for some time, generating "sunk costs"[30] and vested interests as firms and individuals adjusted to it. Most prominent of those likely to have been harmed by export would have been the U.S. maritime industry, which would have lost its monopoly on Alaskan crude shipments to the Gulf Coast. Traffic on the Valdez-to-Gulf Coast route, employing up to seventy tankers, would have declined or ceased altogether. These newly unemployed tankers would have been forced to compete within the domestic shipping market for reduced freight traffic, forcing shipping rates generally to drop.[31] The result would have been that some portion of the domestic tanker

---

[30] In economic analysis sunk costs refer to the costs already incurred that should no longer be considered in determining the costs and benefits of current options. It is held that choices should be made "on the margin," that is, on the basis of expected benefits minus expected costs, and *regardless* of costs incurred in the past.

[31] Some Alaskan trade tankers operated under long-term charter to the Alaskan producers at fixed rates. Others were owned outright by the producers. The remaining tankers, those on short-term and spot market charter, would have felt the adverse market because of exports most quickly and severely.

fleet—those tankers least capable of withstanding the intensified competition—would be laid up or scrapped, and the remainder would be forced to operate at significantly reduced profits. Oil companies, including the major Alaskan producers, that had built up large tanker fleets in response to the export ban would have seen the value of their fleets significantly reduced. These losses would have been partially offset by the gains made on increased netbacks on oil production. Finally, West Coast refiners and consumers would have been faced with higher oil prices to the extent that lifting the ban eliminated the practice of discounting West Coast crude prices.

Much of the analytical debate focused on the effects on federal and state budgets of lifting the export ban. Should lifting the ban have severely depressed the domestic tanker market, the federal budget would have been affected through Title XI Federal Ship Mortgage Guarantees (Title XI).[32] Through the Title XI program, the federal government guarantees debt obligation for U.S. ship owners who build (or rebuild) U.S. flag vessels in U.S. shipyards. Many tankers in the Alaskan oil trade carried substantial outstanding Title XI loan balances, and should their operators have gone bankrupt, the federal government would have taken ownership and become liable for the defaulted loan balance. The amount of loan repayment for which the government would have become responsible depended on the number of shipowners bankrupted and the resale or scrap value of the ships taken into receivership. Estimates of the number and resale value of ships to be bankrupted by exports varied widely. On one hand, bankruptcies may have been limited to tankers displaced from the Alaskan oil trade. Alternatively, removal of the ban might have so depressed the domestic tanker market that *all* Jones Act tankers would have been affected, involving outstanding Title XI loans of nearly $1 billion.[33] Again the issue was fraught with considerable analytical uncertainty.

An additional federal revenue effect of lifting the ban would have been that, as maritime industry profits were diminished, federal tax revenues from the industry would have declined. Because the tax rate on oil production was higher than that applied to merchant shipping, these reductions in tax revenues would only have partially offset the expected revenue gains that would result from exports of Alaskan crude.

Beyond the economic and fiscal considerations noted thus far, two additional noneconomic implications of exports need brief mention here. Among the tankers likely to be bankrupted by lifting the ban were twenty-six small

---

[32] The program was established through Title XI of the "Merchant Marine Act of 1936," June 29, 1936, Ch. 858, 49 Stat. 1985.

[33] From the perspective of the policy analysis paradigm, the losses due to Title XI loan guarantees would be only "budgetary costs," not real resource costs, and therefore should not have been counted as true costs of removal of the ban. Politicians, however, are acutely aware of such costs, and tend to give them considerable weight in decision making.

tankers, capable of carrying clean petroleum products, that were deemed "militarily useful" by the Department of Defense. If a significant number of these tankers were scrapped because of bankruptcy, the military would have faced reduced capacity to provide its forces with petroleum products in a military emergency. Analysts thus had to consider whether lifting the ban would significantly reduce the availability of militarily useful tankers, and if so, what options were available to assure their continued availability.

Lifting the export ban also had important consequences for U.S. foreign policy. Since passage of the TAP Act, the export ban had proved an irritant to U.S.–Japanese foreign relations because the Japanese were eager to find secure, non-OPEC sources of oil. Furthermore, the ban was an embarrassment to the United States' attempts to negotiate reductions in international trade barriers. On these counts, lifting the export ban would have served U.S. foreign policy well. On the other hand, U.S. relations with Panama were likely to suffer should the ban be lifted; Panama received substantial revenues from Alaskan oil shipments through the Panama Canal. Panama had also recently initiated construction of a trans-Panama pipeline designed to carry Alaskan crude from its Pacific to Atlantic coasts. Panama was therefore likely to view elimination of the export ban as harmful to its interests.

The analytical framework and components described above are not intended to exhaust the full range of policy-relevant questions that were—or should have been—considered in the 1981 analysis; the intent is rather to provide the necessary background to understand and appreciate the analytical battles over Alaskan exports. The fact that not all policy-relevant issues were addressed is important in itself, however, and that point is taken up later in this chapter.

_____ 5.3 _____
FORUM, PLAYERS, AND POSITIONS

The analyses examined here took place in the summer and fall of 1981, the first year of the Reagan administration. The administration's formal apparatus for review of major policy issues consisted of six cabinet councils, each of which was made up of a subgroup of the administration's cabinet-level appointees.[34] The export ban was brought before the Cabinet Council on Natural Resources and the Environment headed by Secretary of the Interior James Watt. The council procedure called for convening a cabinet council

---

[34] For an insider's description of the Reagan administration's cabinet council system, see Murray L. Weidenbaum, "Economic Policymaking in the Reagan Administration," _Presidential Studies Quarterly,_ vol. XII, (Winter 1982), pp. 95–99.

working group (CCWG), made up of analysts from departments and agencies that held special expertise or responsibilities with respect to the issue in question. The CCWG provided the analysis for the cabinet council, and determined "what key issues needed debate and resolution at the Cabinet Officer level."[35] Implicitly, the CCWG members were to inform the cabinet council members of those aspects of the issue on which the various analysts were able to reach a consensus, giving the council a base from which to deliberate issues that could not be resolved through analysis. Ideally, analysts were to lay out the policy options and specify the attendant costs and benefits for each, leaving it to the council to weigh the relevant political considerations. In practice, as noted in chapter 4, analysts provide a policy space, delineating a set of dimensions of value on which the analysis is based. And, should the participants of the analytical work group hold opposing policy belief systems, plenty of opportunity exists to engage in analytical strategies and counterstrategies in the pattern depicted in figure 4-1.

The analysts involved in the oil exports decision came from fourteen agencies, councils, offices, and departments throughout the federal government. The principal protagonists came, in order of entry into the debate, from the Department of Energy (DOE) and the Maritime Administration (MarAd).[36] Other analysts who played important roles came from the Department of the Treasury, the OMB, the Department of Defense (DOD), the Department of Transportation (DOT), the Council of Economic Advisors (CEA), and the Department of State. The chairman of the CCWG, whose job it was to coordinate the analyses and see that all the critical issues were addressed, was a senior analyst in the White House Office of Policy Development. The CCWG thus constituted the forum in which an array of analysts worked to shape the oil export analysis.

The CCWG analyses were prepared over a period of roughly four months and moved through numerous iterations of "working paper" drafts and redrafts. It is primarily from this series of drafts, supplemented by documents and interviews provided by analysts involved in the debate, that the data for this case is drawn. Where the data permits, the analysts' perceptions of other participants in the debate, their organizational settings, and the motives behind particular moves and strategies are described along with the analytical positions taken.

During the four months of debate among analysts over whether the export ban should be lifted, four dimensions of value emerged as dominant. These included:

---

[35] Ibid., p. 95.

[36] MarAd was part of the Department of Commerce until the summer of 1981, at which time it was moved to the Department of Transportation.

1. the effect on federal revenues of allowing oil exports,
2. the effect on the U.S. maritime industry of lifting the ban,
3. the foreign policy implications of exports, and
4. the effects on U.S. national defense capabilities of allowing exports.

Other dimensions and subdimensions were raised and dismissed at various points over the period of the analysis. Notably, despite the injunctions of the policy paradigm, *economic efficiency* did not play a major part in the analysis; the efficiency dimension was brought into the analysis only after the initial arguments in favor of lifting the ban had been effectively checked by those opposing exports. By that time the group analysis was too far developed to permit the addition of another major dimension of value.

For the DOE analyst, the primary issue at stake in the analysis was that the ban interfered with crude oil markets in a way that increased the cost of moving crude oil from producers to refiners. These increased costs reduced wellhead revenues, thus lowering federal and state tax revenues and reducing incentives to find and produce additional domestic crude supplies. In his view, the export ban did not result in benefits substantial enough to offset the losses to the economy and the Treasury.[37] The DOE analyst's chief antagonists, analysts from MarAd, were primarily concerned with preserving a policy that provided an infusion of resources to the U.S. maritime industry.[38] In the view of a senior MarAd analyst, he and his colleagues needed to maintain an "advocacy stance" in the face of determined and persistent opposition of numerous federal agencies to the maritime programs. Despite that opposition, "there are laws that say we are committed to a strong maritime industry," and therefore MarAd analysts were obliged to struggle to see to it that the maritime programs were not dismantled.[39] Lifting the ban on exports of Alaskan oil would result in the loss of a major source of employment for U.S. flag tankers. Therefore, MarAd was vigorously opposed to lifting the ban.

The CEA analyst was an unabashed advocate of economic efficiency; when asked if the analysis of the export ban indicated a clearly preferable policy choice, he responded, "Yes—the clear answer is that the ban should be lifted. It's inefficient."[40] The DOT analysts tended to support the MarAd

---

[37] Personal interview, March 19, 1982. The DOE analyst did not characterize himself as a "free marketeer" or a pure efficiency advocate. His use of the free market language was motivated in part by his "sense that it will fly in the current political environment." He added that "where different arguments are acceptable coin, I could see myself arguing against freeing up markets because social goods [in the constrained market] outweighed the efficiency losses."

[38] Operationally, MarAd supported those policy options that would maximize dead-weight tonnage of tanker traffic to be carried aboard U.S. flag ships.

[39] Personal interview, November 1, 1982. The MarAd analyst cited the departments of the Treasury, Justice, and State as being consistently opposed to the maritime programs he favored.

position in favor of the ban, though their analytical positions tended less toward advocacy than did MarAd's.[41] The role of DOT seemed to be one of providing supporting analysis to MarAd, and DOT's contribution to the debate became eclipsed by MarAd's as the debate wore on. The State Department's concern centered on defending the integrity of agreements made with foreign nations. On the whole, the State Department approved of allowing exports because such a policy would "improve U.S. trade posture" by reducing U.S. infringement on free trade, and because it would improve U.S.–Japanese relations. The State Department was bitterly opposed, however, to any policy that would guarantee cargo preference to U.S. flag tankers carrying goods in international trade because such a policy would violate provisons of Friendship, Commerce, and Navigation treaties between the U.S. and its foreign trading partners.

The analyst from DOD was primarily concerned with the effect of lifting the ban on the availability of "militarily useful tankers"—tankers capable of carrying clean petroleum products and able to sail into shallow harbors. The OMB analyst played the role of "guardian of the purse"; his primary contribution to the debate was to question the necessity of proposals to purchase the militarily useful tankers threatened with bankruptcy should the ban be lifted. Finally, the Treasury analysts seemed to come closest to playing the role of neutral objective technicians. They self-consciously restricted their contribution to estimating the size of the federal revenue gains to be made should the ban be lifted. On that question, however, Treasury analysts quite forcefully claimed the prerogative of dominant expertise.

Two points merit emphasis regarding the positions adopted by the various analysts in the debate. First, a range of styles of analysis were evident. Analysts from DOE, MarAd, and CEA each seemed to take on an issue-advocate stance—though, as indicated above, the causes they advocated varied widely. OMB, DOD, and the State Department analysts were primarily concerned with defending or promoting the interests of their host agencies; hence, their roles in the debate approximated the style of the clients' advocate. The Treasury analysts alone attempted to avoid an advocacy stance, which they accomplished by strictly limiting their contribution to the area of their acknowledged expertise.

---

[40] Personal interview, March 16, 1982. Although the "clear answer" was that the ban should be lifted, the CEA analyst noted that the benefits to be obtained from lifting the ban were outweighed by the political costs to the administration should it attempt to permit exports. He added that, in his view, politicians generally discount future benefits of policies like oil exports quite highly, particularly when the politician's term of office is to end before the benefits are expected to accrue.

[41] One of the analysts who favored lifting the ban contended that "there was a clear initial bias in DOT, due to what they are . . . [the DOT analyst] is one of those who supports business, not markets." Personal interview, March 16, 1982.

The second point is that the advocacy positions taken by the analysts in the debate in part reflected the stances adopted in prior interagency analyses of the issue (including the 1977 and 1979 rounds noted earlier). On iterative analytical issues of this kind, contact with advocates from other quarters tends to *harden* adversarial positions. And, as will be shown, over the period of the 1981 oil export study the level of advocacy rose significantly, fueling bitter analytical disputes.

_____ 5.4 _____
THE ANALYSIS

The debate moved through a series of distinct stages. The initial stage was characterized by an aggressive DOE initiative to lift the ban, while MarAd was on the defensive. DOE first emphasized the federal revenue gains to be made through exports, then argued that MarAd's interests (maintaining the market for the Jones Act fleet) would be best served by favoring exports with cargo preference for U.S. flag ships to carry the crude to the Far East. The second round commenced when the Treasury analyst undercut the DOE analysis by estimating a much smaller "federal tax multiplier" for revenue increases on Alaskan crude production. The DOE analyst responded by modifying his analysis to include additional (and less certain) sources of revenue gains. In the third and final round the MarAd analyst mounted a very aggressive analytical assault on the DOE position, and, by virtue of some rather extreme assumptions, was able to predict that the federal government would *lose* revenues should the ban be lifted. DOE responded by highlighting the more dubious of the MarAd assumptions and by attempting to shift the emphasis of the analysis away from the potential revenue gains to the expected economic efficiency gains of allowing exports. The decision—or nondecision—of the cabinet council was to leave the ban in effect, leaving the MarAd position victorious.

In the more detailed description of the strategems and counterstrategems that follows, the focus will be on the streams of events that pertain to the particular strategies in the use of analysis. These streams of events—or episodes—are presented in roughly chronological order, though they frequently overlapped in actual occurrence. The point of this form of presentation is to isolate particular strategems in a way that highlights the general features of the political practice of policy analysis.

DOE takes the high ground.   The DOE analyst began the opening rounds with a vigorous initiative aimed at lifting the ban. The initial force of his initiative was due in part to the fact that, of the participants, only DOE had a quantitative model that linked crude oil shipping costs, flows of crude among

TABLE 5-3

DOE estimates of annual tax revenues and profits if exports were permitted

	Foreign Tankers	US Tankers
Increases in:		
Alaskan State Revenues	$267 million	$102 million
Federal Revenues	$520 million	$197 million
Producer Profits	$30 million	$11 million

Department of Energy, "Issue Paper: Alaska Crude Exports," (unpublished paper, July 21, 1981), p. 4.

various markets, and wellhead netbacks.[42] Thus, at the outset only DOE was capable of making informed quantitative estimates of the effects of lifting the ban on Alaskan oil netbacks. Furthermore, because of its early inclusion in the CCWG analytical process, the DOE model came to be accepted as the primary tool for CCWG discussion of the effect of various policy options on Alaskan oil netbacks. Until DOE's opponents learned to use the model, and how changes in key model assumptions affected the model results, the opponents were in effect handicapped in their debate with DOE.

The initial DOE analysis was couched in the standard benefit–cost framework, though the disparate nature of the benefits and costs deterred attempts to reduce the results to a single net-benefit calculation. Benefits were broken conceptually into economic and political categories, while "costs" included losses to the maritime industry, losses to investors in east-to-west oil pipelines, and possible "national security" implications.

DOE's estimates of the economic benefits of allowing exports were based on the assumption that, should the ban be lifted, between 500,000 and 600,000 barrels per day of Alaskan oil that would otherwise have been shipped to the Gulf Coast would be rerouted to the Far East.[43] As a result of this shift, costs of transporting the Alaskan oil to market would decrease from $5 per barrel to between $0.60 per barrel (at foreign tanker rates) and $3 per barrel (at American tanker rates). Netbacks would rise by $2 to $4 per barrel, depending on whether domestic or foreign flag tankers were used. Overall, DOE estimated that annual Alaskan oil revenues would rise by $310 million to $817 million. Estimating that federal taxes would take roughly 63 percent of the new oil revenues, that the state of Alaska would take 32 percent, and that producers would receive about 4 percent, the revenue breakdown was presented as shown in table 5-3.

---

[42] The model consisted of the system for calculation of netbacks, based on estimated crude transport costs, as described in table 5-1.

[43] In the early rounds of the analysis, the CCWG agreed that to assume that, should the export ban be lifted, roughly 500,000 barrels per day of Alaskan crude would be shipped to the Far East, and none to the Gulf Coast.

Two beneficial economic effects of lifting the ban were highlighted. First, both the federal government and the state of Alaska could expect large revenue gains. At a time of widespread concern over federal government budget deficits, new federal revenues of over $500 million annually, obtainable *without* imposition of new taxes, would look quite attractive to policy makers. Second, by making production of Alaskan crude more profitable, the already considerable incentive for further oil exploration and production in Alaska would be increased.

The DOE analysis also noted "two distinct political benefits" of lifting the ban. The first would be improved relations with Japan, the most probable recipient of Alaskan exports. The second political benefit would be an improved bilateral balance of trade between the United States and Japan. Though exports to Japan would be offset by added imports of crude from foreign sources, "the appearance of a more favorable trading relationship might prove useful in fending off protectionist pressures aimed at Japan."[44]

DOE estimates of the costs of lifting the ban fell into three categories: effects on domestic shipping industry, effects on efforts to build oil pipelines to the east from the western United States, and effects on U.S. energy security. The effect on domestic shippers was seen as dependent on the size of the ship operated. Large tankers—those over 100,000 dead-weight tons (dwt)—that carried Alaskan oil from Valdez to the West Coast and to the Pacific side of Panama, would lose their Valdez-to-Panama trade. The displaced ships would compete for the remaining Valdez-to-West Coast trade, or would join the ranks of subsidized U.S. flag tankers in the less profitable international trade. For all these tankers, rates and profits would decline. However, few, if any, were expected to face bankruptcy; the low operating costs of these tankers suggested that continued operation, even at a loss, would be preferable to the costs of mothballing or scrapping the ships. Medium and small tankers would fare worse: some portion of the twenty-one small tankers that shuttled crude from Panama to the Gulf Coast (many of which were quite old) would be scrapped, along with about nine midsized ships that had been used to move the oil through the Panama Canal.

A second category of costs noted in the DOE analysis concerned the development of various proposed east-to-west oil pipelines. Lifting the export ban would reduce the profitability of all such projects, making their development unlikely. The Northville pipeline across Panama, which was under construction in 1981, would sustain economic losses. In addition, labor unions "recognize the threat that exports pose to potential jobs on pipeline construction" and therefore were likely to oppose lifting the ban.[45]

---

[44] Ibid., p. 5.
[45] Ibid., p. 9.

The final cost of lifting the ban noted by DOE was the effect on energy security, though this was treated as something of a straw man. DOE anticipated the argument that, by allowing exports, the United States would lose 1.5 million barrels per day of crude supplies from a "secure and stable source." DOE argued that this loss would be illusory:

> During a [future supply] disruption, oil prices will be bid up more or less evenly all over the world. In such a situation, the amount of supply available with a ban will be little different from the amount available without the ban.[46]

In addition, fear of loss of supplies during disruptions could be alleviated by inserting "contingency provisions" into sales contracts for Alaskan crude that would allow the United States to terminate the contract in a supply crisis.

In sum, the initial DOE analysis highlighted the economic benefits—particularly the federal revenue gains—expected of allowing exports, while indicating that the costs of allowing exports would be modest. The DOE analyst's strategy was to emphasize the large federal revenue gains expected to result from exports to make lifting the ban a more attractive option to administration decision makers—a strategy he later came to regret. As he put it,

> Early drafts [of the analysis] underemphasized economic efficiency, and overemphasized the revenue gains. I thought then that that would make it fly in government. I would have, in retrospect, put more emphasis on economic efficiency. . . .[47]

Early in the debate the DOE analyst expected little opposition within the administration to his support for exports, and therefore did not view the emphasis on federal revenues as an unduly vulnerable argument.[48] However, as will become clear, other analysts were able to make those gains appear sufficiently uncertain to diminish the attractiveness of exports as a source of federal revenues.

The first serious opposition to DOE came from analysts at DOT and MarAd in late July of 1981. At this stage MarAd worked closely with DOT and relied on DOT for analytical support. According to a senior MarAd analyst, the MarAd representative on the CCWG at that time was new to the Alaskan oil export issue, and was under the direction of a newly appointed maritime administrator who also had little familiarity with the issue.[49]

---

[46] Ibid.

[47] Personal interview, April 23, 1982.

[48] Prior DOE analyses of Alaskan oil exports, done under the Carter administration, had met no significant interagency opposition from MarAd or DOT. In addition (very early in the analysis,) the DOE analyst's office director had said "once you get the administration on board [in favor of exports,] these guys [at MarAd and DOT] will roll over." Thus, initially, the DOE analyst had expected little opposition from within the administration. Personal interview, March 18, 1982.

[49] Personal interview with senior MarAd analyst, May 21, 1982.

The earliest expression of the DOT–MarAd position was made in a memorandum from the office of the secretary of transportation that responded to the DOE position.[50] The tone of the DOT–MarAd analysis was cautious; at no point was the validity of DOE's model of netbacks or revenue calculations directly questioned. Rather, the analysis (1) amplified the expected losses to the domestic shipping industry that would result from exports, (2) introduced some budgetary costs of allowing exports not considered by DOE, and (3) argued strenuously that lifting the ban would seriously harm U.S. national security.

DOT–MarAd's estimates of domestic maritime losses were far more pessimistic than were DOE's. Eighteen of the thirty large tankers in the Alaskan oil trade would be driven out of business, along with nine or ten medium tankers and twenty-two or twenty-three small tankers. This loss of fifty tankers was estimated to reduce U.S. flag tanker capacity by 31 percent, and to eliminate 3,200 merchant seamen jobs.

Though the initial DOT–MarAd analysis did not dispute DOE estimates of changes in netbacks and revenue gains that would result from exports, it did argue that DOE had neglected significant U.S. budgetary costs that would result from U.S. flag tanker bankruptcies. The analysis estimated that U.S. shippers would default on up to $400 million in federally guaranteed Title XI loans. The federal government would be required to assume responsibility for the defaulted loans, partially offsetting the increase in revenues because of increased oil tax receipts.

The most extensive argument made against exports was based on anticipated national security losses. Despite DOE's arguments to the contrary, the DOT–MarAd analysis maintained that U.S. security would be damaged because the United States would be unwilling to break oil trade agreements with Far Eastern trading partners in the event of a future oil supply crisis. Furthermore, if the United States were to allow exports and replace Alaskan crude with other imported crudes, U.S. petroleum refineries would be refitted to refine crude of different gravities and sulfur contents. Therefore, if Alaskan crudes were reacquired by the United States during a supply disruption, U.S. refineries would be forced to retool once again to handle Alaskan crude, a process that would require "a considerable period of time." Finally, DOT–MarAd analysts argued that if exports were permitted, the Alaskan oil "transportation infrastructure" of tanker ships would have dissipated, leaving no capability to deliver Alaskan crude to U.S. refineries in the event that export agreements were terminated.

The early DOT–MarAd strategy was thus to contest DOE's assessment of the results of lifting the export ban on three dimensions of value, while

---

[50] Department of Transportation (Memorandum to the Cabinet Council on Natural Resources and the Environment, July 30, 1981).

avoiding criticism of DOE's model of crude flows and netback changes. Estimates of tanker bankruptcies were roughly twice as high as DOE's estimates. Federal revenues would be $400 million less, according to DOT–MarAd, because of Title XI loan losses that would stem from exports. Finally, DOT–MarAd stressed the national security costs that the DOE analyst had downplayed.[51]

The DOT–MarAd analysis concluded with a recommendation that a decision on the crude oil exports decision "be delayed until a comprehensive analysis of the effects on the merchant marine industry can be completed."[52] Any delay, of course, would serve to maintain the status quo in which the ban would remain in effect. As DOT and MarAd favored retaining the ban, their attempt to use delay occasioned by further "comprehensive analysis" represents one of the more common uses of analysis as a "retrograde tactic" to derail undesirable policy initiatives.[53]

The Northern Tier strategem.   Though the DOE analyst had presented a strong analytical case in the early stages of the analysis, analysts from DOT and MarAd had demonstrated determined resistance to exports. In response, the DOE analyst introduced a strategem designed to convince the MarAd analysts that it was in the interest of the maritime industry to support the removal of the ban contingent on granting U.S. flag ships cargo preference on Alaskan oil shipped to the Far East.

The DOE analyst argued that the construction of west-to-east crude oil pipelines was made economically attractive only because the export ban was in place, increasing the cost of shipping Alaskan oil to refineries in the Gulf Coast and East Coast states. Several west-to-east pipelines had been proposed, the most prominent of which was the Northern Tier pipeline to run from Port Angeles, Washington, to Minnesota and Illinois. If the Northern Tier pipeline were completed, it would be expected to carry virtually all of the Alaskan crude that had previously been shipped by tanker through Panama, leaving U.S. tankers to compete for traffic on the routes from Valdez to Port Angeles and Los Angeles. The resulting loss of U.S. tanker traffic would leave the maritime industry only marginally better-off than would a policy that allowed exports of Alaskan oil.

---

[51] Analysts within and outside MarAd agreed that the "national security" argument was the one most heavily relied on by MarAd analysts to defend the various maritime support programs. Also, see Richard E. Cohen, "Maritime Industry Keeps Afloat in Seas That Are Often Stormy," *National Journal* (September 4, 1976), pp. 1252–1258.

[52] July 30, 1981, memorandum from the Office of the Secretary of Transportation to the Cabinet Council on Natural Resources and the Environment, p. 4.

[53] In analytic circles, this tactic is often referred to as "paralysis by analysis." For examples of this phenomenom see Hank Jenkins-Smith and David L. Weimer, "Analysis As Retrograde Action: The Case of Strategic Petroleum Reserves," *Public Administration Review*, 45(4), (July/August 1985), pp. 485–494, and chapter 6.

The DOE analyst's strategem was to argue that, first, a policy of allowing exports, plus restriction of Alaskan exports to U.S. flag tankers through cargo preference provisions, would leave the U.S. maritime industry better-off than would construction and operation of the Northern Tier pipeline. Second, the existence of the ban on oil exports made construction of the pipeline more likely, while exports would make it economically unviable. Therefore, he argued, the MarAd analysts should support lifting the export ban on the condition that cargo preference be given to U.S. flag tankers on exported crude. The argument was also aimed at Reagan administration policy makers; the administration could reasonably argue that a policy favoring exports on U.S. flag tankers would, in the long run, lead to more U.S. flag tanker traffic than would the ban, thus reducing the political costs that the administration would face in an attempt to permit exports.

Early DOE analyses had shown that U.S. flag cargo preference on oil exported from Alaska would result in substantially smaller revenue gains than would exports on international tankers. However, by mid-August, using revised estimates of tanker shipping rates provided by MarAd, DOE estimates indicated that giving U.S. tankers cargo preference on exported oil would reduce revenue gains by less than 16 percent.[54] Thus the lost benefits that would result from the cargo preference provision did not appear to be excessive.

DOE's mid-August analysis laid out the Northern Tier Strategem in some detail. At the outset, the DOE analysis noted that "large increases in profits and tax revenues will result [from exports] even if U.S. flag tankers carry all Alaskan oil to the Far East." In addition, although allowance of exports would result in losses to the U.S. maritime industry,

> The export ban encourages construction of Pacific-to-midcontinent pipelines which will cut demand for U.S. tankers much more severely than an export regime in which U.S. flag ships carry Alaskan crude to Far Eastern markets.[55]

---

[54] DOE estimates of revenue gains from exports, at world and U.S. flag rates, and for July 31 and August 10 analyses, were as follows:

	World market		U.S. flag	
	8/81	7/81	8/81	7/81
Federal Revenues	$489	$520	$412	$197
Alaskan State Revenues	$251	$267	$212	$102
Producer Profits	$ 28	$ 30	$ 24	$ 11
Total	$768	$817	$648	$310

The primary cause of the large jump in projected revenues under the "U.S. flag" case was a substantial drop in DOE estimates of U.S. flag rates from Valdez to Yokohama. Department of Energy (Unpublished memorandum, August 10, 1981), p. 2.

[55] Ibid., p. 1.

The analysis ranked four scenarios according to how "painful" the effects would be for large U.S. flag tankers. First, and worst, would be the allowance of exports with no U.S. flag cargo preference, leading to sharply falling tanker rates. Some of these tankers would return to the international trades; of those that remained, "it is not clear how many, if any, will go out of business." A second only slightly better case would be one in which the export ban remained in place and the Northern Tier pipeline was constructed. Large tankers that previously carried Alaskan oil to Panama would be left to compete for traffic on the much shorter route to Port Angeles. The third and better case would allow exports and would provide U.S. flag tankers with 100 percent cargo preference on the crude exported to the Far East. U.S. tankers would compete for the 3,500 nautical miles (NM) route to Japan, rather than the 1,820 NM route to Port Angeles. The fourth case, and the best one for the maritime industry, would be the continuation of the export ban and no construction of west-to-east pipelines. The DOE analyst qualified his ranking of the cases by noting that although construction of the Northern Tier pipeline would be "objectively more painful to the tanker industry" than exports with the cargo preference, the expected losses to the tanker industry due to construction of the pipeline

> . . . must be assessed not only in light of some subjective probability of pipeline construction, but also in light of the fact that these costs are postponed [during construction] until the fall of 1984.[56]

The DOE analyst concluded with the argument that the political costs to the administration of a position in favor of lifting the export ban could be mitigated by pointing out that the export ban merely increased the probability of construction of the Northern Tier pipeline. Therefore:

> An administration decision to lift the ban need not be regarded as a "breach of faith" between the administration and the maritime industry. Indeed, such a decision might result in more ton miles of demand for U.S. tankers than would occur if the export ban remained in force.[57]

The MarAd analyst was attentive to this line of argument. In mid-August a MarAd analysis estimated that the Northern Tier pipeline would eliminate the need for 2.7 million dwt, while exports would displace 3.8 million dwt. The analysis notes that the effects of exports on the maritime industry would be minimized by "requiring that some portion of the exchange trade be reserved for the U.S. flag tanker fleet."[58] MarAd estimates of the losses to the

---

[56] Ibid., p. 5.

[57] Ibid., p. 6.

[58] U.S. Maritime Administration, "The Impact of Exporting Alaskan North Slope Oil on U.S. Flag Tanker Employment," (unpublished paper, August 14, 1981), p. 4.

TABLE 5-4

MarAd estimates of the effect of exports, Northern Tier pipeline,
and cargo preferences on U.S. flag tanker employment*
(Thousands of DWT)

	Over 100 DWT	Under 100 DWT	Total
1. Estimated Loss of Employment (No US flag cargo preference):			
A. Due to Exports	2,528	1,087	3,615
B. Due to Northern Tier	1,613	1,087	2,700
2. Potential Recapture of Employment Through Cargo Preference (by route):			
A. Valdez to Japan (500,000 b/d)	1,896	—	1,896
B. Mexico to US Gulf	—	600	600
C. Both			2,496
3. Net Loss in US Tanker Employment:			
Due to Exports Less Cargo Pref	632	487	1,119
Due to Northern Tier	1,613	1,087	2,700
Difference	981	600	1,581

*Estimates taken from Maritime Administration, "The Impact of Exporting Alaskan North
Slope Oil on U.S. Flag Tanker Employment" (Unpublished paper, August 14, 1981).

U.S. tanker trade due to exports plus the cargo preference versus losses due to construction of the Northern Tier pipeline are shown in table 5-4.

According to these estimates, the U.S. maritime industry would lose employment for nearly 1.6 million dwt of tankerage *more* if the Northern Tier pipeline were built than it would under a policy of exports plus cargo preferences.[59] Thus, as long as it was believed that the export ban significantly increased the probability that the pipeline would be built, and as long as the option of providing a U.S. flag cargo preference on oil exports seemed attainable, MarAd analysts were put in a position of favoring exports plus the cargo preference as most advantageous to the maritime industry.

The DOE analyst's Northern Tier Strategem was directed at the DOD analyst as well. DOD was worried that a subset of the tankers in the Alaskan trade deemed militarily useful would go out of business if the ban were lifted. Were this to happen, DOD would have to find up to $190 million to purchase and $2.6 to $3.4 million per year to maintain the tankers. Thus, if the DOD analyst believed that the ban kept the militarily useful tankers in business, his

---

[59] Earlier MarAd papers had been more ambitious; an early August draft had shown that if Alaskan exports to the Far East were replaced by imports of 500,000 barrels per day from the Persian Gulf to the Gulf Coast, and U.S. tankers were given cargo preference on both legs of the transfer, then the U.S. maritime industry would *gain* nearly six million dead-weight tons of new demand.

incentive was to oppose lifting the export ban. By arguing that construction of the Northern Tier pipeline was made more likely by the existence of the ban, however, the DOE analyst could reduce DOD's opposition to oil exports. The most likely effect of the pipeline, once it began operation, would have been elimination of the demand for the small tankers that shuttled Alaskan crude through the Panama Canal and up to the Gulf and East coasts. Those were precisely the tankers that fell into the "militarily useful" category. If it was seen as likely that these tankers would be displaced *even if* the export ban remained in effect, the DOD analyst was less likely to oppose lifting the ban.

For a time the DOE analyst's arguments seemed persuasive with the MarAd and DOD analysts; "They were listening," he said. In retrospect, the senior MarAd analyst affirmed that the Northern Tier Strategem was used "very skillfully" by the DOE analyst.[60] But the strategy failed.

In part the strategy failed because the concessions needed to gain the acquiescence of MarAd and DOD were strongly opposed by analysts representing other agencies. The U.S. flag cargo preference that would be required to make exports less "painful" to the maritime industry was bitterly opposed by the representative of the State Department. According to the State Department, exports would have favorable foreign policy implications, both with respect to U.S. posture on international trade and U.S. relations with Japan, *unless* cargo reservations for U.S. ships were included. The cargo preferences would violate Friendship, Commerce, and Navigation treaties between the U.S. and its allies, and would bring protests and possibly retaliation from those allies.[61] The State Department never budged from that position.

DOD's desire for assurance that, in absence of the ban, funding would be provided to purchase and store the militarily useful tankers ran up against OMB's objective of limiting federal spending.[62] OMB argued that DOD had not demonstrated a need for the tankers and questioned the need for the purchase when U.S.-owned foreign flag tankers, and the tankers of our allies, would in all likelihood be available in a military emergency (as had been the case in the Vietnam War). OMB demanded more analysis from DOD to justify the purchase.

---

[60] Personal interview, November 1, 1982.

[61] DOT and the State Department squared off over the question of cargo preference for the remainder of the working group sessions. DOT contended that ample precedent existed for granting domestic ships cargo preference, citing French practices and U.S. grain deals with the USSR. The State Department retorted that those precedents were irrelevant because they preceded the Friendship, Commerce, and Navigation treaties or were proprietary contracts between governments.

[62] A major role of OMB has been that of guardian of the public purse. See, for example, Larry Berman, *The Office of Management and Budget and the Presidency 1921–1979* (Princeton, NJ: Princeton University Press, 1979). The role of tight-fisted budgeteer was accentuated at the time of this analysis by the federal budget cutting efforts of the Reagan administration.

Another factor in the failure of DOE's Northern Tier Strategem was that the MarAd analysts thought it increasingly unlikely that the Northern Tier pipeline would be built even if the export ban remained in force. Part of this adjustment was, according to a senior MarAd analyst, simply the correction of an initial error of inertia. "Side analyses" on various west-to-east pipelines that had been done by MarAd in the past "were simply pulled off the shelf with no real update." As the analysis progressed, the review process caught up, and the MarAd analysts "came to the conclusion that they should have come to originally"; that the pipeline would not be built.[63] In addition, new information had become available; proponents of the Northern Tier pipeline were meeting stiff opposition from environmentalists, and the Energy Facility Siting Evaluation Council, which was to review the issue for Governor Spellman of Washington had cast a preliminary vote against the pipeline.[64] On that basis the MarAd analysts concluded (correctly) that the Northern Tier pipeline was not a serious threat to U.S. tanker employment. The cumulative effect of MarAd's revised view of the likelihood of construction of the pipeline, the State Department's opposition to cargo preferences, and OMB's resistance to the purchase and storage of the threatened militarily useful tankers was to thoroughly undermine the DOE analyst's Northern Tier Strategem.

The national security dimension.   Discussions of national maritime policy are typically headed by enumeration of the national security benefits that flow from maintenance of a large domestic merchant marine fleet.[65] Since the Arab oil embargo of 1973–1974, policies bearing on the assurance of adequate oil supplies have taken on a similar national security component. Because of its apparent implications for the domestic tanker fleet as well as domestic energy supplies, considerations of Alaskan oil exports have had to confront a range of national security concerns. What is striking, however, is the success with which some of the participants of the 1981 review of the export ban were able to limit the inclusion of the national security dimension, and to channel the

---

[63] Personal interview, November 1, 1982.

[64] The Northern Tier pipeline project never overcame the opposition to construction in the state of Washington. The project was officially abandoned in March of 1983.

[65] In testimony before the House Merchant Marine Subcommittee in August 1975, Maritime Administrator Blackwell quoted Thomas Jefferson as saying that the vulnerable seaboard of the United States can only be protected ". . . by possessing a respectable body of citizen-seamen and of citizens and establishments in readiness for shipbuilding." Cohen, "Maritime Industry," p. 1255. Other testimony in favor of the maritime programs echoed a similar theme. That the national security argument would be carried over into the Alaskan oil export issue was made clear by Frank Drozak, president of the Seafarers International Union, who wrote to the Secretary of Energy in September of 1981 that "chief among our many reasons for opposing the export [of Alaskan oil] is the implications it would have for U.S. security. Export of Alaskan oil would severely cripple the U.S. flag tanker fleet and would disrupt the ongoing development of America's energy system."

discussion into the cost-effectiveness of various alternatives for achieving a given national security objective.

The national security implications of the Alaskan oil export issue stem broadly from (1) the belief that the United States should retain secure supplies of crude oil for domestic use in the face of diminishing world supplies and the possibility of oil supply disruptions, and (2) the need to maintain access to militarily useful tankers for defense purposes.[66] As noted above, an early DOT memo made a fairly extensive case that exports would undermine U.S. energy security by arguing that the United States would lose access to Alaskan oil even in a disruption because the United States would be unwilling to break oil export trade agreements made with its Far Eastern allies. Furthermore, even if those trade agreements were broken and the ban on exports reimposed, it was argued that the West Coast refining region would no longer be fitted to handle the particular qualities of crude characteristic of Alaskan oil. Finally, because of the export policy, the "transportation infrastructure" of tankers required to carry Alaskan oil to the Gulf Coast would have been dissipated, leaving the United States with no means to reclaim Alaskan oil.[67]

The DOE analyst had anticipated much of the energy-security argument and was able to draw on an accumulation of studies of the workings of the world oil market during supply disruptions. These studies had concluded that, in a supply disruption, the price of oil would rise fairly evenly in all oil markets, even if one or more nations were "targeted" by embargoing oil exporters.[68] The result of any reduction in supply, then, would be a general and uniform increase in the *world* oil price, to which the market would respond by (1) a reduction in the quantity of oil consumed, and (2) an increase in oil supplied from nondisrupted oil sources. Because the United States was seen as fully integrated into the world oil market after domestic oil prices were decontrolled, it was assumed that oil prices in the United States would rise to world

---

[66] For a more extensive treatment of the role of energy in U.S. national security, see Donald J. Goldstein, ed., *Energy and National Security*, (Washington, DC: National Defense University Press, 1981).

[67] Department of Energy (Unpublished memorandum from the Office of the Secretary of Energy to the Cabinet Council on National Resources and the Environment, July 30, 1981), pp. 3–4.

[68] The reasoning is well expressed in Thomas Teisberg, "A Model for Simulating World Oil Market Arbitrage During Embargos" (Working Paper, Cambridge, MA: Massachussetts Institute of Technology, November 26, 1979).

> The experience of 1973–74 led to a conclusion that a targeted embargo is not possible. Any attempt to target one country tends to raise prices in that country relative to prices elsewhere. This in turn induces oil flows from low price countries to high price countries, until prices are equalized. The result is that an embargo of one country, with no decrease in total production, has no effect at all; while an embargo of one country with a corresponding decrease in production raises price equally in all countries, and reduces consumption in each country by an amount which depends upon the elasticity of oil demand in the countries. (P.1.)

levels in a supply disruption regardless of the source of the oil. Given this view, there was little point to banning exports of crude oil; restricting Alaskan oil to domestic markets would neither increase aggregate oil supplies available to the United States, nor reduce the expected increase in oil prices in the event of an oil supply disruption.

With respect to DOT's argument that U.S. refinery capacity to process Alaskan crude would be lost if oil exports were allowed, the DOE analyst observed that existing refinery capacity was not likely to be dismantled if Alaskan crude were not used.[69] Furthermore, worldwide oil production trends were toward heavier, more sulfurous crudes, indicating that Alaskan crude would probably be replaced by crudes of comparable quality in Gulf Coast refineries. Finally, during oil supply disruptions, refinery capacity would exceed available crude supplies and would thus allow considerable flexibility in the quality of crudes used to achieve the required mix of products.[70] U.S. refinery capacity was thus not expected to be impaired by allowing exports, even in the event that Alaskan crudes were to be rerouted to the Gulf Coast in some future period.

DOE was equally brusque with DOT's concerns about the energy-security loss due to "dissipation" of the Alaskan oil transportation infrastructure:

> Our analysis suggests that tanker capacity is not likely to be a problem during a disruption. During world oil shortfalls, there will be excess tanker capacity because of the reduced volumes of crude to transport, worldwide. If the U.S. chooses to transport Alaskan crude to the Gulf Coast and domestic capacity is below the required level, therefore, additional tankers can be hired on the world market.[71]

The result of DOE's analysis and persuasive argument was that the energy-security concerns raised by DOT were omitted from the cabinet council paper. In its final form, the cabinet council paper noted that:

> It was the general consensus of the group that in time of disruption, neither shipping nor refinery configurations would be likely to be a problem, even if the Alaskan oil were returned to U.S. traffic.[72]

---

[69] DOE memorandum for the Cabinet Council on Natural Resources and the Environment. August 10, 1981, p. 12.

[70] As refineries reduce operations below capacity levels, they become able to gain a larger portion of light products (e.g., gasoline) from a given barrel of oil by refining the crude more intensively. Utilization of conversion facilities, for example, will result in additional increments of light product. As the number of barrels refined declines, a greater fraction of the total stock of crude can be run through the conversion processes.

[71] DOE memorandum to the Cabinet Council on Natural Resources and the Environment. August 10, 1981, p. 7.

[72] Office of the President (White House Memorandum to the Cabinet Council on Natural Resources and the Environment, November 1, 1981), p. 12.

Thus the accumulation of analysis on the question of energy security appears to have rendered the question sufficiently tractable to dismiss it as a valid concern.

The national defense aspects of the security dimension proved to be more enduring. MarAd analysts estimated that twenty-six militarily useful tankers would be driven out of business and scrapped were the ban to be lifted. In addition, the unemployment of some 2,800 merchant sailors on those tankers would contribute to the decline in the number of trained seamen available to the military in a time of crisis. The costs of such a reduction in military capabilities was highlighted by MarAd and DOD analysts. As stated in the CCWG paper:

> The Joint Chiefs of Staff have constrained existing plans for global conflict scenarios to the existing tanker assets. Therefore, *requirements* equal *available tankers*. If these 26 tankers are lost, military planning requirements would be impacted by about 13%.[73]

The working-group analysis focused on the costs of maintaining access to the twenty-six militarily useful tankers in the event that the ban were lifted and the tankers lost. The MarAd analysts estimated that purchase of the tankers would require approximately $190 million, with between $1 million and $3 million yearly required to maintain the tankers in an appropriate state of readiness. Though such a purchase would maintain access to the tankers, the cost of the purchase would offset gains in federal revenues that would result from exports.

Though conceptually resolved, the implication of lifting the ban on the availability of militarily useful tankers remained a source of contention. Analysts from OMB, in the interest of eschewing unnecessary federal expenditures, argued that:

> [T]he requirement for laying up of these 26 tankers has not been supported with an in-depth analysis and ranking among other Transportation and Defense needs in a manner sufficient to support the acquisition.[74]

DOD analysts rejoined that, though no recent analysis had been completed:

> [A] commitment to some course of action to ameliorate this loss of capability needs to be made in the context of the export decision. . . . Therefore, Defense desires an explicit commitment to acquisition and layup *unless* either an alternative course of action is provided . . . or Defense, in conjunction with OMB, Transportation (MARAD), and other appropriate agencies, decides,

---

[73] Office of the President, Cabinet Council on Natural Resources and the Environment (Working paper, final draft, November 5, 1981), p. 13.

[74] Ibid., p. 14.

after studying the details of the issue, that these tankers are not as essential as previously assumed.[75]

Thus, in OMB's view, the cost of purchase and lay-up should be rigorously justified, then submitted to ordinary budgetary treatment along with other DOD purchases. DOD, on the other hand, wanted explicit commitment of the funds outside of usual budgetary procedures. Analysts from DOD and OMB remained at odds over this issue throughout the period of the working-group review.

Overall, the national security dimension was given less emphasis than would be expected in view of the arguments usually made for maritime programs. The energy-security component was removed—though it could quite possibly have been reinserted had the issue moved beyond the administration to Congress. The primary analytical effect of the national defense component was to partially offset the expected federal revenue gains from allowing exports. Perhaps more importantly for the fate of the issue within the administration, the national defense question pitted OMB's objective of limiting federal expenditures against DOD's desire to have its contingency tanker requirements provided at no cost to its existing budget.

The revenue dimension I: the West Coast discount.   As shown in table 5-1, increased revenues resulting from exports of Alaskan oil stem from decreased shipping costs and higher netbacks to oil producers. The DOE analyst had emphasized that 63 percent of the increase in Alaskan oil netbacks would accrue to the federal government in the form of windfall profits tax and corporate income tax revenues. Thus the DOE analyst had stated that, using foreign flag ships, exports would bring the federal government $520 million per year in new revenues.

The Treasury analyst, in whose province calculation of the tax effects of various policies fell, found fault with the DOE analyst's calculation of federal revenue gains. According to Treasury, the increase in taxable revenues for Alaskan oil production would be exactly matched by losses in revenues by other sectors of the economy.[76] Therefore, increased tax revenues on Alaskan oil profits would be offset by reductions in tax revenues from other industries—namely, the maritime industry. The Treasury analyst argued that the only *net* increase in federal revenues (increase in revenues on Alaskan oil less

---

[75] Ibid.

[76] According to Treasury analysts, the argument that increased revenues in one sector are matched by falling revenues elsewhere amounts to a "rule of thumb" in tax revenue calculations. Implicitly, this means that the change in revenues is assumed to be merely a transfer of wealth from one sector of the economy to another, with no accompanying increase in GNP. Though DOE and CEA analysts consistently rejected that assumption, the Treasury calculation of revenue gains because of exports was used through the remainder of the CCWG analysis.

lost revenues elsewhere) would be because a higher tax rate is applied to the oil industry than is applied to other industries. Thus, even though overall taxable income and profits remain the same, more of that income and profit would be shifted to the heavily taxed oil industry, generating larger tax revenues for the federal government.[77] The result of this approach was to reduce the estimated federal revenue gain expected to result from exports. Instead of DOE's estimate of 63 percent of the increase in gross Alaskan oil revenues, Treasury expected only 30.3% of that increase to accrue to the federal government as net gain in revenue receipts.

Initially the DOE analyst resisted acceptance of Treasury's calculation of the federal revenue gains. He argued, with the support of the CEA analyst, that exports would result in "efficiency gains" to the economy that would increase the gross tax base, and that resources from the maritime industry would be released to earn taxable income in other sectors of the economy. However valid DOE's arguments, the Treasury analyst did successfully claim the dominant expertise on the tax issue. As stated in a Treasury memo to the CCWG leader, though Treasury did not claim to have the expertise to evaluate DOE's and DOT's estimates of oil prices, tanker costs, and the effects of exports on oil prices, Treasury

> [D]oes believe the factor normally applied to such changes in the selling price would provide a reasonable approximation of the changes in federal tax revenues.[78]

The DOE analyst shifted tactics. Instead of debating the fraction of each dollar of new wellhead revenues that would become net new federal revenues, he increased the number of dollars to which that fraction would be applied. He argued that Alaskan oil producers were beginning to discount the price of

---

[77] The Treasury analyst's methodology for computing the net federal tax gain because of exports of Alaskan oil is as follows: assume an increase of $1.00 p/b in gross Alaskan wellhead revenues. The gains and losses would be:

	Oil producers	Other industries	
Change in gross revenues	+ 1.000	− 1.000	
State royalties and taxes	.240	.240	(unknown
	—	—	deductible
Change in WPT base	.760	—	expense
Gross WPT revenue (70%)	.532	—	of .240)
Change in taxable income	.228	− .760	
Change in income tax (43%)	.098	− .327	
Sum of revenue changes	+ .630	− .327	

Net change in federal taxes are thus = .630 − .327 = .303 or 30.3% of gross revenues.

[78] Department of the Treasury (Memorandum on the Crude Oil Task Force, October 20, 1981), p. 3.

Alaskan oil sold on the West Coast below the world market price in order to avoid the expense of the long shipment to the Gulf Coast.[79] He therefore included a range of estimates of the possible sizes of the discount. At one extreme, under full competitive pressure, Alaskan oil producers would have had incentives to discount the price of oil sold on the West Coast to the point that netbacks for oil sold on the Gulf and West coasts were identical. If so, lifting the export ban would cause the price of Alaskan oil on the West Coast to rise by the full amount of the discount. In addition to its effect on the price of Alaskan oil sold on the West Coast, the DOE analyst argued that a discount would reduce the quality-adjusted price of oil produced in California as well. These prices too would rise should the export ban be lifted. At the other extreme, if Alaskan producers were not competitive marketers of crude on the West Coast, Alaskan oil would be sold at the world price, and the prices of neither Alaskan nor Californian oil sold in that market would be expected to rise in the event that oil exports were permitted.

The point of the DOE analyst's inclusion of the discount argument was to increase the size of the estimated federal revenue gains. Should prices of Alaskan and Californian crudes sold on the West Coast rise because of exports, federal and state tax revenues would rise as well. Overall, with the inclusion of the discount argument, the DOE analyst was able to estimate that export of 500,000 barrels per day from Alaska would increase federal tax revenues by between $250 million to $1 billion annually, depending on whether the discount was assumed to be in effect.[80] Thus DOE was able, for a time, to recover from the reduced estimates of federal revenues resulting from Treasury's method of estimating tax gains.

The DOE analyst had included the West Coast discount argument in his earliest drafts of the oil export ban analysis (well before the CCWG was formed), but had later abandoned the argument both because supporting data were not available and because he felt that the argument was too complex to be conveyed to decision makers.[81] However, more recent data had become available that did appear to show a discount on spot market prices of Alaskan crude on the West Coast, though it was significantly smaller than the maximum discount postulated by the DOE analyst.

The issue remained steeped in uncertainty, however. Comparisons of West Coast and Gulf Coast prices were based on uncertain estimates of shipping costs from Valdez. Furthermore, high-priced foreign crude con-

---

[79] See section 5.2.

[80] Office of the President, Cabinet Council on Natural Resources and the Environment (Draft of the Working Paper, September 23, 1981), p. 4.

[81] Personal interview, March 18, 1982.

tinued to be imported to the West Coast, a phenomena not readily explained if the discount argument were accepted.[82] Despite the uncertainty, the DOE analyst decided to include the discount argument late in the CCWG analysis. The primary motivation for including the argument was the setback on the federal revenue dimension because of Treasury's tax calculations. As the DOE analyst put it, once Treasury revised the tax calculations, he saw "no reason to be generous and understate the case [for exports] and make it look less strong."[83]

The net result of Treasury's reduced estimate of federal tax receipts per dollar of increase in oil revenues and the DOE analyst's addition of the discount argument was to increase the upper extreme of possible federal revenue gains, while expanding the range of uncertainty concerning how large those gains would be. However, the tactic of capitalizing on analytical uncertainty in order to make the results of the analysis more to one's liking can typically be used by *both* sides of the debate.

The revenue dimension revisited: MarAd's counterassault.   Subsequent to the DOE analyst's introduction of the West Coast discount argument, the tone of the CCWG analysis became increasingly adversarial. The MarAd analyses in particular became more aggressive, introducing new assumptions that strengthened the case against allowing oil exports and even making forays into the analysis of energy markets. The change stemmed in part from MarAd's perception of the seriousness of the threat to U.S. maritime programs that was implicit in the DOE analysis. A more aggressive and experienced analyst assumed control of the MarAd analyses, one who was deeply committed to the maintenance of a strong U.S. maritime industry. In his view,

> We [MarAd analysts] need to be concerned with maintaining an advocacy stance. Some of it is self-interest. At the same time, there are laws that say we are committed to a strong maritime industry. If you allow yourself to lose these fights [among federal agencies over maritime policies], you're not doing your job. . . . We are obliged under law to see to it that a strong maritime industry exists. *That's* what we're hired for.[84]

---

[82] A straightforward economic argument would hold that, in order to reduce the price of crude sold on the West Coast, discounted Alaskan crude would have needed to first displace all of the more expensive foreign crudes imported to the West Coast. The demand for the imported crudes would thus have been taken to mean that crude still brought the world price on the West Coast. On the other hand, it could have been argued that, because of differences in refining costs, *some* of the high-quality imported crudes would have been demanded even though Alaskan oil was discounted. In that case one would have expected to see the volumes of imported crudes gradually dropping off as Alaskan crude captured a greater share of the market—a pattern that has been observed over the past few years.

[83] Personal interview, March 18, 1982.

[84] Personal interview, November 1, 1982.

The change in tone also reflected a change in tactics. MarAd analysts no longer believed that the Northern Tier pipeline would be built, and were thus able to concentrate their efforts on demonstrating the ill effects of lifting the export ban. In addition, MarAd's criticisms of the DOE analysis became more incisive as the driving assumptions behind DOE's modeling efforts became more widely known, and hence more manipulable.

The new MarAd analyses dramatically enlarged estimated losses to the maritime industry that would result from allowing exports of Alaskan oil. The new estimates were based on the assumption that, should exports take place, reduced tanker demand would suppress tanker rates throughout the domestic market to the point that the *entire tanker industry* would face bankruptcy.[85] Combined Title XI loan defaults in that instance would result in losses to the federal government of nearly $1 billion, all of which would offset the federal revenue gains expected to result from export of Alaskan oil.[86] At the same time, MarAd analyses showed decreased estimates of federal revenues due to exports. One means by which this was accomplished was a successive reestimation of oil tanker rates in ways that reduced the increase in netbacks that would result from exports. Noting again the effect of shipping rates on netback estimates as described in table 5-1, either *increased* shipping rates from the Persian Gulf to the Gulf Coast or *decreased* shipping costs from the Persian Gulf to Japan would reduce the size of the netback gain due to exports.

Over the period of the CCWG analysis, MarAd provided three sets of shipping rates, each of which reduced the netback gain expected from exports. Between August and October of 1981, MarAd's tanker rate revisions reduced the expected netback increase from export of oil that would otherwise have gone to the Gulf Coast by between $0.70 and $0.80 p/b. The shipping rate estimates and resultant netback changes are shown in table 5-5. Applied to the 500,000 barrels per day that were expected to be exported, the change in netbacks reduced estimated revenue gains to the federal government by $39 million to $43 million per year.

MarAd analysts also sought to undermine the West Coast discount argument by asserting that California crude oils were not substitutable for

[85] One clear message in MarAd's analysis was that, in proposing a policy that favored export of Alaskan oil, the administration would face serious opposition from the politically powerful maritime interests. This message was also being delivered along other avenues, including "letters of concern" sent to the president and members of his cabinet by maritime groups and members of Congress. The political clout of the maritime lobby was manifest in one letter, dated October 30, 1981, that rejected exports as contrary to the "national interest," and that contained the signatures of 76 members of the House of Representatives.

[86] MarAd analysts made estimates of Title XI loan defaults of that magnitude in a number of papers prepared for the CCWG between late September and e arly November of 1981. In their final estimates, however, MarAd analysts reduced projected Title XI losses to about $700 million.

TABLE 5-5

Comparison of DOE and MarAd Estimates of Tanker Rates and Netback Estimates
(Amounts shown are in dollars per barrel)

Source	Date	PG-USGC	PG-JPN	AK-USGC	AK-JPN	Netback increase*
DOE	7/81	$1.70	$1.04	$5.00	$0.57	$3.77
MarAd	8/81	$1.20	$0.74	$4.00	$0.41	$3.13
MarAd	10/81	$2.03	$0.96	$4.00	$0.51	$2.42
MarAd	10/81	$2.33	$1.52	$4.00	$0.84	$2.35**

* The increase in netback attributable to export of one barrel of Alaskan crude to Japan that would otherwise have gone to the Gulf Coast.

** The last row represents MarAd's estimates of netback gains for 1986. Netbacks were reduced because MarAd assumed that international tanker rates would rise over time, while domestic tanker rates would remain constant.

Alaskan crudes because of their very high sulfur content and low gravity. Because of these quality differences, they argued, California crude prices would not rise in the event that lifting the export ban caused the price of Alaskan oil sold on the West Coast to rise.[87] Thus, the MarAd analyst projected no increase in federal revenues because of changes in California crude prices should the ban be lifted. Furthermore, the MarAd analysts argued that the DOE analysis exaggerated the size of the discount on Alaskan crudes sold on the West Coast. MarAd data showed an average discount of $1.81 p/b, which was assumed to drop to $0.81 p/b as soon as the Northville pipeline across Panama began operation. Thus, rather than using a range of estimates of the discount as the DOE analyst had done, MarAd analysts opted for a point estimate and implicitly assumed that it would hold constant in future periods should the ban remain in effect.

Two other arguments were raised that reduced projected federal revenues. First, MarAd analysts contended that, in order to make the sale of Alaskan oil attractive to the Japanese, the Japanese would require a "price concession" of about $0.60 per barrel on Alaskan oil. That assumption alone reduced projected federal revenues by nearly 25 percent. Second, it was noted that the three major Alaskan oil producers had signed "through-put" agreements[88] for

---

[87] To bolster this argument, the MarAd analysis compared the spot price of heavy imported PG crudes with the posted price of California oil, showing them to be roughly equal. Spot and posted prices are not comparable, however. Spot prices tend to respond rapidly to changing market conditions, and may be well above or below posted prices at a given point in time.

[88] Through-put agreements commit oil producers to pay for the shipment of a stated amount of crude through a pipeline, regardless of whether the crude is actually shipped.

TABLE 5-6

Estimated federal budgetary effects of lifting the ban on oil exports
(dollars in millions)

	FY 83	FY 84	FY 85	Total 83–87
High Revenues/Low Outlays:				
Revenues	$365	$364	$363	$1798
Outlays	$200	$ 50	$ 50	$ 33
Net	$165	$314	$313	$1467
Low Revenues/High Outlays:				
Revenues	$134	$133	$132	$ 643
Outlays	$300	$130	$130	$ 700
Net	− $166	− $ 3	− $ 2	− $ 57

shipment of 300,000 barrels of oil per day with the Northville pipeline across Panama; therefore, oil producers would not be likely to export the full estimated 500,000 barrels per day to Japan. Lower levels of exports would further reduce projected tax revenue gains to the federal government.

The net effect of MarAd's assumptions showing increased costs of lifting the ban in conjunction with decreased tax revenue gains was to project a net federal revenue *loss* of $232 million in 1982, and a cumulative loss (discounted at 10%) of $613 million through 1986.[89] As a result, the CCWG analysis showed an enormous range of uncertainty regarding the effect of lifting the ban on federal revenues. Table 5-6 shows the range of revenue estimates provided in the final draft of the CCWG analysis.

The lower bound on revenue estimates, assuming no West Coast discount and that *all* Title XI ships default, approximates MarAd's position. The upper bound on revenue estimates, assuming a West Coast discount of $1.19 per barrel and that only Title XI ships employed in the Alaskan trade default on their federal loans, represents the DOE estimate. The result was an enormous range of estimates of the revenue gains that would result from exports—a range of over $1.5 billion in present value.[90] In view of the fact that all prior working-group drafts had projected that exports would result in substantial net federal revenue gains, MarAd's accomplishment in showing sizable revenue losses is most impressive.

The DOE analyst responded to the MarAd counteroffensive in a number of ways. Considerable effort was devoted to rebutting specific elements of the MarAd analysis. For example, the DOE analyst noted that, despite MarAd's

---

[89] Maritime Administration (Unpublished paper, October 16, 1981).

[90] Both high and low estimates were made using MarAd's shipping rate estimates. Using the rates preferred by the DOE analyst, the "upper bound" estimate would have been $2 billion, and the range of estimates would have been about $2.1 billion.

assertions, heavy crude oils do indeed compete for sales with lighter crudes; therefore, California crudes would necessarily be suppressed in price in order to compete with the discounted Alaskan crudes. In addition, the DOE analyst took issue with MarAd's assertion that the Japanese would require a $0.60 p/b price concession to be induced to take Alaskan crude. He argued that the Japanese would need to compete with other Far Eastern buyers for the Alaskan crude, including Korea, Taiwan, and Singapore, and would therefore be compelled to pay the full world price for the oil. Furthermore, he noted, the Japanese showed no evidence of being able to extract price concessions on the oil received from other sources, so there was little reason to believe that they could do so with Alaskan crudes.[91]

A point-by-point rebuttal would not suffice, however. As noted earlier, the DOE analyst had given a great deal of weight to the revenue dimension in making his case for exports on the assumption that the Reagan cabinet would be attracted to the large federal revenue gains available through exports. Once the MarAd analysis had increased the uncertainty about the receipt of those revenue gains, and even made revenue losses seem plausible, the DOE analyst's central strategy was seriously undermined. His response was to reemphasize the *economic efficiency gains* that would flow from allowing export of Alaskan oil and to argue that the federal revenue gains, though significant, were merely the fragment of the efficiency gain captured by the federal government. The DOE analyst announced his shift in a memorandum to the Treasury analyst dated October 21:

> First, this memo underscores something fundamental. The decision on whether or not to lift the ban should not be contingent upon the effects of this action on federal revenues. The U.S. economy stands to gain from a more efficient use of domestic economic resources if the ban on Alaskan exports is lifted. The more efficient use of domestic resources will lead to a higher national income for all Americans to enjoy. The amount of this increased income that will be received by the federal Government is significant, but of secondary importance when compared to the increased health of the U.S. economy, overall.[92]

The increased national income was to result from increasing the economic resources devoted to the discovery and production of oil, and from decreasing the resources devoted to the transport of Alaskan crudes to the Gulf Coast on inefficient Jones Act tankers. Had the DOE analyst been successful in shifting the primary emphasis of the analysis from the revenue to the economic

---

[91] These and other objections to the MarAd analysis were presented in a memorandum addressed to the working group leader that was produced in late October, 1981.

[92] Department of Energy (Unpublished memorandum to Treasury analyst, October 21, 1981), p. 1.

efficiency dimension, he would have been able to mount an argument for lifting the export ban that was less susceptible—though by no means immune—to emasculation through exploitation of analytical uncertainty.

The DOE analyst was only mildly successful in his belated attempt to shift the weight of the analysis away from the revenue dimension to the efficiency dimension. Subsequent working group drafts of the analysis contained a clause intended to reduce the stress on the revenue implications of oil exports:

> The primary reason for lifting the export ban would be our general commitment to free trade and a deregulated economy, with the resulting economic benefits. The extensive attention given to tax revenues [in the CCWG analysis] should not be taken to mean that the purpose of lifting the ban is to raise more taxes.[93]

Despite this disclaimer, both the executive summary and the body of the analysis continued to give central attention to the federal revenue implications of lifting the export ban. Both the summary and the body were broken into four sections, focusing on implications of lifting the ban for the maritime industry, the federal budget, U.S. foreign policy, and national defense. The federal revenue section was by far the largest. Discussion of the economic efficiency benefits of lifting the ban—which was limited in space to one short paragraph—was subsumed under the discussion of the federal budget. A genuine shift of analytical emphasis to economic efficiency benefits, as called for by the DOE analyst, would have required the reverse; budgetary gains would have been subsumed under the broader category of economic efficiency gains. Thus, while the DOE analyst was able to include some new language in the analysis, he was unable to alter the dimensions of value in which the analysis had previously been cast.

_____ 5.5 _____

STRATEGIES IN ADVERSARIAL ANALYSIS

On November 5, 1981, the Cabinet Council on Resources and the Environment met and voted to take no action on the Alaskan oil export ban. Though it is not possible to isolate the effect of the CCWG analysis on the decision to maintain the ban, it is possible to reconstruct the strategies employed by the principle analysts, and to observe in detail the process of analysis in the bureaucratic context.

The oil export study well illustrates the process of analysis depicted in chapter 4. The DOE analyst, with support from analysts at the CEA, mounted an initiative to encourage the administration to lift the oil export ban; analysis

---

[93] Final draft of the CCWG working group analysis, November 5, 1981, p. 1.

was used to drum up support within the administration. Analysts at MarAd and DOT, perceiving the initiative to threaten progams (support of Jones Act tankers) and values (national security) that they championed, quickly developed counteranalysis to discourage lifting the ban. Intense analytical conflict ensued, with both sides committing extensive analytical resources over the four-month exercise. Professed analytical beliefs rapidly became fixed, and analytical strategies were tailored to making and refuting analytical claims that would entice decision makers to preferred policy choices. In the end, with the exception of the question of energy security, little headway was made toward a consensual analytical basis from which a policy choice could be made.

The analysis *did* suggest the existence of a common policy space, made up of a set of key dimensions of value, through which participants to the debate understood and struggled over appropriate conception of the issue. The federal revenue dimension, initially conceived as a value of prime importance to decision-making clients, became the focus of primary contention. Also of importance was the degree to which an export policy would damage the domestic maritime industry. Of secondary importance, but still of significance, were the foreign policy and national security implications of exports. Neither the DOE or MarAd analysts limited the use of analysis to the pursuit of the objectively "best" policy option, as prescribed by the policy paradigm. Instead, both adopted the role of the issue advocate, who seeks to shape the policy space in ways designed to attract decision makers to the analysts' preferred policy choice. The clients to whom the competing analysts sought to appeal were in this case the cabinet-level members of the Reagan administration. The strategies used reflect a sensitivity to what were believed to be the administration's interests; the administration's budget problems led both the DOE and MarAd analysts to give a great deal of weight to the revenue dimension. The strategies of both analysts also gave due consideration to the administration's desire to avoid confrontation with the politically powerful maritime lobby. Furthermore, in working to advantageously shape the policy space, both analysts made extensive use of analytically intractable aspects of the issue to press their claims for their preferred policy positions and to undermine the opponent's case.

The DOE analyst's strategy reflected his view that this issue constituted a conflict between a concentrated, highly mobilized interest and a diffuse and unorganized "public interest." The Reagan administration's avowed interest in deregulating markets did not appear to him to provide a sufficient impetus to push forward with a proposal to permit oil exports. The only concentration of interest that favored lifting the ban stemmed from the additional tax revenues that were expected to result from exports. With the first phase of the administration's tax cut policy in force, and the looming threat of annual federal budget deficits in excess of $100 billion, the revenue gains expected of exports seemed to be just the issue with which to harness the administration to an effort to lift the ban. For this reason the DOE analyst gave primary weight to the federal revenue dimension in making his case for allowing export of Alaskan oil.

The DOE analyst was aware that a primary concern of the administration, in making a decision on this issue, would be the opposition of the maritime lobby to any policy proposal that permitted exports. He also became aware early in the analysis that key members of the CCWG—the MarAd and DOT analysts—would be unwilling to concur with *any* policy that was deemed harmful by the maritime interests. Furthermore, the DOD analyst was likely to oppose exports unless it could be shown that exports would not threaten the availability of militarily useful tankers. Faced with this situation, the DOE analyst sought to show that allowing exports could well be in the maritime industry's best interest, via his Northern Tier Strategem. At a minimum, he provided a line of reasoning that would allow the administration to argue that, in favoring exports, it had not abandoned the interests of the maritime lobby. To the DOD analyst, his message was that the export ban could not be counted on to maintain the availability of the desired tankers.

Unfortunately for the DOE analyst, the Northern Tier Strategem was undermined by the conflicting interests of the various agencies involved (MarAd versus State, and DOD versus OMB), while the appeal of the federal revenue dimension to the administration was undermined by the vigorous analytical opposition of the MarAd analysts. The DOE analyst was therefore forced to attempt to shift the focus of the analysis to the economic efficiency gains that would stem from oil exports as a larger and less analytically intractable category of benefits. Faced with the inertia of the previously established dimensions of the CCWG analysis, the DOE analyst was able to make only superficial progress toward such a shift.

For the primary champions of the export ban, analysts from MarAd, the strategy recognized and made use of the fact that the benefits of the ban accrued to a highly concentrated group—the maritime industry. The standard defense of the maritime programs rests on the contention that the nation as a whole benefits from the existence of a robust domestic ocean shipping industry, primarily through the enhancement of national security. Much of this argument was eliminated from the analysis in its early stages, however, and the remaining defense arguments were cast in cost-effectiveness terms that did little to favor maintaining the ban. The MarAd strategy therefore focused on undermining the DOE federal revenue arguments through the mobilization of analytical uncertainty. By adjusting the assumptions used in the DOE revenue calculations, MarAd could argue that exports would result in *net losses,* rather than gains, in federal revenues. The intractable nature of tanker rate projections assured that such estimates would remain within the pale of analytical plausibility.

In addition to undermining the prospect of large revenue gains, the MarAd analysis emphasized the very certain political costs to the administration should exports take place. MarAd's assertion that exports would bankrupt the entire domestic tanker industry, although disputed by others in the working group, kept the assurance of bitter maritime opposition to an export policy prominently in the forefront of the analysis. The effect of the strategy was to signal to the administration that, while allowing exports could result in either losses or gains in federal revenues, the political costs of such a policy were large and assured.

For both the DOE and MarAd analysts, strategy was in part a function of and response to the perceived behavior of *other* analysts. The DOE analyst became willing to introduce the admittedly uncertain West Coast discount argument only after the analyst from Treasury had (in the DOE analyst's view) unreasonably understated the federal revenue gains to be had from exports. To have *neglected* to introduce the discount argument, he felt, would have resulted in a biased collective analytical result. The MarAd analysts also acted in response to the behavior of other analysts. The vigorous and compelling arguments made by the DOE analyst spurred the intense rebuttal and counterarguments made regarding the massive tanker bankruptcies and extensive Title XI loan defaults. Thus, as noted earlier in chapter 4, an important element of the policy context driving the political uses of analysis is the perception of the roles played by other analysts. From the analyst's perspective, provision of balanced composite advice often *requires* attempts to wrest the shape of the policy space toward a more reasonable depiction of the implications of the policy options under consideration. The participation of one advocate analyst thus leads other analysts to adopt an advocacy role. Advocates beget advocates.

5.6
CONCLUSIONS AND CAVEATS

Advocacy analysis must be tailored to the policy arena in which it is applied. The 1981 analysis of the Alaskan oil export ban provides a particularly clear illustration of the process of adversarial analysis because that process was contained to an unusual degree within a single, fairly well-defined policy forum.[94] The analytical strategies and dimensions of value employed in the analysis were carefully fitted to that arena. Much of the debate reflected the

---

[94] The fact that the analysis was conducted entirely within the administrative branch should not obscure the *use* of other, potential fora to shape the dimensions of that analysis. Letters from Congress and the maritime interests, for example, served to reinforce the argument that the political costs of lifting the export ban were large and certain.

competing policy beliefs and preferences represented by the MarAd and DOE analysts. In pursuit of these beliefs and preferences, the dimensions of value on which the analytical strategies hinged were tuned to the perceived interests of the administration and the political context of the moment as much, if not more, than the generic analytical considerations of the issue.

No attempt was made to reduce the multiple dimensions of the analysis to a single dimension, such as net changes in economic surplus. Rather, the various dimensions of value remained discrete, each measured in its own metric—e.g., tax dollars gained, tankers lost, foreign policy good will, and credibility gained. The dimensions used—and those left out—reflected the constellation of actors and interests involved in the narrowly circumscribed forum. The absence of concern for the environmental effects of the export ban—such as increased oil tanker traffic along U.S. coastlines or the increased prospect of west-to-east oil pipelines—reflected the low priority such concerns had within the administration, while the centrality of the revenue dimension reflected the administration's pressing budgetary problems. Had the administration carried the issue to Congress, the new and more open forum would have called for a markedly different set and weighting of dimensions. Letters and statements from Congress, as well as past Congressional action, indicated that energy security, and the national security implications of U.S. flag tanker losses, would have been promoted to primary concerns. The environmental dimension may well have found a constituency here, and the question of the sanctity of the compromise deal that allowed construction of the trans-Alaska pipeline only on the condition that exports be barred may have become a factor. The policy space in which analyses of the Alaskan oil export ban would be cast, and the analytical strategems used, were thus likely to have been substantially different had the issue reached the Congress.

<hr />

5.7
THE LIMITATIONS OF POLICY CONTEXTS

Overall, the oil export case study well depicts the process of policy analysis in the bureaucratic context. The limitations of this case study for purposes of illustrating the more general practice of policy analysis stem from its conduct within a fairly stable policy context. It remains, therefore, to illustrate the process of policy analysis across an *array* of issues spanning *differing* policy contexts. That task is undertaken in the next chapter.

CHAPTER 6

Analysis as a Component of the Policy Process

Concern with the implications of policy analysis for democratic governance transcends concern with the particular roles and strategems of analysts; it requires assessment of the broader processes by which analysis affects public decision making over a *range* of policy contexts. The praise and criticisms of policy analysis, as described in Part One, are at considerable variance over how analysis is applied in policy making. Does (or can) analysis make an independent, influential contribution to the beliefs—and therefore the choices—of policy elites? Alternatively, is analysis a sterile endeavor, unable to dent existing preconceptions? Still worse, is analysis merely a tool employed in the pursuit of preconceived policy preferences, used to legitimate such choices and deceive the unsophisticated?

In chapter 4, I presented a conceptual model of the process of analysis in policy subsystems that suggests answers to some of these questions. Proponents and critics of the policy analysis paradigm have tended to view the world in which analysis is practiced as either unimportant or homogeneous; the factors affecting the role played by analysis in shaping beliefs and policy preferences of elites, the likelihood that analysis can replace more traditional politics, and the likely institutional alterations because of analysis will be irrelevant or constant. In contrast, the view of the practice of analysis developed here holds that the uses and influence of analysis vary systematically with the context in which analysis is employed and with the nature of the issue to which it is applied. Of chief importance are: (1) the *level of conflict,* as derived from the tension between competing belief systems within the policy subsystem; (2) the degree of *analytical tractability* attending the issue under debate; and (3) the characteristics of the *forum* in which the analytical debate is conducted.

The following sections will apply this conceptual model to a set of case studies of the practice of analysis. The intent is to provide illustration and enrichment of the model by application across a set of instances of the use of analysis in which important factors in the policy environment vary considerably. A large fraction of the important *combinations* of environmental factors can be illustrated with the cases; where the cases do not provide such illustration, an attempt is made to draw from other descriptions of the application of analysis available in the literature.

_____ 6.1 _____
ANALYSIS IN PRACTICE: CASES-IN-BRIEF

Four cases of the use of policy analysis provide the grist for depiction of the processs of analysis. Included are: (1) analytical debates over the appropriate size of the Strategic Petroleum Reserve, (2) the natural gas deregulation debates in 1978 and 1983, (3) the oil refinery policy debates conducted late in the Carter administration, and (4) the 1983 round of the oil export policy debate—the round subsequent to the one recounted in detail in the preceding chapter.

In the paragraphs to follow, each of the cases of policy analysis are described in brief, providing background and a skeletal overview of the players and the progression of the analytical debate, in order to facilitate the illustration of specific points made in later sections.

The strategic petroleum reserve size debate.[1]   In the mid-1970s a broad political consensus had developed in favor of building a large, publicly owned

---

[1] Much of the data on the following case is drawn from David L. Weimer, *The Strategic Petroleum Reserve: Planning, Implementation, and Analysis* (Westport, CT: Greenwood Press, 1982); and Hank Jenkins-Smith and David L. Weimer, "Analysis as Retrograde Action: The Case of Strategic Petroleum Reserves," *Public Administration Review,* 45(4) (July/August 1985), pp. 485–494. Reprinted with permission from *Public Administration Review,* © 1985 by the American Society for Public Administration (ASPA), 1120 G St. NW, Suite 500, Washington, DC 20005. All rights reserved.

strategic petroleum reserve (SPR) to be drawn down in times of oil supply disruptions (such as the 1973–1974 Arab oil embargo). Among energy analysts in the energy-security subsystem, it was believed that the benefits of the SPR would include a reduction in the price rise in time of disruption, and therefore lessened macroeconomic disturbances such as inflation and unemployment. It was also argued that the SPR would act as a deterrent to future oil embargos such as occurred in 1973–1974. The presumption widely shared among officials during the Carter administration was that one billion barrels of oil would be stored in the completed SPR.

The SPR size debate developed when analysts in the OMB criticized the proposed size of the SPR, arguing that such a size could not be justified on the basis of benefit–cost analysis. For these analysts, minimizing government expenditures took precedence over possible future economic benefits. Joined by economists in the CEA, these analysts took analysts at DOE to task over the arguments and analyses made for building a large SPR, resulting in repeated interagency studies.

In early stages of the debate (1977–1978), OMB analysts were able to focus on demonstrable weaknesses in the DOE analyses. As the debate progressed, however, and as the approach and techniques used were improved, OMB's repeated rejection of results justifying a large SPR gradually took on a more obvious—and less justified—advocacy tone.

Natural gas price deregulation debates.[2]   In the aftermath of the oil price increases in the 1970s, the regulation of natural gas was redesigned to provide distinct price controls for various categories of gas. The categories were constructed according to perceived costs of production, with older developed sources accorded low pre-1973 price levels, and more recent and expensive sources allowed relatively higher prices. The intent was to limit price increases to consumers for old inexpensively produced gas (thus avoiding "windfall profits" for producers) while allowing higher prices as necessary to induce exploration and development of new gas fields.

The complexity of the natural gas price regulations, and the perception of serious market defects caused by the price controls, have resulted in vigorous debate on many aspects of the gas regulation issue.[3] Particularly

---

[2] Sources particularly useful for this case were: M. Elizabeth Sanders, *The Regulation of Natural Gas: Policy and Politics, 1938–1978* (Philadelphia: Temple Press, 1981); Michael Malbin, "Congress, Policy Analysis, and Natural Gas Deregulation: A Parable about Fig Leaves," in *Bureaucrats, Policy Analysts, Statesmen: Who Leads?*, ed. Robert Goldwin, (Washington, DC: American Enterprise Institute, 1980), pp. 62–87; and John Weyant, "Is There Policy-Oriented Learning in the Analysis of Natural Gas Policy Issues," *Policy Sciences*, vol. 21, nos. 2-3 (1988), pp. 239–262

[3] See Edward Mitchell, ed., *The Deregulation of Natural Gas* (Washington, DC: American Enterprise Institute, 1983); and Hank Jenkins-Smith, ed., "Natural Gas Regulation in the Western States: Perspectives on Deregulation," *Natural Resources Journal*, 27(4) (Fall 1987), for a range of subissues and viewpoints within that debate.

useful are the debates over the responsiveness of quantities of natural gas supplied and consumed to changes in price—a debate that has continued since early consideration of the Natural Gas Policy Act (NGPA) of 1978. In a more recent continuation of that debate, substantial attention has focused on the effects of price controls on "old gas," gas that had been discovered and developed prior to 1978 and is therefore subject to very low controlled prices.

Two broad coalitions of subsystem actors have faced off over these issues. Government analysts at the federal level can be found on both sides, with much of the difference in positions matching ideological positions (of the analyst or the analyst's client). Analysts from oil companies, consumer groups, and academic institutions have also been drawn into the fray.

Particularly interesting has been the transition of the characteristics of the debate over time. While the level of subsystem conflict has remained high, the tractability of the issue—or at least subparts thereof—has increased. The result has been a narrowing of the bounds within which analysis can be employed as a tool in the pursuit of a predetermined policy perspective.

The refinery policy debate.   During the mid to late 1970s the price of crude oil was subject to price controls designed to cushion the shock of rapidly rising world crude prices to U.S. consumers.[4] Under these controls, with domestic oil prices held far below the price of imports, oil refiners that had access to substantial domestic crude supplies—mainly the larger integrated firms— were at a substantial competitive advantage over those refiners that relied on higher-priced imported oil. To redress this imbalance, an elaborate set of regulations designed to equalize the cost of crude for all domestic refiners at the national average crude price—called the crude oil entitlement program— was introduced. In essence, this program required a transfer of funds from firms with greater-than-average access to domestic supplies to those that had less-than-average access.

Coupled with the entitlements program were a set of provisions, dubbed the "small refiner bias," that gave disproportionately large entitlements to smaller refiners—those capable of processing less than 175,000 barrels per day (bpd). As entitlements were being phased out in the late 1970s, numerous analysts, in and out of government, called for tax and tariff provisions as a new form of small refiner protection to replace the entitlements-based small refiner bias. These analysts argued that the existence of large numbers of small refineries, kept in business by the bias, were essential to maintenance of national security; that the bias was justified on equity grounds; and that the small refiners constituted a competitive force that put downward pressure on

---

[4] For an excellent description of the oil price control policy and its effect, see Joseph Kalt, *The Economics and Politics of Oil Price Regulation: Federal Policy in the Post-Embargo Era* (Cambridge, MA: MIT Press, 1981).

petroleum product prices. Opponents of continued small refiner protection—including some government analysts, several oil companies and petroleum trade groups, and a scattering of academic economists—countered that U.S. national and energy security were not served by protection of the small refiners, and that such protection resulted in an inefficient allocation of resources.

The locus of conflict of primary interest here was within the DOE, where analysts in the Office of Policy and Evaluation (PE) prepared a major study favoring complete elimination of the small refiner bias. Other analysts within DOE, along with some high-level DOE officials, strongly opposed removal of the small refiner bias and fought a long battle within DOE, first to change the study conclusions and second to indefinitely postpone its publication and release.

The oil export ban debate—1983.[5]   The debate within the Reagan administration over the Alaskan oil export ban recounted in chapter 5 was but one round in what has become a biennial event. This repetition is due to the fact that the ban is legislated in the Export Administration Act, which must be renewed every two years. Analytical battle over the ban was therefore waged in 1977 and 1979 under the Carter administration, and again in 1981 and 1983 under the Reagan administration. The 1983 round is the basis for the fourth case study of the process of analysis.

As had been the case in 1981, the debate concerned the virtual prohibition of export of Alaskan crude. With export markets in the Pacific Rim forbidden, Alaskan producers ship what they can to the West Coast market and must ship the excess—up to half of the 1.7 mmbd production—over the long and relatively expensive route to the Gulf and East coasts. Shipment of Alaska crude has provided the largest single source of employment for domestic Jones Act tankers—ships wholly owned and crewed by American citizens and by law given exclusive right to carry trade between U.S. ports—utilizing well over 50 percent of total tonnage.

The recent (and ongoing) adversarial debate was initiated by analysts in the DOE and elsewhere who argued that the oil export ban resulted in waste of domestic economic resources, that it lessened incentives to produce additional crude in that region, and—most importantly—that enforcement of the ban provided no national security benefits to the nation. Analysts at MarAd rejoined that energy *and* national security would be jeopardized by removal of the ban. As in 1981, analysts from DOE, MarAd, and other agencies were

---

[5] For a technical discussion of the 1983 analysis, see Terrence Higgins and Hank Jenkins-Smith, "Analysis of the Economic Effects of the Alaskan Oil Export Ban," *Journal of Operations Research,* 33(6) (November/December 1985), pp. 1173–1202.

brought together to provide an interagency analysis in the Reagan administration's cabinet council process.

Primary changes from the 1981 debate were (1) the introduction of a large computer simulation model of the world oil market with which to assess the effect of various oil export policies on oil trade and prices, and (2) the restriction of the debate to a small set of participants through security classification of the proceedings of the analysis. As shall be described below, both of these factors affected the way the analysis was employed.

In each of these cases, initiatives mounted by members of a policy subsystem were vigorously supported by analysis. Other members of the subsytem, perceiving important interests to be threatened, mobilized a thoroughgoing rebuttal of the specific proposal and the underlying belief system. It is this process, through its many iterations, and imbedded in a larger political environment, that I wish to analyze in more detail. In particular, my interest is in the relationships between a set of important factors bearing on the subsystem debate and the prospects for policy learning. These factors are (1) the degree of fragmentation and conflict characterizing the subsystem, (2) the analytical qualities of the policy issue, and (3) the characteristics of the particular forum in which the subsystem debate is conducted.

6.2
LEVELS OF CONFLICT

The conceptual model of the policy process developed earlier places primary importance on belief system conflict within policy subsystems. As depicted in figure 4-1, when debate over an initiative threatens the core beliefs, values, and causal assumptions of competing coalitions, analysis will be characterized by high-level conflict. Where the issue is peripheral to the belief systems of competing coalitions, there will be little or no conflict. Furthermore, as conflict rises, willingness of subsystem participants to commit analytic resources should rise, while—in the upper ranges of conflict—willingness to change belief systems in light of analytical results is diminished. Thus, the model would predict that it is in the midrange of conflict—where some incentive exists to mobilize resources for analysis yet change in belief systems would be tolerable—that the results of analysis could be expected to affect the beliefs of policy elites. Low-level conflict would be expected to draw little analytical attention, and when conflict is high, analysis will tend to be deployed primarily as a political tool to promote, justify, and defend a predetermined policy position.

Instances of high, moderate, and low-level conflict are drawn from the four cases outlined above (and, where appropriate, from the case presented in chapter 5). In each case, to the extent possible, I will identify the competing belief systems of the contending coalitions and indicate the implications of the issue under study for those belief systems.[6]

High-level conflict. One debate characterized by high levels of conflict between opposing subsystem coalitions raged over the merits of some kind of economic protection for small domestic refiners to replace the small refiner bias being eliminated with the crude oil entitlements program. A loose coalition made up of small refiner groups, analysts, and agency heads in the federal bureaucracy and in Congress proposed and supported legislation for such protections, arguing that

1. the small refiners were necessary to maintain a flexible crude processing base sufficiently large to avoid dependence on foreign—and particularly OPEC—sources for refined products;
2. government incentives were necessary to ensure that adequate domestic refining capacity was available to meet domestic demand;
3. small refiners were necessary to maintain a competitive refinery industry; and
4. large numbers of small refiners would be bankrupted should some kind of protection not be made available.

Tax breaks of various kinds and an oil import fee were the primary policy proposals made toward this end.[7] The proposals were put into legislative form as Senate Bill 1684 by Senator Johnston of Louisiana.

The coalition behind the initiative for new refiner protections was driven in part by a healthy dose of economic self-interest. While most larger refiners embraced decontrol, many of the small refiners, accustomed to operation under the protection of the small refiner bias, foresaw reduced profit margins or bankruptcy unless a new form of the small refiner bias were devised.[8] Particularly alarmed were a group of very small refiners, dubbed the "bias babies," that came into business and prospered primarily because of the

---

[6] The data for these cases were collected from a number of sources. Included were: a systematic review of the public policy literature on the issue, a review of federal agency documents regarding the specific analyses (provided by analysts at DOE, MarAd, and other agencies), and—where possible—interviews with the participants of the analyses. Specific sources are cited where relevant.

[7] See Henry Schuler, *The National Security Implications of Increased Reliance Upon Importation of Refined Products* (Washington, DC: Conant and Associates, 1979), which was provided for the Domestic Refiners Group (DRG). The DRG was composed of those segments of the refining industry most likely to be harmed by elimination of the small refiner bias. Also see *APRA Tax Proposals,* (Washington, DC: American Petroleum Refiners Association, July 1980), and see Tom Alexander, "Day of Reckoning for Oil Refiners," *Fortune* (January 12, 1981), pp. 38–41.

[8] Christopher Madison, "The Minors Fear for Their Lives When Federal Controls are Gone," *National Journal* (July 19, 1980), pp. 1172–1176.

subsidies afforded under the small refiner bias.[9] But coupled with those who had direct self-interest at stake were many who apparently had no direct personal stake, and who seem to have acted on the belief that the national interest was best served by retention of some form of the small refiner bias. In particular, several high-level officials—including the deputy secretary of energy—and office directors argued strenuously for creation of refiner protections.[10] Whatever the reason for support of the initiative, these participants uniformly adhered to the beliefs that retention of ample domestic refining capacity was essential to (a) protection of U.S. energy security, (b) healthy competition among refiners, and that (c) elimination of the small refiner bias would result in seriously diminished U.S. refinery capacity.[11] These beliefs— particularly (a) and (c)—formed the core of the coalition's belief system.

An opposing group of subsystem participants, from positions in DOE, the Treasury Department, industry groups, and reporters for trade publications opposed the continuation of protections primarily on the grounds that small refiners—particularly those requiring subsidies to survive—were often highly inefficient; many of such plants were unsophisticated "teakettle" refineries capable only of distillation processes that produced a high percentage of low-grade residual and boiler fuels. Maximum yield of the more valuable high-quality products requires more technically sophisticated processing that is cost effective only in larger refineries.[12] Furthermore, these analysts argued that the proliferation of small refiners contributed nothing to energy security, and that the international refinery industry was highly competitive and sufficient to keep domestic refiners competitive.[13] At base, this coalition opposed the extension of refinery protections and the small refiner bias on efficiency grounds; such an extension would result in the continued flow of economic resources to refiners whose product was less valuable than that of their larger competitors. Furthermore, the program would be costly—to consumers if a tariff were used, and to taxpayers if the tax incentives were used.[14] Finally, this coalition acknowledged that many small refiners would suffer economic

---

[9] Ibid., and Alexander, "Day of Reckoning."

[10] See the testimony of Jack O'Leary, Deputy Secretary of Energy, in U.S. Senate, *Domestic Refinery Development and Improvement Act,* Part I. Hearing before the Subcommittee on Energy Regulations, Committee on Energy and Natural Resources (Washington, DC: U.S. Government Printing Office, September 11, 1979), pp. 62–76.

[11] This argument is most succinctly stated in Schuler, *National Security.* Also see O'Leary, op. cit.

[12] For a description of these processes, see William Leffler, *Petroleum Refining for the Non-Technical Person* (Tulsa, OK: Pennwell, 1974).

[13] See Department of Energy, Office of Policy and Evaluation, *Costs and Benefits of a Protective Tariff on Refined Petroleum Products After Crude Oil Decontrol* (Unpublished paper, DOE/PE-0028, December 1980). Also see Department of Treasury, Office of Tax Analysis and Department of Energy, Office of Policy and Evaluation, *Evaluation of Certain Proposals to Aid Domestic Refiners* (Unpublished study, Washington, DC: January 16, 1981).

[14] *Evaluation of Certain Proposals to Aid Domestic Refiners.*

loss or bankruptcy after decontrol but argued that these losses would not significantly diminish the ability of U.S. refiners to meet domestic product needs in a future oil supply crisis.[15] These propositions constituted the core beliefs of the antiprotection coalition.

Analysts in the PE office at DOE who opposed continued protections produced and circulated within the department a draft analysis of the proposed tariff that found such a tariff to be unnecessary and costly.[16] The study was "stomped on" (in the words of one of its authors) by Deputy Secretary of Energy Jack O'Leary, who actively sought protections for small refiners. O'Leary repeatedly asked for revisions in the report, requests that were passed along by a compliant Assistant Secretary for PE, Alvin Alm.[17] O'Leary, attorneys in DOE's general council (GC), and several program offices strongly opposed release of the study with its negative findings.[18]

Analysts in PE continued to refine the study but resisted changing the study conclusions. In that form, copies of the document were leaked to the press, initially drawing mixed but mostly negative reviews from the oil-industry press.[19] Apparently undecided on the issue, the Carter administration then released the study to twenty-seven oil refining companies, all members of the advisory National Petroleum Council (NPC), in order to test the industry response.[20] The response was interestingly (and predictably) divided; smaller independent refiners favored tax protections for small refiners by a large margin, while larger and integrated refiners tended to oppose tax protection. The same split was evident, though with a decidedly more favorable tilt in both groups, over questions of whether a tariff should be levied on product

---

[15] In the course of my interviews, it was evident that an additional, though less-often stated, belief of many members of this coalition was that the protection and bias were *inequitable*. It was seen as directing economic resources to a politically powerful group (the small refiners) at the expense of the economy as a whole.

[16] See DOE, *Costs and Benefits of a Protective Tariff on Refined Petroleum Products After Crude Oil Decontrol*. The study was initially prepared in mid-1979, and was ultimately released—ten months later—under the above title.

[17] Interview with PE staff analyst, August 1984.

[18] See O'Leary, U.S. Senate, *Domestic Refinery Development*, pp. 62–76. The internal DOE debate is documented in Department of Energy, "Action Memorandum: Refinery Policy" (Unpublished memorandum from Lynn Coleman, General Council, DOE, to William Lewis, PE, DOE, March 3, 1980); Department of Energy, "Discussion of Whether Federal Subsidies Should Be Provided to Encourage Domestic Refineries to Upgrade Existing Capacities" (Unpublished memorandum from R. Dobie Langenkamp, Resource Development and Operation, Resource Applications, DOE, to William Lewis, PE, DOE, April 11, 1980); Department of Energy, "Refinery Policy—Previous FEA/DOE Positions" (Unpublished memorandum from Craig Banburger, General Council, DOE, to William Lewis, PE, DOE, April 15, 1980).

[19] John Jennrich, "DOE Refinery Policy Draws Fire," *Oil and Gas Journal*, 78(33) August 18, 1980, pp. 66–70.

[20] See Department of Energy, Office of Policy and Evaluation, *Comments on the Refinery Policy Study/Summary of Analysis* (Unpublished paper, August 1980).

imports (which would benefit *all* domestic refiners, regardless of size). The divided industry did little to resolve the analytic dispute.

The issue reached a standoff in DOE, with PE analysts refusing to modify the results of the analysis, and O'Leary and other DOE office directors refusing to concur with release of the study.[21] A long series of internal DOE study rejections and rejoinders ensued. The process was punctuated by emergence of new data, which tended to support the PE view that refiners were sufficiently flexible and responsive to price changes to meet shifts in domestic petroleum demand without government protections or incentives. One article providing such new data was routed from PE analysts all the way to the energy secretary.[22] In the face of such evidence, the tenor of the defense of protection for small refiners changed; more frequently the argument was based on "political reality." In a January 1980 memo to the secretary of energy summarizing the critiques of the PE study, the undersecretary wrote: "It is important that you are aware that refinery policy is politically very sensitive— refiners, particularly small refiners, will be required to adjust to decontrol and the PE analysis does not adequately examine the difficulties they will encounter in this transition."[23] One of the PE analysts commented that the position of O'Leary and others opposed to the study had been ". . . that there *will be* small refiners. They didn't *defend* the issue via equity, but rather as a *political matter;* (they said) there will always be small refiners and we can't have a report that says otherwise."[24]

Little compromise was evident on either side. Though proponents of continued refinery protection had shifted the focus of the debate from the analytical arguments over energy security and costs to political reality, neither had modified their analytical claims; there was no convergence of analysis over time.[25] When the issue finally broke in favor of the PE analysts it was linked more to a change in personnel, and finally a change in administrations, than to changing belief systems. Late in the Carter administration, O'Leary

---

[21] For the PE position in late 1979, see Department of Energy, "Analysis of the Costs and Benefits of a Protective Tariff on Refined Petroleum Products" (Unpublished memorandum from William Lewis, PE, DOE, to the Secretary and Deputy Secretary of Energy, December 31, 1979).

[22] Greg Clock, "Refining, Petrochemical Construction on Upswing," *Oil and Gas Journal*, 78(20) (May 19, 1980), pp. 43–46. The article was sent to the secretary, attached to Department of Energy, "Refinery Investment," (unpublished memorandum from William Lewis, PE, DOE, to the Secretary and Deputy Secretary of Energy, June 4, 1980).

[23] U.S. Department of Energy, "Release of Policy and Evaluation Protective Tariff/Refinery Study" (Unpublished memorandum from Undersecretary of Energy to Secretary of Energy, January 14, 1980), p. 1.

[24] Personal interview, August 20, 1984.

[25] For a snapshot of the positions of the various sides to the debate a year later, see U.S. Congress, Senate, Committee on Finance, *Incentives for Domestic Refining*, (Hearing before the Subcommittee on Energy and Agricultural Taxation, Washington, DC: U.S. Government Printing Office, March 27, 1981).

and Alm left DOE and were replaced by officials more sympathetic to the approach and findings of the PE study. Pressure outside DOE for release of the full study accumulated as the concurrence battle within DOE dragged on. The study was finally released in December 1980—more than a year after the completion of the first draft—over the objections of the deputy secretary.[26] As a necessary compromise to those opposed to the study conclusions, the study was headed by an introduction stating that the report was merely a draft in an ongoing study. Finally, the crude oil entitlements program was allowed to lapse without creation of new small refiner protections as the new Reagan administration took control in 1981 with its distinctly antiregulatory bias. Thus, the change in policy (or rather: the refusal to change the previously adopted policy) was a function of turnover of personnel within the policy subsystem, which in turn reflects a change in the broader governing coalition.

The refinery study illustrates an instance in which intense subsystem conflict between competing coalitions leads to commitment of extensive energies to analysis of the issue over a considerable period of time. Despite that commitment, little or no modification of important policy-relevant beliefs or aims was evident on either side. The role of analysis was essentially stalemated through conflicting claims, leaving more decisive policy developments to such factors as personnel and electoral change.

A similar instance of high-level conflict was evident in the Alaskan oil export debate—particularly the issue of the effect of exports on tax receipts—described in detail in the preceding chapter. It is interesting to note how the belief systems of the competing coalitions had developed into the deadlocked, inflexible postures that generated the conflict. In this instance, underlying the debate lay the intense interest of the maritime industry in maintenance of the export ban, which strongly conflicted with the free-trade, free-market belief system held by economists and analysts at DOE, CEA, the State Department, and elsewhere. The development toward intense conflict was spurred by the pattern of participation in the issue; the authorization of the ban, extending that in the TAP Act, was written into the Export Administration Act of 1977 (EAA), which must be renewed every two years. Renewal of the EAA has provided repeated opportunities for opponents of the ban to try to block renewed inclusion of the ban and for those favoring the ban to defend it. A cyclical pattern of activity on the issue has thus developed, marked by President Carter's ill-fated attempts to ease the ban in 1977 and 1979, and with cabinet-level reviews (and no legislative action) by the Reagan administration in 1981 and 1983. Through this cyclical process the various subsystem participants have taken fairly fixed positions on the issue and have come to view opponents' positions and policy statements with some prejudice. As described in the previous chapter, this rigidification was well advanced in the

---

[26] Interview with PE analyst, August 19, 1984.

1981 round of the debate, in which the question of the effect of lifting the ban on federal tax receipts played a prominent role.

In the 1983 round of that debate, an effort was made to overcome some of the uncertainties that plagued the 1981 analysis.[27] Instead of the simple net back calculations employed previously, a sophisticated nonlinear programming model of the world oil market was used to estimate crude oil flows, prices, and petroleum product prices under various oil export policy scenarios.[28] Estimates of oil tanker prices on relevant routes, expected world oil prices, and the policy scenarios were agreed upon by MarAd and DOE analysts early in the debate. Repeated runs of the model were performed, projecting each scenario over time to 1995. Based on changes in crude oil and product prices between a base case (continued ban) and various export options, reductions in tanker traffic, changes in tax revenues, and energy-security implications were calculated.[29] The estimates showed large tax revenue gains under all scenarios. In addition, analysts from the Interior Department estimated that the value of federal oil leases in north Alaska would increase significantly because netbacks in the region would be higher; from that source alone, estimated revenue gains (discounted present value) were about $4.5 billion.[30] At least on the basis of tax receipts, then, the initial analyses clearly favored an export policy.

Analysts from MarAd and the DOT immediately and vigorously denounced these results. Long lists of "problems and concerns" with the model, the data used, and the results were compiled and circulated.[31] Though several minor errors in calculation were unearthed and corrected, the primary contention was over the appropriateness of the model itself; one MarAd analyst characterized the model as a complicated "black box" that shed no light on the policy problem.[32] Though the model techniques and formulation

---

[27] This author was a DOE analyst involved in that debate, and much of this case is drawn from notes and recollection of the analytical proceedings. Because the analysis, drafts, and memoranda involved were classified, none of these can be cited here.

[28] For a description of the model and of the results of that analysis, see Terrence Higgins and Hank Jenkins-Smith, "Economic Effect."

[29] One interesting conclusion was that the Windfall Profits Tax (WPT) on crude oil *increased* incentives to ship Alaskan crude to the Gulf and East coasts. Thus, the planned phaseout of the WPT by 1991 would reduce shipments of Alaskan crude to the Gulf and East coasts *even though* the oil export ban remained in effect. See ibid.

[30] Department of the Interior (Unpublished memorandum from Nicolai Timines, Jr., Deputy Director, Office of Policy Analysis, Department of the Interior, to Jackson Silvey, Associate Director, Office of Policy Planning and Analysis, Department of Energy, September 22, 1983).

[31] See Higgins and Jenkins-Smith, "Economic Effect," for a more detailed discussion of these criticisms.

[32] Though the model specifications were provided to the MarAd analysts, those specifications relied heavily on the algebraic formulation of the model. The MarAd analyst complained that these were "unintelligible."

were widely used and well understood among practitioners, the MarAd analysts correctly observed that this was the first major application of this particular model, and therefore contended that its results should be taken "in the presence of a small salt mine."

Members of the analysis working group representing DOE, the Interior Department, the State Department, and OMB continued to use the model results in completing the analysis. Analysts from DOT and MarAd continued to participate, though they dissented from the model results in footnotes throughout the report. Though repeated attempts were made to resolve these analytical differences, no progress was made. The paper, including the dissenting footnotes, was presented to the cabinet council in the fall of 1983. Once again, the cabinet council voted to take no action on the issue, thus assuring that the ban would remain in effect.

Again, high-level conflict between competing subsystem coalitions resulted in analytical stalemate. Factors other than analysis thus take overriding importance in the issue—in this case, strong opposition to removing the ban in Congress and the general bias in the legislative process in favor of status quo.[33] In this setting, analysis takes the role of support and legitimization for competing claims and policy positions by policy elites.

Moderate conflict.   Fortunately, not all analysis fits the pattern described in the preceding paragraphs. The case studies provide several examples of moderate levels of conflict, permitting genuine learning and belief system change on one or more sides to the debate. In each of these cases the focus of argument was over an issue related to, but not decisive for, the belief system core. They provide a more optimistic assessment of the application of analysis in subsystem conflict.

The debate over natural gas (de)regulation has become a major preoccupation in the energy policy subcommunity in Washington since the late mid-1970s. In its largest dimensions (that of whether continued price controls, or deregulation and reliance on market forces would better serve the American economy), the debate has been mired in very high levels of conflict, generating volumes of studies but apparently little substantive change in the belief systems of the protagonists; the Reagan administration continues to favor deregulation, and Chairman of the House Energy and Commerce Committee John Dingell proclaims "old gas" prices will be deregulated "over my dead

---

[33] Removal of the oil export ban required *changes* in the EAA, while the Act itself was virtually assured of legislative renewal. Extending small refiner supports, described above, required new legislation because the old program was based on a program legislated to expire. In both cases, then, the initiative that lost was the one requiring greatest legislative change from the status quo. For a formal explanation of how the legislative process gives advantage to the status quo, see William H. Riker, *Liberalism Versus Populism* (San Francisco: Freeman, 1982), pp. 69–73.

body."[34] But within this larger deadlock, progress *has* been made toward resolving many of the underlying analytical and technical questions. One area of such progress has concerned the size of the supply response to be expected from lifting price controls on certain categories of old, low-priced gas.

Opponents of deregulation have long contended that removal of gas price controls would result in little new-gas production and a large price increase; those favoring decontrol have argued, conversely, that in the absence of controls, supply would expand significantly with only moderate price increases.[35] In combination, the claims that (1) a large supply response would occur in combination with (2) a small or moderate price increase are threatening to the core beliefs of those in favor of continued controls; such assertions, if believed, would strongly support the case for decontrol.[36] In the case to be discussed here, however, the level of conflict attending this issue was attenuated; by decoupling the supply response and the expected cost to consumers, the issue was made less threatening to beliefs of the antidecontrol coalition, allowing some adjustment of beliefs with respect to supply response.

One category of price-controlled gas—those wells that under the NGPA would never be deregulated—was brought under close analysis in 1983 in the context of the Reagan administration's initiative to deregulate the gas industry.[37] An analyst at Shell Oil Company, the holdings of which include large domestic gas fields, produced a study that concluded that should prices of these "forever regulated" gas supplies be allowed to rise to an estimated "market clearing" level of $3.50 per million Btu (mm/Btu), a total of 52 trillion cubic feet (tcf) of gas would be added to domestic reserves of natural gas.[38] This was a significant claim, because total domestic consumption of natural gas was slightly more than 17 tcf in all of 1983.[39]

The argument of the Shell study was that, at low regulated prices, the production cost per cubic foot of gas extracted would exceed the regulated price long before reserves recoverable at a moderately higher cost ($3.5 per mm/Btu) would be exhausted. Using a representative sample of seventeen gas

---

[34] See the *Washington Post* (June 6, 1983), p. A14.

[35] See Malbin, "Congress, Policy Analysis, and Natural Gas Deregulation," and Weyant, "Natural Gas Policy," for descriptions of earlier analytical positions on this issue.

[36] In the language of economics, such a result would allow the efficiency gains accompanying consumer and producer responsiveness to price without an excessive transfer of wealth from consumers to producers. For a succinct case against that view, made by a subsystem participant favoring continued price controls, see Mark Cooper, "Commentary," in *The Deregulation of Natural Gas,* ed. Edward J. Mitchell (Washington, DC: American Enterprise Institute, 1983), pp. 151–153.

[37] Included were NGPA categories 104, 105, 106(a), 108, 109, and portions of 103.

[38] C.S. Matthews, *Increase in United States "Old Gas" Reserves Due to Deregulation* (Houston, TX: Shell Oil Company, April 1983).

[39] See *Monthly Energy Review* (Washington, DC: Energy Information Agency, U.S. Department of Energy, May 1984) p. 58.

fields, four sources of added recoverable reserves were identified: the higher price would make it profitable to continue production of gas wells at lower natural pressure, extending the life and production of the well; "infill drilling"—placing new wells between existing ones in hopes of tapping new supplies—would increase as higher prices made the necessary expenditure profitable; replacement of abandoned wells; and investment in "stimulating" (through fracturing and acidifying) current gas production would become economically feasible at the higher market price. The estimated result of these added activities would be the production of 52 tcf that otherwise would have been left in the ground to dissipate beyond recovery.

Opponents of deregulation were quick to attack the Shell study. The staff of the House Subcommittee on Fossil and Synthetic Fuels produced a critique of the Shell study, which argued that any addition to reserves would come at great expense to consumers because, in order to stimulate marginal new production, the price of *existing* reserves (gas that would be produced anyway) would rise along with that of the new marginal reserves.[40] The subcommittee staff estimated the marginal cost of the new production to consumers to be $7.48 per thousand cubic feet (mcf). Joining in criticism were the Independent Gas Producers Committee (IGPC), a group of producers specializing in production of gas in the high-cost categories of the NGPA, and a group called the Consumer Federation of America (CFA). These groups contended that Shell drastically overestimated expected new reserves; 5.67 tcf, rather than Shell's estimated 52 tcf, would be added to old gas reserves because of decontrol.[41] Furthermore, because the price increase on *all* old gas reserves would result in a meager 5.67 tcf addition to these reserves, the IGPC/CFA calculated that the marginal cost of these new reserves to consumers would be a *very* expensive $30–35 per mcf.

Shell defended its study through its own critiques of the subcommittee staff analysis and of the IGPC/CFA criticisms.[42] In particular, Shell buttressed its claims that deregulation would be beneficial by pointing out that much of the increased revenue from price increases on existing reserves would be taxed away by state and federal governments; therefore it was inaccurate, Shell argued, to count all of that increase in revenues as a windfall profit for producers. In addition, Shell quickly acquired allies on the issue: DOE

[40] U.S. Congress, House of Representatives, Subcommittee on Fossil and Synthetic Fuels, "Cost to Consumers of Producing Added 52 TCF of Old Gas Reserves Under Deregulation" (Unpublished staff analysis, May 6, 1983).

[41] Independent Gas Producing Committee and Consumer Federation of America, "Joint Independent Gas Producers Committee—Consumer Federation of America Analysis of Shell Old Gas Study" (Unpublished paper, Washington, DC, May 16, 1983).

[42] See *The Costs and Benefits to the U.S. Economy of Additional Gas Resulting From 'Old' Gas Decontrol* (Houston, TX: Shell Oil Company, May 1983).

weighed in with its own analysis of reserve additions expected from decontrol, estimating a total increase of 8.4 to over 11.1 tcf.[43] ARCO Oil and Gas Company, another major domestic gas producer, joined with its own estimate that reserves would increase by 38 tcf.[44]

The most interesting strategic move, perhaps, was a request by Shell that a highly respected, independent group of petroleum consultants review the Shell study to confirm the methodological adequacy of the Shell study. The group found the Shell methodology to be "applicable and reasonable," and in applying their own alternative approach reached comparable conclusions regarding reserve additions.[45] Shell circulated the review to all participants in the debate.

The debate over the volume of old gas reserve additions attributable to price deregulation did not alter the course of the struggle over new natural gas regulation; too many additional risks were at stake for such an outcome.[46] It is nonetheless significant that a new and important factor in the policy debate—reserve additions from old gas supplies—had been raised and received acknowledgment from all sides. Even the most vehement opponents of deregulation, the IGPC/CFA, estimated *some* increase in this supply category (5.67 tcf) and adjusted its projections accordingly. The admission of this new factor into all belief systems was possible in large part because such acknowledgment did not decisively threaten the core of any coalition. As described above, the "decoupling" of supply quantity and price factors served to diffuse the intensity of conflict involved. A further reason, to be discussed more fully in a later section, was that the issue was a relatively tractable one analytically; the engineering and geological study performed by Shell was based on well-proved and widely accepted methodologies, and had been reviewed and endorsed by an "honest broker" and acknowledged specialist in the area. In that situation, outright rejection of the new factor would prove costly in terms of damaged credibility—something to be avoided unless other avenues to protect the core of the belief system are exhausted. Opponents of deregulation found that other avenue; they agreed that an old gas supply response would occur but argued that the marginal cost of those supplies would be excessive.

Another debate in which modification of belief systems was apparent was the struggle between analysts at DOE and OMB over the appropriate size of

---

[43] Department of Energy, Office of Policy, Planning and Analysis *Supplemental Analysis of Natural Gas Consumer Regulatory Reform* (Unpublished paper, May 1983).

[44] Contained in a letter from Stuart Mut, Senior Vice President, ARCO Oil and Gas Co., to U.S. Congressman W. J. Tauzin, May 16, 1983.

[45] Comments from a letter from H. J. Gruy and Associates, Inc., to D. G. Russell, Vice President, Production, Shell Oil Company, April 4, 1983.

[46] See, for example, the range of natural gas issues and positions presented in Mitchell, *Natural Gas.*

the SPR.[47] In that case, the analytical positions taken by analysts at OMB in part reflected their institutional role: that of guardian of the purse.[48] Coupled with the OMB's overriding objective to cut budget expenditures was the fact that, for several reasons, the SPR makes a particularly inviting target for budget cuts:[49] the SPR fill is a very costly budget item, and therefore attracts scrutiny from those with budget oversight responsibilities; while the benefits of the SPR are uncertain and expected to accrue in future years, the costs of the program all accrue *now;*[50] the benefits of the SPR are widely dispersed throughout the economy, and therefore the program is unlikely to obtain an intensely committed constituency that would vigorously fight a move to cut the program budget. Beyond reasons endemic to the program, OMB had considerable cause for requesting reevaluation of policies established in the urgent days following the 1973–1974 Arab oil embargo: the approach and techniques previously used to assess the program were questionable, and oil market conditions had changed sufficiently to warrant review.

If these factors made the SPR an attractive target for cuts, the political context in the late 1970s made it a truly enticing one: as the 1980 election drew closer, the budget deficit was increasingly seen as a political liability for the Carter administration. OMB analysts thus had sound reasons to look to the SPR for cuts.

Manning the trenches on the other side were analysts at DOE who remained committed to construction of the large SPR. Carter's first Secretary of Energy, James Schlesinger—an ardent proponent of a large SPR as a means to enhance U.S. national security—persuaded President Carter to work toward a billion barrel SPR. Analysts working at DOE could draw on a series of earlier studies estimating that the optimal SPR size was well over one billion barrels in defense of Schlesinger's position.[51] In making that defense, the DOE analysts' position was based solidly within the policy analysis paradigm:

---

[47] The following description draws heavily on Weimer, *Strategic Petroleum Reserves* and Jenkins-Smith and Weimer, "Retrograde Action."

[48] On the role of OMB, see Hugh Heclo, "OMB and the Presidency—The Problem of Neutral Competence," *The Public Interest,* vol. 38 (Winter 1975), pp. 80–89; and Bruce Johnson, "From Analyst to Negotiator: The OMB's New Role," in *Journal of Policy Analysis and Management,* 3(4), 1984, pp. 501–515.

[49] These and other reasons are noted in Weimer, *Strategic Petroleum Reserves,* pp. 112–113.

[50] The implicit assumption here is that OMB analysts have a higher discount rate over time than do analysts who support the large SPR size initiative.

[51] A partial list of such studies would include: Robert Keunne et al., "A Policy to Protect the U.S. Against Oil Embargoes," *Policy Analysis,* 1(4) (Fall 1975), pp. 571–597; Randall Holcombe, "A Method For Estimating GNP Loss from a Future Oil Embargo," *Policy Sciences,* 8(1) (June 1977), pp. 217–234; and Egan Balas, *The Strategic Petroleum Reserve: How Large Should It Be?* Management Science Research Report No. 436, (Pittsburgh, PA: Graduate School of Industrial Administration, Carnegie-Mellon University, June 30, 1979). For a more exhaustive list, see Weimer, *Strategic Petroleum Reserves.*

creation of a large SPR would reduce the expected economic surplus loss attributable to a future oil supply disruption.

OMB first used its budgetary authority to cut funding for phases Three and Four of SPR construction (that is, for the third and fourth 250 million barrel installments) in the FY 1979 budget in the fall of 1977. Schlesinger managed to restore the cuts for Phase Three planning by direct appeal to the president. OMB reopened the issue in 1978, organizing an interagency task force to review the size question. Analysts from OMB, CEA, and DOE were included in the group. At this stage, a variety of macroeconomic models were used to assess the economic benefits and costs of the SPR; the assumptions employed in the models were to be developed jointly by the task force. While some of the assumptions necessary for modeling the use of SPR were jointly ageed upon, DOE and OMB analysts remained at odds over many others. Of particular importance were their disagreements over the "scrap value" of the SPR at some future date, the likelihood of future oil supply disruptions, and the assumed relationship between probabilities of disruptions and optimal SPR size. OMB raised these and other questions with DOE analysts but upon failing to get satisfactory answers, submitted their own analysis to the president, which recommended that phases Three and Four of the SPR be cut. The early joint analyses thus failed to achieve consensus.

OMB called for a new joint study in early 1979. By this time, wary from past experience, DOE analysts resisted involvement in yet another task force with OMB. As stated by one DOE analyst in an internal memo:

Problem with OMB Re SPR Size

DOE *will establish its work plan* after considering OMB proposals. DOE must be responsible for use of its resources.

No joint effort with OMB. We will do our work plan and inform OMB of results and DOE position. Experience last year with a "joint effort" was unacceptable. OMB staff continuously attempting to manage the studies, but not responsible for the results or costs. Then OMB went to the President without any previous consultation with DOE.

Do not expect to reach agreement on all assumptions of "facts." In the past we have had irreconcilable differences with OMB staff. We see no reason for that to change. Most of the differences about assumptions cannot be resolved by analysis because they are projections or predictions of potential future considerations. No reason to expect OMB staff to agree to any assumption that might support a SPR size larger than 750 MMB.[52]

Nonetheless, DOE agreed to another joint study. Again the task force members sought to achieve consensus on assumptions used in macroeconomic

---

[52] Ibid., p. 120.

models. Though initial agreement was reached, OMB and CEA frequently requested modifications. Despite apparent attempts by OMB analysts to find assumptions congenial to a reduced SPR size, the study results suggested a minimum SPR of 1 billion barrels, and an optimal size of up to 6 billion barrels. OMB strongly objected to these results and—despite their earlier concurrence on the modeling assumptions—raised serious objections regarding (1) the disruption probabilities used, (2) the fiscal and monetary assumptions employed in estimating GNP loss, (3) the salvage value attributed to the SPR if no disruption occurred, and (4) the assumption that the SPR drawdown would replace imports lost to the disruption on a barrel-for-barrel basis. In each case, OMB wanted the assumptions adjusted in a direction that diminished the projected value of the SPR, thereby reducing the estimated optimal size.

Based on these criticisms, OMB was once again prepared to recommend elimination of *both* Phase Three and Phase Four funding. Realizing this, the DOE analysts retrenched to defend only Phase Three (up to 750 million barrels). At the same time, analysts elsewhere in DOE were able to make considerable use of the uncertainty and dissensus in the DOE–OMB debates; OMB's more valid critiques took aim at the inherent shortcomings of the macromodeling approach used in the debates to that date. In particular, the handling of the uncertainty surrounding the likelihood of future supply disruptions, and the variability of the oil market state (from conditions of excess supply, to "tight" markets, to various magnitudes of disruptions) made the static results of the macromodels vulnerable to critique. An alternative methodology was developed within DOE, by MIT economist Thomas Teisberg, that permitted a more adequate conceptual handling of uncertainty. This was a computerized dynamic programming model—based on a set of probabilities of transition from one market state to another—that calculated the optimal stock fill or drawdown rate over a period of years based on changes in social surplus resulting from alterations in world oil prices.[53]

DOE employed the Teisberg model in a major stockpile size study in December 1979. Looking at a range of "optimistic" and "pessimistic" probabilities of disruptions, the study indicated that the optimal stockpile size ranged between 800 million and 4.4 billion barrels.[54]

---

[53] See Thomas Teisberg, "A Dynamic Programming Model of the U.S. Strategic Petroleum Reserve," *Bell Journal of Economics*, 12(2) (Autumn 1981), pp. 526–546. The model finds an optimal solution by maximizing the net present value of social benefits—or net *reductions* in economic surplus loss due to disruptions brought about by stockpile drawdowns—over all possible future conditions, calculated probabilistically on the basis of the market–state transition probabilities.

[54] U.S. Department of Energy, Office of Policy and Evaluation, *An Analysis of Acquisition and Drawdown Strategies for the Strategic Petroleum Reserve*, by Glen Sweetnam et al. (Unpublished paper, December 1979).

Once again, in late 1979, DOE agreed to work with OMB and CEA on the SPR size question. In initial discussions over methodology, OMB and CEA raised a number of objections to the new Teisberg model, finding fault with specific assumptions employed (which were easily altered) and with the apparent complexity of the model. OMB and CEA eventually rejected the Teisberg model and proposed yet another, more comprehensive study with the previously used macromodels. DOE analysts resisted; past experience with attempts to arrive at mutually satisfactory assumptions, and the inherent limitations and vulnerabilities of macroeconomic modeling when employed on this issue (as evidenced by OMB's earlier dissatisfactions), made yet another round of macromodel analysis an unwelcome prospect. By mid-1980 a compromise was reached: DOE would provide staff and contractor support to the OMB/CEA study if, in return, the CEA would provide an acceptable set of assumptions for use in the Teisberg model. DOE would use its own study with the Teisberg model to support its SPR budget request.

Once the macromodel study commenced, it became clear that the results, based on CEA assumptions (and agreed to tacitly by OMB), indicated an optimal SPR size well in excess of 1 billion barrels. OMB and CEA never finished the study and refused to provide a copy to DOE (even though it was conducted with DOE funding). With the apparent failure of the macromodels to provide acceptable results, OMB finally expressed interest in the Teisberg model. As this study progressed, OMB indicated at last that they would not oppose Phase Three funding.

Though neither side in this debate was fully persuaded to alter their policy positions, each apparently did—after considerable effort and expense—modify understandings of the SPR policy issue on the basis of the analytical exercises described here. The repeated frustration of the DOE analysts in attempts to find acceptable model assumptions, and the particular vulnerability of the static macroeconomic models, led them to try to find a more generally valid and defensible approach to the problem. Their success in this instance is evident from the continuing widespread use of the Teisberg model within DOE and the central role the model has played in establishing DOE's SPR policy.[55] DOE's later analytical understanding of the issue, and the technical means with which the SPR was analyzed, were undoubtedly superior to the efforts of a few years prior.

The OMB analysts' persistent objections were partly responsible for the improvement in DOE's analytical capabilities on this issue. It is less easy to determine, however, what effect the repeated rounds of analysis had on the beliefs and policy positions of the OMB analysts. It is useful to speculate on

---

[55] U.S. Department of Energy, Office of Energy Emergencies, *Issues and Analysis of the Use of the Strategic Petroleum Reserve: Staff Paper on the Department of Energy Approaches and Current Status of Studies* (Unpublished paper, DOE/EP-0075, December 1, 1982).

what might have occurred had OMB been able to produce a joint OMB/CEA/DOE analysis that *had* shown the budget cuts to be justified. Had that occurred, OMB would have been in a position to push much more vigorously for reductions in the planned SPR size. In all likelihood, too, they would have been more successful because DOE would have had less analytical ammunition with which to resist.[56] From that standpoint, it would appear that the repeated analytical findings justifying a large SPR served to inhibit both the vigor and the success of OMB's drive to cut the SPR budget.

It is also possible that, for a time at least, OMB's failure to obtain analytical results justifying reduction in the SPR size finally led to a reevaluation of their policy position. Early in the Reagan administration, some of the same OMB staffers that had previously sought to reduce the SPR size directed an interagency study considering how to *accelerate* Phase Three of the program. It is more likely, however, that OMB was responding to other factors; a changed political environment, in which David Stockman (who was on record as an ardent supporter of the SPR) had been appointed director of OMB, may have made the OMB analysts less willing to seek analysis supporting cuts and further delay in SPR expansion through yet another interagency study.[57]

Low-level conflict.   When an issue is of only peripheral concern to all sides in subsystem debates, it is most likely to be ignored or treated only superficially. As evidenced by the SPR case described above, it is often the persistence with which opponents protest methods, data, and conclusions that drives analysts to improve their understanding of the issue and their capability of applying that understanding to policy questions. When issues are peripheral, the motive for such efforts is lacking.

It is probably the norm that issues of very low levels of conflict are either resolved by quiet consensus among the interested few or are ignored altogether. Thus, the most notable feature of issues of low-level conflict may be their *absence* in analysis. One example of the inclusion of such an issue that *did* receive attention was the treatment of the environmental implications of alternative Alaskan oil export policies. Environmental concerns had held a central place in the early arguments over construction of the Alaskan oil pipeline, resulting in court action to block the construction and, in 1973, passage of the TAP Act overriding that court action.[58] Once the pipeline was

---

[56] This point is made in Jenkins-Smith and Weimer, "Retrograde Action," p. 19.

[57] Recent events seem to support this latter, less charitable view. Once again in 1984, under intense pressure to cut the budget deficit, OMB and DOE considered reducing the ultimate SPR size to 500 million barrels, eliminating phases Three and Four. See "Hodel Sees Risks in Oil Price Slide," *The Dallas Morning News* (December 12, 1984), p. D-1.

[58] See chapter 5, section 5.1.

constructed and it became apparent that an ecological disaster was not forthcoming, ecological concerns dropped from sight to be replaced by national security, efficiency, and budgetary considerations. In the 1983 discussion of the issue, in keeping with the policy analysis paradigm, the environmental issue was resurrected in the interest of making the analysis as comprehensive as possible.[59] Analysts from the Department of the Interior performed a limited (three or four pages in length) review of the issue, noting that maintenance of the oil export ban resulted in extensive oil tanker traffic along the U.S. and Latin American coastlines as crude was hauled from Alaska to destinations on the West and East coasts. This coastline traffic exposed coastal lands to some (unspecified) risk of oil spills. On the other hand, lifting the ban, and the resulting increase in profitability of new Alaskan production, would have the effect of increasing exploration and development activity in North Alaska and the Beaufort Sea, thus raising the risk of environmental damage in those areas. The review concluded that these effects were offsetting—"a wash."

It is clear that, had analysts on either side of the debate invested sufficient effort, a great deal more could have been learned about these and other environmental factors.[60] The point is not that the analysts involved were remiss; rather, it is simply the case that given limited time and analytical resources, issues that are peripheral to the belief systems of all major subsystem coalitions admitted to the forum are likely to claim little—if any—priority. The substantive contribution of analysis in such instances, and the resulting effect on beliefs of policy elites, can be expected to be quite limited.

One point needs mention here: the fact that the environmental concerns were peripheral to all sides included in the 1983 debate over oil export policy should not be taken to mean that such issues were peripheral to all factions in the subsystem at large. The analysis was conducted exclusively among selected participants from federal administrative agencies for the Reagan administration cabinet council. Furthermore, the entire proceedings were classified to minimize leakage of information. For these reasons, only selected viewpoints were represented. Those of an environmentalist bent, in particular, were absent from the forum. Had such individuals been included, both as analysts

---

[59] The analysis and working drafts were classified, and cannot be cited here. The points made here are drawn from this author's recollection and notes.

[60] Two additional factors that come readily to mind are (1) that many of the tankers hauling crude from Panama to the Gulf and East coasts were very old (called "rust-buckets" by some), and therefore may have posed more than the usual risk of spills, and (2) that continuation of the ban made construction of west-to-east pipelines more likely. In the process of off-loading crude from tankers, large volumes of hydrocarbon gas are usually released into the atmosphere. Therefore, construction of a west-to-east pipeline terminus in the San Francisco or Los Angeles regions (which are frequently proposed sites) would have substantially increased air pollution problems in those areas. These and other issues were informally raised, but not included in the written analysis.

and as the clients for whom the analysis was written, it is likely that the environmental concerns would have received more attention. This point is discussed at greater length in a later section.

6.3

ANALYTICAL TRACTABILITY

Of the cases considered here, none were characterized by the complete absence of common standards of validity; in each case, considerable overlap of theories, data sources, and techniques existed across competing subsystem coalitions. Perhaps the most demonstrable case of a highly tractable issue, one that served to limit the range of plausible disagreement among analysts, was evident in the natural gas debate concerning the old-gas-supply response to changes in price. The basis for understanding the problem was extensive industry experience with the geologic structure, natural well pressure, and the expected lifetime of gas fields. Based on this understanding, the engineering approach used by the Shell analysts to assess the likely effect of higher prices on gas production was—though still subject to a degree of uncertainty— widely understood and accepted among industry experts. Shell underscored this acceptance through employment of their "honest broker," whose report stressed the validity of Shell's method and the similarity of Shell's results to those achieved in alternative studies within the industry.[61] Given the widespread acceptance of the techniques used, opponents of decontrol were forced to choose between conspicuously disregarding a claim widely perceived to be valid, or accepting the claim (albeit only partially) and attempting to deflect its importance. As described above, they chose the latter course.

Much analytical conflict falls into the midrange of analytical intractability where considerable overlap of belief systems exists, but the issues are sufficiently intractable to permit analysts to promote uncertain claims on behalf of their preferred positions, or to refute or ignore threatening claims made by other analysts. The great uncertainty attending the discovery of existing and projected tanker rates, so central to the oil export debate described in chapter 5, permitted each side to produce plausible estimates that improved prospects for adoption of their preferred policy option. Once the prerogative of producing tanker rates was conferred on the MarAd analysts—a conference based on considerations of bureaucratic and analytic turf—the rates were successively revised in a direction that decreased the estimated economic benefits of exports (see table 5-5). Thus, the MarAd position was considerably enhanced.

Another instance for which the policy issue was sufficiently intractable to permit significantly differing yet still plausible analytical conclusions was the

---

[61] Gruy and Associates, letter to D. G. Russell, pp. 1–2.

1977–1978 natural gas deregulation debate in Congress.[62] The central question concerned the expected change in the price and quantity of the total supplies of natural gas made available to consumers should price controls be removed. In these debates little data was available concerning such a supply response; natural gas prices had remained fairly stable in preceding decades, producing neither data on supply responsiveness (price elasticity of supply), nor great interest in analyzing the question. When the question did become of interest, conflicting interests and an atmosphere of mistrust made arrival at consensus on techniques for making such estimates—let alone the estimates themselves—a difficult task at best.[63] Without such consensus, characterization of responsiveness of gas supplies to changes in price became a matter of the input assumptions made by the individual analyst. With little conclusive research available to narrow the range of plausible assumptions, analytical assumptions (and results) congenial to the full range of preferred policy options were made available with impunity. Thus, those favoring continued controls fielded analyses showing that decontrol of gas prices would result in large price increases and little increase in supply, while those favoring decontrol relied on studies showing large increases in supply accompanying moderate price increases.[64]

The nearest example of complete dissension across belief systems within the policy subsystem is evident in the case of the refinery policy study. Analysts within DOE had made a persuasive argument, based on microeconomic analysis, that over most foreseeable future conditions a tariff on petroleum-product imports would impose large economic costs on the economy while providing only slight (if any) national security benefits.[65] Within the microeconomic framework, the results of the study were fairly conclusive. As the debate wore on, critics of the PE study conclusions began to attack the analysis (and the analysts responsible) for perceived flaws in the microeconomic approach to energy analysis and for the failure of that approach to incorporate political reality.[66] The most biting and public of such critiques was lodged by

---

[62] The players, positions and circumstances of that debate are described admirably in Sanders, op. cit. Also see Malbin, "Congress, Policy Analysis, and Natural Gas Deregulation," for a more detailed view of the analyses performed in that debate.

[63] Aaron Wildavsky and Ellen Tenenbaum, in *The Politics of Mistrust: Estimating American Oil and Gas Reserves*, (Newbury Park, CA: Sage, 1981), argue that competing interests and uncertainty virtually precluded consensus. In particular, see chapter 8.

[64] See Malbin, "Congress, Policy Analysis, and Natural Gas Deregulation," pp. 69–80.

[65] The completed DOE report was released under the title *Costs and Benefits of a Protective Tariff on Refined Petroleum Products After Crude Oil Decontrol.*

[66] Much of the criticism took place strictly within DOE. See Department of Energy, "Release of Policy and Evaluation Protective Tariff/Refinery Study" (Unpublished memorandum from Undersecretary of Energy to Secretary of Energy, January 14, 1980), p. 1.

a high-level DOE official in Congressional testimony in September 1979. Referring to DOE's own analysts, Deputy Secretary of Energy John O'Leary had this to say:

> Our analysts tend to be classically educated. They tend to be educated in operations research and economics, not in politics, and what I am describing here [the world petroleum product market and the role of OPEC] is really the manifestation of a political phenomenon. None of the analysts, none of the pure analysts, predicted the success of OPEC. All of them . . . took the view that surplusses would result in ever stronger downward pressure on the price of crude over time, and they were caught aback by the politics, the political incursion that forged the real world in which we live today. And it seems to me that if we let the same view dictate our refinery policy, that is to say, if we take the view that this is a classical world that obeys the classical rules and the best thing to do is save money in the short run and let the refineries develop willy-nilly where they will . . . we may find ourselves in a tragic position a decade from now. . . . [67]

O'Leary's argument, then, was that the set of assumptions and techniques underlying the PE analysis were flawed—"a completely unsophisticated laissez-faire view"[68]—and therefore the conclusions of that analysis were not to be believed. By denying that the approach of microeconomics provided a consensual basis for assessment of analytical claims, O'Leary could plausibly argue that the (to him) unpalatable conclusions drawn from that approach should be heavily discounted.

From these examples we can draw the following tentative conclusions: the greater the analytical tractability (meaning the degree of consensus regarding the bases for assessing the validity of analytical claims) with respect to a policy issue, the more likely it is that learning and adjustment of belief systems will occur among competing subsystem coalitions. On the other hand, intractable issues permit a wide range of plausible analytical positions, allowing subsystem participants with conflicting belief systems to promote and defend their conflicting analytical claims with relative impunity. Thus the more tractable an issue the broader the range of conflict within which belief system adjustment and policy learning would take place.

Several supplemental points need mention here. Analytical tractability of an issue can be expected to *change* over time. One plausible argument is that, all other things being equal, the greater the time and analytical resources devoted to a particular policy question, the more analytically tractable the

---

[67] O'Leary, U.S. Senate, *Domestic Refinery Development*, p. 75.

[68] Ibid., p. 33.

issue is likely to become.[69] The natural gas deregulation debate provides some support for this argument. In that debate, what were tremendous differences among competing analyses regarding the effect of deregulation on gas prices in the 1977–1978 period had been reduced substantially by 1983–1984.[70] In part this narrowing was attributable to the emergence of new data; analysts had been able to track the response of suppliers and consumers to changes in gas prices over a period of years.[71] This narrowing had occurred despite the fact that competing coalitions had remained tenaciously and vociferously wedded to their opposing policy preferences—tractability increased despite the fact that intense conflict continued unabated.[72] Thus, over time the analytical tractability of the issue has increased, enhancing the prospects for learning and belief system adjustment.[73]

If policy concerns remained constant, the foregoing would provide room for optimism that, eventually, belief systems would be *forced* toward agreement on the basis of validating analytical claims and, therefore, toward a narrowing of analytical disagreement. Militating against such a progression, however, is the tendency of the focus of policy concern to shift, and of policy objectives to change, in a manner that often precludes sustained analytical attention over periods of time sufficient to render the issue analytically

---

[69] Edward Banfield disagrees. He argues that "... an analytical society may increase its problems while decreasing its ability to cope with them." See his "Policy Science as Metaphysical Madness," in *Bureaucrats, Policy Analysts, Statesmen: Who Leads?* ed. Robert Goldwin, (Washington, DC: American Enterprise Institute, 1980), p. 14. Banfield argues that this is because analysis tends to discover ever greater complexity in social phenomena.

[70] See Weyant, "Policy-Oriented Learning."

[71] Ibid. A partial list of the studies conducted after passage of the Natural Gas Policy Act in 1978, and before the 1983 debate described here, includes: U.S. Department of Energy, Office of Policy, Planning and Analysis, "Issues in the Debate Over the Natural Gas Policy Act of 1978," by Catherine Abbott (Unpublished paper, November 13, 1981); James Johnson, "Decontrol of Natural Gas at the Wellhead" (Unpublished paper, Standard Oil Company of Indiana, June 1981); Department of Energy, Division of Oil and Gas, Office of Energy Source Analysis, "The Natural Gas Market Under the Natural Gas Policy Act," by Mary Carlson, Nancy Ody, Richard O'Neill, Mark Rodekohr, Phil Shambaugh, Richard Throsser, and William Trapmann (Unpublished paper, Energy Information Administration, June 1981). For a summary of these studies, see Richard Cooper, "A Note on the Deregulation of Natural Gas Prices," *Brookings Paper on Economic Activity*, vol. 2, (Washington, DC: Brookings Institution, 1982), pp. 371–394.

[72] For an interesting review of the positions of some important congressional players in that conflict, see "Competing Interests Snarl Gas Debate," *Washington Post*, (June 26, 1983), p. A1.

[73] This optimistic assessment should not be taken to mean that, eventually, disagreement within policy subsystems will be eroded as analysts and scientists close in on the correct understanding of the policy issue. Serious doubt has been raised as to whether the progress of science (let alone analysis) ought to be seen as a steady progression toward an ultimately correct understanding of the phenomenal world. See Thomas Kuhn's *The Structure of Scientific Revolutions* 2nd ed. (Chicago: University of Chicago Press, 1970). If Kuhn's view is correct, fundamental understandings of phenomena can be expected to undergo periodic shifts as a branch of science experiences

tractable. Often, once legislation has been passed in response to a perceived problem, interest—and comittment of analytical resources—quickly wanes.[74] Reflecting on this tendency in the health area, one government analyst remarked:

> People told me before I came here, and it's absolutely true, that Congress legislates something, and then there's a great tendency to say that has solved the problem. That means that they don't pay attention to it after that. You might sometimes prefer *not* to have legislation, because then it keeps attention focussed on the problem.[75]

Even should analytical attention be maintained, however, for sufficiently complex issues the enhanced understandings provided by research and analysis may do little to foster the type of epistemological concensus within subsystems necessary to resolve the competing analytical claims underlying (or justifying) policy differences. One thorough study of the effect of analysis of the causes of poverty and racism in the 1960s and early 1970s concludes that the findings of such analyses served to erode away the "simple faiths" on which the political movement of the Great Society was based.[76] Demonstration of the complexity of social phenomena served to *weaken* consensus within subsystems regarding the validity and substance of analytical claims.[77] In such cases, though learning (as the refutation of simple faiths) clearly takes place, the range of plausible analytical claims may actually be *broadened,* thus, permitting subsystem participants wider latitude in employing analysis to support preferred positions and in responding to threatening analytical claims from other quarters.

Thus, the effect of time on the level of analytical tractability appears to be indeterminant. This is highly significant; as noted in chapter 3, both proponents and critics of analysis have argued from the premise that improved knowledge and techniques of analysis will one day permit analysts to hone in on the one best answer to perceived policy problems.

---

a "paradigm shift." Israel Schefler argues cogently for the more traditional view of science and the development of knowledge in *Science and Subjectivity* (Indianapolis, IN: Bobbs-Merrill, 1967).

[74] Anthony Downs argues that this is because people learn that the pursuit of one value through legislation often means sacrifice of some other value, leading to reduced interest in the original policy concern. See his "Up and Down with Ecology—The Issue Attention Cycle," in *The Public Interest,* vol. 28 (Summer 1972), pp. 38–50.

[75] John Kingdon, *Agendas, Alternatives and Public Policies* (Boston: Little, Brown, 1984), p. 109.

[76] Henry Aaron, *Politics and the Professors,* pp. 152–159.

[77] Banfield, "Policy Science," makes the same arguments regarding the effect of analysis on education policy. See pp. 13–14. Also see Martin Rein and Sheldon White's seminal "Policy Research: Belief and Doubt," in *Policy Analysis,* 3(2) (Spring 1977), pp. 239–271.

_____ 6.4 _____

THE ANALYTICAL FORUM

In addition to the analytical tractability of an issue, prospects for substantive contribution for analysis are affected by the nature of the forum in which the analytical debate is conducted. Most important is the *degree of openness* of the forum; to what degree are subsystem participants screened from active contribution to the policy debate. Three kinds of fora were identified: (1) *open fora,* in which all active subsystem participants within the subsystem have ready access to the debate; (2) *professionalized fora,* in which participants are screened on the basis of professional training and/or technical competence; and (3) *closed fora,* in which one or more policy elites screen participants for reasons of national or political security. While the cases examined here did not provide examples of all types of fora, important illustrations of several types are evident.

Open fora.   These are fora in which all mobilized participants within the subsystem are actively engaged in the debate. Among the cases employed here, the open forum is best typified by the natural gas deregulation debates. With the locus of the debate in Congress, nearly all major points of view could and did find opportunity for expression in testimony before committee hearings or in proposed legislation.[78] Given the large number of participants, and the divisive nature of the issue, it was only natural that a diverse array of beliefs would be represented concerning such underlying factors as the ultimate volume of recoverable gas reserves,[79] the likelihood of exercise of producer "monopoly power," and (most importantly) the nature of political justice that ought to guide choice.[80] This diversity was compounded by the fact that expert analysts could be found to champion virtually all of the major positions taken on the issue. (See section 6.3 on analytical tractability.) Given these diverse beliefs, held by persons of widely varying backgrounds, it should not be surprising that the participants expended little effort trying to arrive at consensus based on either the results of analysis or the fundamental assumptions on which the analyses were based. Rather, in the words of then-Congressman David Stockman (who was a participant in the debate), the

---

[78] The plethora of analyses provided to Congress on the natural gas deregulation issue is staggering. Malbin, "Congress, Policy Analysis, and Natural Gas Deregulation," describes a range of the analyses presented and used in the 1977–1978 period of the debates. For a partial list of subsequent analyses, see section 6.2, above, and Weyant, "Policy-Oriented Learning."

[79] This question alone is the basis for tremendous disagreement over appropriate policy. See John J. Schantz, *Oil and Gas Resources—Welcome to Uncertainty,* Reprint No. 58 (Washington, DC: Resources for the Future, 1978).

[80] See Malbin's interesting discussion of the "real issues," "Congress, Policy Analysis, and Natural Gas Deregulation," pp. 81–84.

results of analyses were used as "fig leaves" to cover basic beliefs and values in public debate.[81] The reason, at least in part, was that there existed no common basis in training or accepted theory upon which to weigh competing claims. The result was that analysts and decision makers alike could make and rely on a wide range of apparently plausible analytical assertions with relative impunity.[82] Within an open forum, then, uncertainty tends to be fully exploited by the competing subsystem coalitions in defense of existing belief systems.

Professionalized fora.   Most of the cases developed for this study involved debate among energy experts—and even specialists within some subfield in energy policy. Yet, by the definition of professionalized fora employed here, none occurred within a professionalized forum. Though for that reason I cannot provide a case example to illustrate the process described in chapter 4, it is important to make clear *why* none of these debates were conducted in what could be called a professionalized forum.

The criteria defining a professionalized forum are that the analysts involved share a common basis for assessing analytical claims—that is, the rules for making and verifying analytical assertions are known and shared among the participants. Deviation from these norms would be readily observable, resulting in quick exposure and loss of professional credibility among peers.[83] Furthermore, credibility among peers is a prerequisite to influencing the beliefs and policy positions of policy elites. These are demanding criteria and are probably rarely achieved in close proximity to the policy-making process.[84]

In practice, I suspect, professionalized fora are at best only approximated in the run of policy debates, wherein the commonality of training and experience serves to eliminate the more spurious of analytical claims without foreclosing the opportunity for honest professional difference of opinion. The rarity of the natural occurrence of such fora in the policy-making process has motivated those who seek a more influential role for analysis to attempt to

---

[81] Quoted in ibid., p. 85.

[82] Even in an open forum, however, there are limits to analytical plausibility. In 1977 the Carter administration released a study supporting its natural gas policy recommendations that subsequently was found to significantly understate current (and, by implication, future) gas prices. The error made the costs of the policy to gas producers appear to be smaller than would be the case with more accurate price estimates. As a result of the obvious error, the administration's analysis was discredited and ignored for the remainder of the debate. Weyant, "Policy-Oriented Learning."

[83] As stressed above, this practice could be likened to the practice of Kuhn's (*Scientific Revolutions*) "normal science."

[84] An exception is the case provided by Richard Barke, "Technological Change and Regulatory Adjustment: The FCC and Technical Standard Setting" (Paper delivered at the meetings of the Association for Policy Analysis and Management, New Orleans, October 1984). In that case, engineers and technicians in the telecommunications industry working in the forum of a technical advisory committee to the Federal Communications Commission (FCC) were able to resolve policy issues (the setting of technical standards) despite the existence of intense conflict of interest.

institutionalize such fora as "science courts."[85] Others, also disenchanted with
the lack of professionalized fora, have called for the development of "medi-
ating institutions," funded independently of government and modeled on the
Brookings Institution and the American Enterprise Institute, to increase the
frequency with which policy debates occur in something like a professionalized forum.[86] Nevertheless, the rarity persists. It is not surprising, though no
less unfortunate, that such fora are absent from the cases examined here.[87]

Closed fora.   Various stages of the Alaskan oil export debate, described
above, were conducted within rigidly closed fora. In part because the issue
involved assessment of the need for certain militarily useful tankers and the
likely effect of various export policies on the availability of those tankers,
participants in the administration's working group assembled in 1983 to
study the question were limited, and all working group papers (including
drafts) were classified. Part of the intended value of the closed forum was that
the group could, in principle, study a wide range of policy options—some
quite unpopular with affected interests—without raising the wrath of those
wedded to particular policies. For that reason, the range of options given
serious assessment may have been broader than would have been the case in
an open forum.[88] However, the closed forum also created unanticipated
problems; as the analysis progressed, competing coalitions within the group
arrived at an analytical impasse over the data used, the key assumptions
employed, and the modeling techniques used to analyze the problem.[89]
Because the forum was closed, it was difficult (if not impossible) for decision
makers to discern whether the impasse reflected idiosyncrasies within the
group or broader dissension within the analytic community.[90] Issues that
might have been resolvable in a broader, open forum—such as the adequacy
of the modeling techniques used—were therefore left at a standoff.

---

[85] Murray Levine, "Scientific Method and The Adversary Model: Some Preliminary Suggestions," *Evaluation Comment,* 4(2) (June 1973), pp. 1–3; and Marilyn Kourlisky, "An Adversary Model for Educational Evaluation," *Evaluation Comment,* 4(2) (June 1973), pp. 3–6.

[86] See Martin Greenberger, et al., *Caught Unawares,* pp. 288–290; and Martin Greenberger, et al., *Models in the Policy Process* (New York: Russell Sage, 1976), pp. 231–234.

[87] This lack of cases may soon be ameliorated. John Weyant and others at Stanford University's Energy Modelling Forum (EMF) are working to assemble a case study of the proceedings of an EMF debate among scholars—all respected energy economists and operations research analysts—sponsored to review the natural gas deregulation issue.

[88] Several members suggested early in the proceedings of the working group that the range of options considered should be limited on the basis of "political feasibility." In my view, such a move would have defeated a primary purpose of the closed forum: allowing an unrestricted review of options.

[89] See Higgins and Jenkins-Smith, "Economic Effect," pp. 33–35.

[90] The Reagan administration cabinet council, for which the analysis was prepared, voted to endorse the study but took no policy action. Ibid.

More serious, however, was the potential for outright exclusion of certain viewpoints and interests from the forum altogether. For example, few of the high-level Reagan administration officials were concerned with the possible environmental implications of export policies. As noted earlier, because the issue was peripheral to the core concerns of the coalitions represented, little serious analysis of environmental factors was performed. While the low level of concern for this issue within the group might well have reflected a consensus within the broader subsystem that the environmental implications of export policy were unimportant,[91] it is conceivable that important subgroups of the policy subsystem can be excluded in this manner, distorting the outcome of the analysis.[92]

These concerns require some qualification, however. Typically, the closed forum represents but one arena in which the policy is debated. In the Alaskan oil export case, the working group analysis was part of the process of developing an administration position on the issue. Once completed, the issue would be taken up in a subsequent forum—Congress. Within the very open Congressional forum, the administration's analysis would be open to inspection from many sides and viewpoints.[93] Potential problems because of closed fora would therefore seem to loom larger in the analytical debates of regulatory agencies; when closed analysis provides the basis for decisive administrative rule making, subsequent fora for debate of the issue may not be readily available.[94]

6.5
SUMMARY

The cases reviewed here provide considerable support for the conceptual model of the process of policy analysis provided in chapter 4. Where high levels of analytical conflict were evident, as in the oil refinery debates and over the question of federal tax receipts in the Alaskan oil export debates, compet-

---

[91] That seems to have been the case. In the nearly exhaustive expression of views and analyses presented at Congressional hearings on the issue, environmental concerns were notably absent. See Congress, Senate, Committee on Foreign Relations, *Export of Alaskan Oil*, Hearings before the Subcommittee on East Asian and Pacific Affairs (Washington, DC: U.S. Government Printing Office, July 19–20, 1983).

[92] For example, see Mark Rushefsky, "The Misuse of Science in Governmental Decision Making," *Science, Technology, and Human Values*, 9(3) (Summer 1984), pp. 47–59.

[93] For a nearly exhaustive collection of views and analyses of the oil export issue, see Congress, *Export of Alaskan Crude Oil*.

[94] Even in these areas, however, the presence of "whistle blowers," analysts who leak information to the press, and access to information under the Freedom of Information Act may serve to contain the most excessive abuses. The fate of Ann Gorsuch Burford is testimony to the effectiveness of such factors.

ing subsystem coalitions fought one another to an analytic standstill. Neither side in the debate felt compelled to adjust beliefs or policy positions on the basis of analytical conclusions. Cases of more moderate conflict—including the debate over the supply response of old gas and (to a lesser extent) the SPR size issue—evidenced a greater influence of analysis on the beliefs and policy positions of the participants involved. Where analytical conflict is low, illustrated here by the environmental implications of the oil export issue, few analytical resources are committed to the question.

The analytical tractability of the issue under study also seems to have important bearing on the use of analysis. When questions of basic framework underlie the conflict, as was the case in the refinery policy debate, analysis can be expected to provide little help in resolving differences in belief and policy preference. Even on more moderately intractable issues, such as the natural gas price–quantity relationship in the early Congressional debate on that issue and the tax revenue issue in the oil export debate, analysis tends to be mobilized in defense of preconceived policy positions. In such instances, particularly in combination with intense conflict, analysis is more frequently employed as a political tool than as an avenue for learning and persuasion. On somewhat more tractable issues, like the question of the old-gas-supply response, analysis has a greater chance of modifying policy relevant beliefs and, perhaps, policy positions.

Though the cases developed here provided no instance in which analysis took place in a professionalized forum, they do support the argument that the characteristics of the forum can systematically affect the ways in which analysis is employed. Open fora, illustrated by the natural gas debate, seem to afford wide opportunity for use of analysis in defense of preconceived policy positions. Implicitly, this would be compared with a forum restricted by professional or technical training—a professionalized forum—in which analytical claims would be subject to a more restrictive, consensual basis for validation. Though no such fora were evident in the cases recounted here, the scant evidence from the literature tends to support this hypothesis. Closed fora, such as the 1983 round of the Alaskan oil export debate, have mixed implications for analysis; though necessary for security reasons, and efficacious for political reasons, closed fora may also inhibit assessment of analytical claims (and differences) from the subsystem at large. More importantly, such fora may permit exclusion of important values and beliefs through selective screening. As noted, these problems appear to loom larger in policy arenas that do not have a succession of fora for debate through which voices excluded at one stage may be heard at another.

It is not intended that these findings be taken as conclusive or as the final word on the issue of the role of analysis in the policy process. The nature of the questions addressed, and the type and volume of data required, preclude the kind of research design that could permit such pretensions. Nevertheless, as applied to the case studies, the conceptual model of the policy process does provide a strong basis from which to reassess the claims made for, and the critiques of, policy analysis in democratic decision making. It is to that issue that the next chapter is addressed.

PART THREE

THE PRUDENTIAL
PRACTICE OF
POLICY ANALYSIS

CHAPTER 7

Policy Analysis and Democratic Politics

This volume has had two goals: first, the claims made for policy analysis, and the critiques of policy analysis as a threat to democratic politics, were developed in Part One. Analysis was praised by its more ardent proponents as holding potential for providing a more accurate mapping of citizens' preferences into public policy and as a corrective for the inefficiences and inequities of politics-as-usual. Critics have rejoined that, far from improving democracy, the widespread promulgation of policy analysis will create a new and unrepresentative policy elite, that analysis will distort citizen preferences, and that attempts to employ analysis will mire existing policy processes in ever-greater complexity and indecision.

Second, in Part Two, an attempt was made to provide a realistic appraisal of policy analysis *as practiced* in the bureaucratic institutions of the American political process. Analysis departs considerably from the characterization of its advocates. I have argued that analysis must be seen as an interactive, collective process within policy subsystems. The particular uses to which analysis is put, and the nature of its contribution to the content of public policy, must be understood in terms of the *context* in which the debate is waged and of the analytical qualities of the issue under review. Despite the wide currency of the objective technician style of analysis in the policy literature, the exigencies of the policy environment tend to push analysts into various advocacy roles from which they participate in the process of analysis within subsystems.

It remains for this chapter to knit these parts together. In concrete terms, what are the implications of the practice of analysis for democratic governance? Given the practice of policy analysis depicted here, does analysis constitute a threat to the practice of democratic politics? And, if so, in what form? I will argue that, rather than condemn analysis generally, it is the practice of analysis in particular kinds of institutional and political situations that calls for close and critical scrutiny.

Also of importance, however, are the implications of politics for analysis. Is the potential contribution of analysis rendered moot by its necessary adjustment to the patterns and conflicts of policy making? Put differently, is analysis necessarily and regularly doomed to play handmaiden and mandarin to the exercise of power politics? Again I will argue that the answer is contingent on the characteristics of the issue and the policy setting.

Finally, based on this study of analysis in practice, can policy analysis be institutionalized in the policy process in a manner that makes the most of its virtues while containing its potential abuses? How can the key elements of the policy context be harnessed in this effort? What styles of analysis would be appropriate in such an institutionalized practice of policy analysis?

_____ 7.1 _____

DOES POLICY ANALYSIS THREATEN DEMOCRACY?

The major critiques of policy analysis, detailed in chapter 3, each contain an implicit view of the characteristics of the practice of analysis. The force of the critique depends in large part on whether those presumed characteristics obtain with sufficient generality to uniformly affect the practice of policy analysis. Interestingly, the characteristics presumed to be predominant by the various critics differ; critics who contend that the analysts themselves will acquire unrepresentative political power have in mind a policy-making context in which analysts are relatively free of the yoke of their political clients and in which analysts are able to specify the one best answer to a perceived policy problem. Alternatively, those who see analysts primarily as mandarins, who apply a legitimating technocratic sheen to the dictates of the politically powerful presume a context in which analysts are largely unconstrained in making analytical claims and in which the client is able to maintain tight control over the analyst. To back up these various views, critics are able to find instances of the practice of analysis that seem to support *each* of the claims made.

The critics (and proponents) of analysis can be likened to the blind men of the fable who, upon encountering an elephant, each seized on one part as descriptive of the whole. While the particular critique may be cogent for the perceived part of the policy context, fuller assessment of the critique requires that it be viewed in light of the full range of policy contexts. With this end in mind, the pages that follow will review the critiques of analysis with particular attention to the kinds of contexts in which analysis will—and will not—generate the kinds of threats perceived by the critics. In this way, it is hoped, the applicability of the several critiques to the more general process of analysis can be tested.

Analysis and undue influence.   One of the primary themes of criticism, drawing from the broader strains of the anti-technocracy literature, holds that policy analysts will obtain (or have obtained) unrepresentative political power by virtue of their technical prescription of the best solution to policy problems. Jacques Ellul made the argument most succinctly, when he wrote:

> When the expert has effectively performed his task of pointing out the necessary ways and means, there is generally only one logical and admissable solution. The politician will then find himself obliged to choose between the technician's solution, which is the only reasonable one, and other solutions, which he can indeed try out at his own peril but which are not reasonable. At such a moment, the politician is gambling with his responsibility since there are such great chances of miscarriage if he adopts the technically deviant solutions. In fact, the politician no longer has any real choice; decision follows automatically from the preparatory technical labors.[1]

The critique of unrepresentative influence stems largely from the liberal democratic concern with the dispersion of power in political systems; technically optimal solutions are valued far less than are policies legitimately derived from democratic or representative institutions.[2] The provision of technically optimal solutions becomes a threat when the political tasks of perceiving policy problems, valuing outcomes, and bounding the range of legitimate and acceptable solutions are turned over to a technical elite while political officers merely rubber-stamp the technicians' optimal choice. What are the prerequi-

---

[1] Jacques Ellul, *The Technological Society* (New York: Vintage Books, 1964), pp. 258–259.

[2] See chapter 3.

sites to such an influential role by policy analysts? What would the process of analysis, and the policy environment of the individual analyst, need to be like to make such influence possible?

This threat of policy analysis presupposes that the use of analysis is able to fundamentally shape the policy-relevant beliefs and values—or belief systems—of policy elites. That, in turn, requires that the policy elites do not have strong commitments to preexisting belief systems in the area of concern; such elites must be willing to adjust existing beliefs in accordance with the findings of analysis. Such willingness best fits the pattern of low analytical conflict, in which no significant coalition in the policy subsystem finds its core beliefs and values threatened by the analytical claims made. As noted above, however, rarely are extensive analytical resources mobilized for issues characterized by low levels of analytical conflict; more typically, as illustrated by the review of environmental implications of oil exports, such issues receive at best cursory analytical attention. Analytical resources tend to be committed most extensively precisely where conflict among competing core beliefs and values is highest, and therefore, willingness to adjust beliefs in light of analytical findings is slight. The early analytical brawl over natural gas deregulation, for which analysis was fielded by many sides in the debate, is a case in point.

The greatest prospects for analysis to significantly alter the beliefs (and policy preferences) of policy elites exist where analytical conflict is moderate, allowing not only some flexibility in belief systems but also incentives for subsystem participants to commit the requisite analytical resources. The necessary preexistence of *some* analytical conflict, and therefore *some* resistance to change in belief systems, would seem to diminish (though not eliminate) the prospect for overriding influence by policy analysts.

But the critique of analysis as an unrepresentative power argues further that the influence of analysis stems from the *uniformity* of analytical findings; political decision makers will be confronted by provision of the one best answer to the policy problem. Such a situation is imaginable; a highly tractable analytical issue—such as how to handle communication flows in fire stations to minimize bottlenecks[3]—will allow for a substantial degree of consensus among policy analysts regarding analytical findings. Such consensus will make the conclusions of analysis more persuasive and restrict the ease with which those who dissent can mobilize analysis for an opposing set of claims. As indicated in the review of the old gas analysis, the well-developed technical basis for estimating the relationship between prices and recoverable reserves in known gas fields was such that even those who had a large stake in denying

---

[3] Martin Greenberger et al., *Models in the Policy Process* (New York: Russell Sage, 1976), chapter 8.

that reserve increases would occur under decontrol had to admit to *some* such increase.

It is important to consider, however, what kinds of issues are likely to admit of high levels of analytical tractability. As discussed earlier, the imputation of meaning and value to events—an imputation that must occur before "problems" can be specified—cannot be reduced to a technical process.[4] In order to map citizens' preferences into public policy, as called for by the dominant policy paradigm, such preferences must already exist; until they exist there is ample room for analysts to differ over what the appropriate objectives are. On large-scale policy questions, and where objectives are in conflict, there will inevitably be ample room for analytically plausible yet opposing policy positions.[5] It is therefore on the narrower technical questions, for which clear goals are established, that it is possible for analytical tractability to narrow the range of admissible conflict.

The scale or narrowness of analytical issues is only part of what determines tractability. Analysis is a collective activity, fundamentally based on the existence of consensual bases for assessment of the validity of analytical claims. Therefore, while the characteristics of the issue itself are important determinants of tractability, so are the range and kinds of *participants* in the analytical debate. When the participants share common training, techniques, and tests of validity of analytical claims, the range of plausible analytical claims is likely to be considerably narrowed. Thus, maximum consensus on the analytical question is likely to be achieved when the debate is held in a professionalized forum, where the participants are screened by virtue of professional training or technical proficiency. When, on the other hand, the forum is wide open to all subsystem participants, the broad range of professions and levels of analytical sophistication represented admit much more tenuous bases for consensus on the validity of analytical claims. In such open fora, as seen in the refinery policy debates recounted in chapter 6, there exists tremendous room for plausible dissent from analytical findings.

Finally, the argument that analysts will acquire significant unrepresentative political clout presumes that analysts will be able to develop and employ analysis independently of their political clients. In the terms developed here, these critics assume that analysts will be subject to little organizational allegiance and can therefore propose and effectively advocate an optimal solution even should that solution conflict with the interests of the client. Such circumstances are not the norm. In the refinery-policy case, for example,

---

[4] See chapter 3.

[5] The possibility that analysts as a group are bearers of an implicit or covert ideological perspective, therefore permitting consensus within their ranks on questions of this sort, will be addressed below.

analysts at DOE struggled for well over a year to release a study indicating that new refinery supports were unnecessary; high-level officials in DOE who favored such supports successfully squelched the study for an extended period.[6] Release of the study awaited the arrival of more receptive clients.

Overall, then, analysis can be expected to have decisive influence of the kind feared by Ellul only under a fairly restrictive set of conditions: the level of analytical conflict must be low, but somehow *still* sufficient to mobilize necessary analytical resources to conduct the study; the issue must be highly tractable; the forum in which the issue is debated must be sufficiently professionalized or otherwise restricted to permit common bases for assessment of analytical claims; and analysts must be relatively free of organizational allegiance to clients already committed to a policy position. In none of the cases of the use of analysis employed in this study—nor in any of the uses of analysis in my experience—has this set of conditions been fully met. Furthermore, because policy development and implementation in the American political process typically moves through a *series of stages,* there are multiple opportunities for the undue influence of analysts at one stage to be corrected at another. For these reasons, in my judgment, the general usurpation of political power by policy analysts is not to be greatly feared.

The distortion of public preference.   A separate but related set of criticisms of policy analysis is based on the contention that analysis will distort the expression and valuation of preferences employed in formulation of public policy. One frequent argument is that, because analysis stresses the reduction of all values to a common metric, so-called hard values that can be readily measured in dollar amounts will be emphasized at the expense of less-readily measurable values (such as market externalities and intangibles). Furthermore, in the zeal to quantify, those applying policy analysis will reduce heterogeneous values to a structureless mass, ignoring complex interrelationships and orderings among values. In particular, the status of perceived rights and obligations will be rendered comparable to that of marketable goods. And finally, policy analysts working within the policy analysis paradigm are not equipped to assess the "standing" of the disparate preferences that may be expressed in society; because analysts eschew reference to grounds of equity and justice in favor of efficiency, *all* expressed preferences (those of criminals as well as victims) are accorded equal legitimacy.

Critics also point out that application of the policy paradigm seeks reliance on expressed preferences—ideally "willingness-to-pay" as determined from market prices, shadow prices, or surveys—in a fashion that ignores the formative process of politics. Preferences are assumed to be static

---

[6] By the time the refinery study was released, in fact, two of the original primary authors had moved on to other jobs.

and fully developed at the outset, waiting to be measured and mapped into public policy. Such a process, the critics charge, bypasses a most crucial step in politics: the *formulation* of preferences through public debate. Furthermore, until such a process has taken place preferences are likely to be superficial and volatile, rendering any assessment of willingness-to-pay misleading at best.

Defenders of policy analysis have rejoined that the critics have overblown the importance of analysis in shaping public policy; in fact, they contend, analysis is but one all-too-insignificant force within the tumult of politics, more likely to be overwhelmed than to dominate the process. In this view, analysis strives to play a modest corrective role in rationalizing the allocation of resources in a process otherwise riddled with self-seeking special interests. As noted earlier, both critics and defenders are able to point to instances of the use of analysis that support their claims.

It is useful to ask, in the view of the criticisms made, what must be the nature of the process in which analysis is employed to so distort public values and preferences? If, as I have argued, analysis is used to define the shape and content of the policy space, the critics' contention is that analysis will systematically affect that policy space in ways that undermine certain kinds of values while inflating others, and will provide only infrequent reassessment of existing political preferences. Under what conditions would the process of analysis be conducive to such practice?

Foremost among the prerequisites would be a restriction of analytical conflict within the policy subsystem. When, on the contrary, an array of competing subsystem coalitions debate an intractable policy issue, various analysts would admit and defend a variety of conflicting policy positions. That is illustrated with a vengeance by the natural gas deregulation debates described in chapter 6. However, the systematic bias feared by the critics *could* occur in a subsystem narrow and specialized enough that only directly affected interests have sufficient incentives to mobilize analysis.[7] Within regulatory policy, "client politics"—in which benefits are provided to a small concentrated group while costs are dispersed over a wide population—would fit this scenario.[8] In that case, expression of values and beliefs in the subsystem itself will have a decided tilt that is likely to be carried over into the provision of analysis.

---

[7] Even when the benefits to some group from participation are large, the dispersion of those benefits across a large number of beneficiaries will often render collective action by the group "irrational." Smaller groups, with more concentrated benefits, are systematically better able to pursue collective action. See Mancur Olson, *The Logic of Collective Action* (Cambridge, MA: Harvard University Press, 1965). Thus on issues characterized by potential for concentrated benefits for a small group, and diffuse costs for a larger group, the former is likely to be well represented in the subsystem while the latter will have little or no representation.

[8] See James Q. Wilson, ed., *The Politics of Regulation* (New York: Basic Books, 1980).

In a scenario of this kind, generation of balanced aggregate analysis on the issue would require that government analysts take the role of issue advocates—advocating the dimensions of value and positions of the more diffuse, indirectly affected groups. It may be that there is a tendency on the part of analysts to play such a balancing role. The oil export debates, described in chapter 5, were characterized by a dynamic of this sort. In that analytical debate, the DOE analyst perceived the MarAd analysts as serving the narrow interests of the maritime industry. Partly because of that apparent advocacy, the DOE analyst stridently sought to provide analytical support for a policy that would permit exports and thereby (in his view) benefit the economy at large. Evidence from the airline and trucking deregulation debates, in which recent policy has moved *decidedly* against the concentrated interests usually predominant in the subsystems, also suggests that such a role can be played by policy analysts.[9] Despite such instances, however, the evidence of such phenomena as "capture" of regulatory agencies by the regulated industry suggests that agency analysts cannot be regularly counted on to play this balancing role.[10]

Even within a subsystem of more inclusive representation, analysis might take on the value-distorting characteristics as charged by the critics if the particular forum for debate were appropriately screened. The flaws peculiar to the policy analysis paradigm might be expected to reach fullest form in a narrowly circumscribed professionalized forum, and other kinds of bias could be achieved through screening on the basis of policy preferences. The general lack of consideration of environmental issues in the closed debates over oil export policy in 1981 and 1983, when such issues had played a pivotal role in initial debates over the issue, indicates that screening *can* make a considerable difference in the content of analysis.

In many cases, however, this concern must be tempered by the fact that the political process presents a *succession* of fora in which the policy is debated. In the oil export case, for instance, had the Reagan administration decided to pursue an export policy, the forum would have moved to Congress—opening the debate to virtually all interested parties. Concern should focus, therefore, on fora that may permit screening and not provide for correction of potential bias through debate in subsequent fora.

---

[9] See Martha Derthick and Paul Quirk, *The Politics of Deregulation,* (Washington, DC: Brookings, 1984), and Anthony Brown and Joseph Stuart, Jr., "Competing Advocacy Coalitions, Policy Evolution, and Airline Deregulation" (Unpublished manuscript, 1988).

[10] On regulatory capture, see Marver Bernstein's *Regulating Business By Independent Commission* (Princeton, NJ: Princeton University Press, 1955), chapter 3. Also see Sam Peltsman's "Toward a More General Theory of Regulation," *Journal of Law and Economics,* 19(2) (August 1976), pp. 211–240.

According to the critics, values may be further distorted by the inability of the policy analysis paradigm to come to grips with the issue of *standing* among preferences. As discussed in chapter 3, the policy analysis paradigm provides no means by which analysts can distinguish between legitimate and illegitimate preferences, leading to a propensity to accord all preferences equal status. In the terms developed in chapter 4, *any* expressed dimension of value would merit inclusion in the policy space. However, at least in contentious policy disputes, the chief characteristic of analytical strategies may well be the struggle by analysts to include or exclude competing dimensions of value in the policy space. In the oil export policy dispute, for example, the DOE analyst sought to preclude the traditional national security dimension from dominating the policy space, and substituted the budget dimension in its stead. When MarAd analysts succeeded in wresting the placement on the budget dimension to an unfavorable (and highly uncertain) position, the DOE analyst sought (and failed) to shift emphasis to the economic efficiency dimension. The recognition that analysis is often the locus of competing dimensions of value is sufficiently widespread that leading proponents of the policy analysis paradigm have sought to enshrine efficiency as the preeminent dimension championed by analysts in order to assure that it is not *altogether* eclipsed by the press for other (special interest) dimensions of value.[11]

However, the fact of contention among analysts over dimensions of value is not sufficient grounds for complaisance regarding the issue of standing. Short of a wide open analytical forum, analysts cannot count on the analytical debate to sufficiently probe the matter of the legitimacy of the various expressed preferences for decision makers.[12] It is in closed or professionalized fora, in particular, that the process of analysis per se cannot be counted on to fully develop and grapple with the issues of the legitimacy of competing preferences. The problem is compounded if, once made, a decision will not be subject to further analytical scrutiny in an additional, more open forum. It is in such contexts, then, that the critics' claims take on greatest force and urgency.

A further important contention by the critics of analysis is that, because analysis relies on existing preferences (via prices or surveys) to attribute value to policy outcomes, analysis skips the crucial *formative* role of debate in the policy process. This view, based as it is on the model of analysis prescribed by

---

[11] See, for example, Charles Schultze, *The Politics and Economics of Public Spending* (Washington, DC: Brookings Institute, 1968).

[12] Even in an open forum, analysis may well omit inclusion of certain legitimate but politically impotent preferences. It is here that the objective technician's penchant for exhaustive inclusion of all preferences is an essential corrective to unbalanced political muscle. This issue is discussed explicitly in section 7.4.

the policy analysis paradigm, seems to assume that policy choice will be based on a *single analysis* produced at a single point in time. As the depiction of the policy process and cases in this study have shown, analysis is more aptly understood as a collective activity in which analytical resources are diffused throughout the policy subsystem and employed in the interest of many policy preferences. Furthermore, on larger political issues, analysis tends to be mobilized in many successive fora, and is readily adapted to incorporate new information and changing preferences. The natural gas deregulation and the oil export debates, for instance, have continued over a series of years, adapting to new information and the rise and fall of political interests. This characteristic of analysis is not so much an intended practice as it is a necessary adaptation of the use of analysis to the American political process; political decision is rarely if ever made at a discrete point in time. Even once made, ample opportunity exists for review and delay through the use of analysis. In the SPR size study reviewed in chapter 6, for example, analysts at the OMB were able to repeatedly call for reevaluation of an issue that had been shown to be justified on the basis of net social benefits. Thus, analysis rarely takes the form of a one-shot conclusive study as depicted by the critics; the norm, on the contrary, is that analysis is iterative, reflecting (and sometimes contributing to) the development and realignment of political preferences.

Overall, then, in what ways and under what conditions can analysis be expected to distort the expression of values and preferences on which policy choice is based? As I have argued, the conditions under which much of analysis is employed—significant analytical conflict, open fora, and analysis conducted in iterative stages—serve to inhibit these kinds of abuses and biases. When the forum is open and analysis is mobilized in the interest of numerous competing positions, analysis can be employed by all sides in the debate. Even when the forum is closed, the availability of subsequent fora typically assures that analytical positions shorted in the earlier round can find expression in a later one. This is particularly relevant for the large-scale, controversial issues that may take decades to work their way through the political process.

Nonetheless, there are regions of the policy environment for which the fear that reliance on analysis may distort the policy space holds considerable credence. The matter of which dimensions of value to count, and at what weight, is most serious in closed and professionalized fora. More threatening still are issues debated within agencies and bureaus concerned with narrower, more complex issues, such as regulatory policy. The participants of the policy subsystems surrounding such issue–areas may ill represent those affected by the policy, leading advocate analysts to weight the provision of analysis in favor of the interests of the better mobilized groups. Furthermore, because regulatory agencies have acquired extensive administrative rule making authority, the forum for analytical debate within these regulatory agencies (usually in the form of administrative hearings) may be the one and only forum before authoritative policy choice is made. Although parties injured by the resultant policy might be able to seek redress in later hearings, before Congressional oversight committees, or in the courts, as long as the distribution of costs and benefits continues to reflect the pattern of client politics the aggregate provision of analysis can be expected to continue to be weighted in favor of the better mobilized groups.

Analysis as a strain on the democratic process.   The third major theme of criticism of policy analysis centers on the contention that the use of policy analysis will overwhelm American political institutions and processes. The hurdles in the way of citizens and politicians who would engage in meaningful policy debate are increased when debate is drawn to technical complexities and buried under the jargon of the expert; in a self-generating cycle, the increasing demands on the time and cognitive abilities of decision makers for digestion of analysis leads to increased reliance on the analysts and their advice, and the complexity and uncertainties introduced by analysis serve to further complicate an already burdened decision-making process, causing that process to grind at an ever-slower, less-deliberate pace.

In large part, these contentions bear on the manner in which *complexity* of the issue under consideration is addressed in analysis. How is such complexity treated in analytical debates, and does complexity regularly serve to confuse and prolong policy deliberation? Treatment differs according to several factors, the most important being the analytical tractability of the issue and the level of conflict in the debates. When the issue is intractable and subject to high levels of conflict, the attending complexities are frequently treated much as the critics contend: advocate analysts capitalize on uncertainty—and even strive to generate greater uncertainties—to make their claims seem plausible and to undermine those of their opponents. In the process, the debate is clouded with uncertainty.

The Alaskan oil export case described in chapter 5 provides good illustration of the use of strategies that capitalize on uncertainty by advocate analysts. Because estimation of future period tanker rates proved highly intractable, analysts from MarAd were able to repeatedly revise rate estimates in a direction that reduced estimates of oil price increases—and therefore tax receipts—in North Alaska. Such a result served their purpose of making an oil export option look less attractive to Reagan administration officials. The DOE analyst, who sought to improve prospects for exports, had employed a similar strategy in adding to the analysis a new and uncertain category of tax receipt gain—those attributable to increases in expected West Coast crude prices. The net result was successively greater uncertainty; over the course of the debate the apparent range of possible effects of export options on tax receipts was widened dramatically.

The 1977–1978 natural gas debates show a similar phenomenon: because little was known about the responsiveness of gas supplies to changes in prices, analysts advocating different policy options were able to select assumptions that cast their preferred position in the most favorable light. Coupled with the open forum, the highly analytically intractable issue effectively created an open season on wild claims. Again, strategies employing uncertainty served more to obscure than to enlighten with regard to the issue in question.

It is useful to inquire what the effects of such unconstrained use of uncertainty in adversarial analysis are on the clients for whom the analysis is produced. In the Alaskan oil export case, at least, both analysts and clients were well aware of the advocacy bent of those involved. In most cases, this is to be expected; analysts who see their opponents as advocates will say as much to their clients in order to forewarn and inure them to unwarranted bias. Analysis in such cases quickly loses the luster and sheen of objective neutrality. Experience with biased or flawed analysis appears to have made most decision makers skeptical of analysis employed in divisive issues—particularly when presented by someone with a direct stake in the outcome.[13] Though good analysis may thus be discounted with the bad, and though such analysis may be used as a political resource, it is likely that advocacy analysis of highly conflictual issues fools few decision makers.

Not all issues admit the unrestrained use of strategies that capitalize on uncertainty. When the issue is more tractable, analysts have less latitude in making analytical claims. In the old-gas-supply debate, conducted after the accretion of considerably more information on the responsiveness of gas supplies to price than had been available in the 1977–1978 debate, all participants were compelled to accept the claim that price deregulation would result in the addition of significant volumes of gas reserves that would otherwise never be recovered. Useful information was provided through the use of analysis *despite* high levels of conflict.[14] Thus, there are limits on the generation and use of analytical uncertainty.

Given that the employment of uncertainty is bounded in some instances, what is the likely *systematic* effect of the use of such strategies in political institutions? For a number of reasons, the properties of analysis as applied in the political process tend to *inhibit* the successful promulgation of political initiatives.[15] In part this property of analysis stems from the inherent vulner-

---

[13] John Kingdon, *Congressmen's Voting Decisions* (New York: Harper and Row, 1973).

[14] Even on less tractable, high conflict issues *negative sanctions* on analysts and their product can serve to limit unjustifiable analytical claims. In the 1977–1978 gas deregulation debates, for instance, President Carter's staff analysis was repudiated and (more importantly) ignored because their assumed price estimates were incorrect. See chapter 6.

[15] This idea is developed in slightly different form in Hank Jenkins-Smith and David L. Weimer, "Analysis as Retrograde Action: The Case of Strategic Petroleum Reserves," in *Public Administration Review*, 45(4) (July/August 1985), pp. 485–494.

ability of analysis—and of quantitative analysis in particular—to critique. Analysis by definition requires abstraction and simplification of complex real-world phenomena. Typically, too, theories are not fully developed, and data is incomplete or absent. Therefore it is always possible for critics to contend that the theory, the model, the technique, or the data are flawed and thereby fault the analytical conclusions. Another reason for the systematic effect of analysis stems from the nature of the political process. American politics is characterized by innumerable veto points and successive fora for analytical debate. At each step, opportunity exists for opponents to challenge a political initiative, to criticize analysis that supports the initiative (because analysis is always vulnerable), and to call for the provision of new analysis to justify the policy.

Various institutional relationships within the political process further enhance the use of analysis to stall or reverse the initiative; the position of oversight agencies, such as OMB and (within departments) policy analysis divisions, provides strategic placement to call for justifying analysis. The role of such agencies and their analysts in reviewing programs and making budget recommendations for the program offices gives them considerable clout in making demands for new or revised analyses.

Of the cases used in this study, the SPR size issue best illustrates the use of analysis to block or delay political initiatives. In that case, even though the initiative to fund construction of a large oil stockpile had received broad political support,[16] analysts from OMB were able to repeatedly delay the commitment of funds through demands for new analysis to justify the policy. In the Alaskan oil export case, the initiatives mounted by DOE in 1981 and 1983 to remove or modify the oil export restrictions in the Export Administration Act (EAA) were successfully blunted by the repeated criticisms and counteranalyses provided by analysts for MarAd.[17] The refinery-policy study found analysis playing that role as well: because the small refiner supports were scheduled to end with oil decontrol, those in favor of continuation of supports were required to press for legislative change. Analysts at DOE mobilized analysis arguing that such changes would be costly and provide no energy-security benefits.[18] Documented cases of the widespread

---

[16] Ibid., and chapter 6.

[17] In that case, passage of the EAA was virtually assured, thus requiring that those in favor of exports make the initiative for change.

[18] One of the chief differences between the natural gas debates and the SPR size study has been the inability of any initiative in the gas issue to achieve the widespread support afforded the large SPR initiative. Thus, the use of analysis to blunt initiatives in the former have been far more diffuse, as various sides to the debate promote analyses that undermine the initiatives of their opponents and support their own. See Michael Malbin, "Congress, Policy Analysis, and Natural Gas Deregulation: A Parable about Fig Leaves," in *Bureaucrats, Policy Analysts, Statesmen: Who Leads?* ed. Robert Goldwin (Washington, DC: American Enterprise Institute, 1980), pp. 62–87; and John Weyant, "A Decade of Natural Gas Policy Analyses: Economic Foundations, Political

use of analysis to blunt political initiatives can be found elsewhere in the literature.[19]

For these reasons, it is appropriate to think of the widespread use of analysis as analogous to an institutional bias that inhibits political initiatives. As indicated by cases reviewed here, criticism of, and demand for, supporting analysis can provide an effective means to blunt or reverse political initiatives. In playing that role analysis may complement the ranks of institutional arrangements created explicitly for that purpose. The establishment of stringent standards and procedures for review of regulatory policies under the Carter and Reagan administrations were deliberate attempts by those administrations to create an institutional bias *against* the creation of unjustifiably costly new programs.[20] The creation of the OMB itself, as an institutional guardian of the public purse, was in part an effort to force the justification of particular initiatives in view of overall budget priorities. Thus, one of the systematic effects of policy analysis is to reinforce existing institutional biases toward restraint in adoption of new programs.[21]

Such restraint is a two-edged sword, however. Analysis as an inhibitor of political initiatives is indiscriminate with respect to inhibiting policy initiatives that *expand* government programs and regulations and those that *contract* them. The use of analysis by MarAd to undermine efforts to lift the Alaskan oil export ban, for example, was a case in which persistent criticism of analysis was used to torpedo removal of government regulations. Thus, those who see analysis as a tool for the diminution of government action are likely to be disappointed.[22] In effect, the bias implicit in such tactical uses of analysis—

Orientations and Organizational Designs" (Discussion paper, Energy Modelling Forum, Stanford University, Palo Alto, CA, September 1983).

[19] See, for example, Eugene Bardach and Lucian Pugliaresi, "The Environmental Impact Statement vs. the Real World," *The Public Interest,* vol. 49, (Fall 1977), pp. 22–38. Also see the discussion of analysis as a purveyor of the "nothing works" refrain, deferring social welfare initiatives, in Martin Rein and Sheldon White, "Policy Research: Belief and Doubt," *Policy Analysis,* 3(2) (Spring 1977), pp. 239–271.

[20] See James C. Miller, III, and Bruce Yandle, eds., *Benefit–Cost Analysis of Social Regulation* (Washington, DC: American Enterprise Institute, 1979); Susan Tolchin, "Presidential Power and the Politics of RARG," *Regulation,* 3(4) (July/August 1979), pp. 44–49; and George Eads, "Harnessing Regulation: Evolving White House Oversight," *Regulation,* 5(3) (May/June 1981), pp. 19–26.

[21] Mark Moore of the Kennedy School of Government contends that policy analysis will have a restraining influence for yet another reason: the rules of social science evidence are themselves conservative and will therefore militate against the proliferation of unwarranted policy initiatives. See his "Statesmanship in a World of Particular Substantive Choices," in *Bureaucrats, Policy Analysts, Statesmen: Who Leads?* ed. Robert Goldwin (Washington, DC: American Enterprise Institute, 1980), pp. 20–36.

[22] Mark Moore argues that analysis will serve to restrain government action, ibid.

much like that of the plethora of veto points sprinkled throughout the political system—is toward maintenance of the status quo.

Overall, then, analysis may well have a cumulative, encumbering effect on the political process. Though the tendency of analytical debate to generate uncertainty on more intractable issues appears to be self-limiting because it becomes an obvious tactic to decision makers, the aggregate effect of analysis appears to have been to provide political actors with yet another tool to block, delay, or reverse the political initiatives they oppose. Such a result is somewhat ironic in light of the reformist tradition from which the policy analysis paradigm is derived.[23]

Is democratic politics threatened by the practice of policy analyis? On the whole, the threats anticipated by the critics of analysis have not been realized. Analysis has been *transformed* as it has been integrated into the political process and dispersed among its halls and denizens. Except perhaps in rare instances, it has not been applied as prescribed by the policy analysis paradigm. Rarely does policy analysis acquire significant independent influence in the shaping of public policy although, on occasion, it can alter the beliefs of policy makers. Furthermore, the interactive and often iterative process of analysis serves to limit unbridled distortion of the expression of values and beliefs on the part of any particular analyst.

Rather than indict policy analysis generally, the criticisms of policy analysis hold greatest force when applied to the use of analysis in specific contexts. When the forum is open, and many sides have cause and resources to mobilize analysis, the threats to the democratic process are slight; it is when applied in less visible and less open fora, and particularly when the issue under review is subject to "client politics," that advocacy analysis may do most to distort policy and mislead decision makers. The critics of undue influence and distortion would do well to concentrate their concern on these areas.

The most general effect of analysis appears to be its surprising tendency to inhibit political initiatives, thereby reinforcing the policy status quo. Critics who feared that the mobilization of analysis would lead to radical change in policy and in political institutions should be reassured. If anything, the provision of another tool with which to resist political initiatives serves to *reinforce* the decanting and slowing of political power that for liberal democrats is so essential. Participatory democrats, on the other hand, will find little to celebrate; though policy analysis poses little threat to direct decision makers, its tendency to inhibit change on larger issues may reduce the ease

---

[23] See chapter 2, and Robert Nelson, "The Economics Profession and the Making of Public Policy," *Journal of Economic Literature,* vol. 25, (March 1987), pp. 42–84.

with which popular expression can work its way through the policy process to new policy.

In sum, the diffusion of policy analysis throughout the political process has not wrought fundamental political change. Despite the high hopes of the advocates of the policy analysis paradigm, and the dire fears of the critics, analysis has been diluted and transformed through application to impart only modest, incremental change in the patterns of politics.

———— 7.2 ————
DOES DEMOCRACY THREATEN ANALYSIS?

Politics has proved resilient, and it is policy analysis that has had to adapt. Has analysis sold its soul in the process? Some of the critics of analysis have held that policy analysts will be mere handmaidens to the politically powerful, legitimizers of predetermined choices. Others, more sympathetic with the aims of policy analysis, have worried that analysis is ineffectual, more often ignored than abused in the political process. Have these claims been borne out?

As was true of several of the apparent threats of analysis, the validity of these concerns depends in large part on the context in which analysis is applied. Analysis is most likely to serve primarily as a political resource when the issue under review is subject to higher levels of conflict. In such instances, the application of analysis bears directly on beliefs and values of core concern to subsystem participants. For that reason, these participants will be loathe to consider the findings of analysis unless those findings corroborate their previously held beliefs and values. From the perspective of the individual analyst, a context of this kind is one in which the client or clients (and perhaps the analyst as well) are committed to a predetermined policy option and are likely to demand analysis that serves as ammunition in the political debate.

Further enhancing the use of analysis as a political resource would be the review of a highly intractable policy issue. The more intractable the issue, the greater latitude the individual analyst has in shading analysis one way or another without moving beyond the pale of analytical plausibility. In the 1977–1978 natural gas debates, for example, the intractability of the supply-response question allowed analysts on all sides of the debate to pick analytical assumptions that best served their preferred position. Likewise, the uncertainty about future oil tanker rates allowed MarAd analysts to repeatedly revise estimated rates in a direction that reduced the attractiveness of an initiative they sought to reverse—the export of Alaskan crude oil.

The forum in which the issue is debated will also affect the propensity to employ analysis as a political resource. When contentious issues are reviewed in an open forum, the wide array of participants, with varying professional training and levels of analytical sophistication, reduces the likelihood of finding shared bases for verification of analytical claims. This was evident in the refinery-policy case, in which economists, operations researchers, and other "pure analysts" were written off as "naive." The 1977–1978 natural gas deregulation debates also demonstrated the lack of such common bases.

Closed fora, in which decision makers restrict access to the debate, have a less clear-cut relation to use of analysis as a political resource. Clients sometimes erect closed fora, with screening based on ideology or policy preference, in order to obtain compliant analysis.[24] But such fora can also be erected with the intent to widely survey possible policy options without public exposure or to permit use of sensitive national security data. For these reasons, the relationship between closed fora and the prospects for contribution by analysis is indeterminate.

Thus, it is in analytical debates characterized by high levels of conflict, over analytically intractable issues, and in open fora that analysis is most likely to be employed primarily as a political resource. The expectation that analysis will provide neutral and independently influential policy advice in contexts of this sort is likely to be met with frequent disappointment.

Fortunately, not all policy contexts are of this kind. Under the right circumstances, analysis can significantly modify the policy-relevant beliefs of policy elites, and the content of analysis can be narrowly constrained by prevailing theory and data within professional circles. Of particular importance is that the issue be subject to moderate levels of conflict, sufficient to encourage the mobilization of the necessary analytical resources, yet not sufficient to lead policy elites to refuse to consider analytical findings that depart from their preconceptions.

Also of importance, the more analytically tractable issues restrict the range of plausible analytical claims. The old-gas-supply issue provides good illustration: the issue was rendered relatively tractable by the accumulation of theory, data, and (above all) experience with the price–quantity relationship of the particular gas categories, and the moderate conflict over the issue (because those threatened by the claim were able to rely on other, less-assailable reasons to justify continued opposition to decontrol) permitted widespread adjustment of beliefs to accomodate the new findings.

Professionalized fora, in which participants to the debate are screened by virtue of professional training or technical competence, also contribute to restriction of the use of analysis as a political resource. The available literature on such fora suggests that, in combination with an analytically tractable issue,

---

[24] See chapter 4, section 4.3.

the professionalized forum may be able to obtain consensual adjustment of policy-relevant beliefs even in the face of high levels of conflict.[25]

In sum, in a policy context of moderate conflict, on analytically tractable issues, and in fora approximating the professionalized forum, policy analysis can be expected to make a substantial contribution to the ways that policy elites perceive policy issues and options. Of course, most policy contexts are neither of this kind—completely hospitable to the provision of analysis—nor of the kind wholly conducive to the use of analysis as a political resource, but rather, will fall somewhere between these extremes.

_____ 7.3 _____

IMPLICATIONS

What are the implications of this view of the practice of analysis for practitioners? First and foremost, it is a mistake to view analysis as a discrete act, in which a problem is analyzed, options reviewed, and advice given. Viewed in abstraction from the *process* of policy analysis, "success" or "failure" of analysis is too often seen as wholly contingent on the technical perfection of its content and whether clients accept or reject the conclusions of the analysis. Such a view may well fail to recognize that a particular analysis is more often one part of a many-sided, ongoing exchange about the way issues should be perceived, what values are affected and how, and what policy options merit consideration by policy elites. Such a view may also fail to recognize that what counts as the success of a particular analysis must be at least partly contingent on the policy context; to expect a scrupulously objective, technically precise analysis to make a substantive dent in a highly conflictual, intractable policy debate is to ask for disappointment and frustration.[26] On the other hand, to write a partial, even adversarial, analysis that makes the case for an important but neglected policy perspective can be a significant corrective when the debate is conducted in a closed forum.

A further implication of the view of the process of analysis developed here is that practitioners can learn under what circumstances to expect more from analytical effort.[27] Analysts frequently have considerable discretion over how

---

[25] See Richard Barke, "Technological Change and Regulatory Adjustment: The FCC and Technical Standard Setting" (Paper delivered at the meetings of the Association for Policy Analysis and Management, New Orleans, October 1984).

[26] Arnold Meltsner quotes one analyst, an objective technician who was frustrated by the reception of his work at the Office of Equal Opportunity (OEO) as saying: "that's what drove me out of OEO; the leadership simply didn't understand the proper role of evaluation." *Policy Analysts in the Bureaucracy* (Berkeley, CA: University of California Press, 1976), p. 23.

[27] See H. Theodore Heintz and Hank Jenkins-Smith, "Advocacy Coalitions and the Practice of Policy Analysis," *Policy Sciences*, vol. 21, nos. 2–3, (1988) pp. 263–277, for a more extended discussion of these issues.

they address the issues or over how they allocate their efforts over the subelements of a given issue. If the objective is to change perceptions on policy issues or to generate consensus, the analysts would do well to avoid expending resources directly on problems mired in fixed, highly conflictual, and intractable issues. A good strategy is to pick a subelement of that issue that, being out of the direct line of fire of clashing interests, may permit some consensual learning. The focus of the Shell analysts on a *subset* of gas reserves—old gas categories—rather than on the overall question of the expected market price for gas under decontrol permitted the addition of significant and widely accepted new data that were directly relevant to the policy question. To pick a contrary example, in the next round of the oil export debate (for there is sure to be a next round) a direct focus on the likely effect of exports on federal tax receipts is unlikely to bear fruit.[28] Thus, attention to the context of analysis would not only forewarn the analyst of when analytical effort is unlikely to be successful, but it can provide a guide to more effective allocation of that effort as well.

—————— 7.4 ——————
ANALYSTS AS DEMOCRATIC CITIZENS: A PRUDENTIAL STYLE OF POLICY ANALYSIS

More broadly still, the view of analysis as a process speaks directly—though not comfortingly—to the question of which of the various styles of analysis is most appropriate for practitioners. As described in chapter 4, three dominant styles of policy analysis are offered up in the policy analysis literature as appropriate guides for professional behavior. The *objective technician* is to provide neutral, objective analysis—along the lines specified in the policy paradigm—and then retire from the field. Advocacy is not the objective technician's game. The *issue advocate,* on the other hand, does not object to joining into the political fray and will use analysis to pursue some conception of the good cause. It is probably the case that most issue advocates, by dint of training in the fundamentals of policy analysis, are efficiency advocates. The *clients' advocate,* in contrast, uses analysis to make the best case for the clients' preferred policy option.

As described earlier, and as illustrated through the case studies, each of these styles has strengths in particular kinds of policy contexts and fatal weaknesses in others. The objective technician may do well with regard to a low-conflict issue debated in a professionalized forum, but would be utterly

---

[28] A better target might be to perform a more extensive analysis on the effect of changes in the price of Alaskan crude on recoverable oil reserves in the region—an issue that has received only cursory attention in previous analyses.

at sea in an analytical brawl over a high-conflict intractable issue in an open forum. Furthermore, the advocate styles of analysis may be appropriate for analytical debates in which analytical conflict is sufficient to assure that all relevant viewpoints are represented, but they may actually undermine the credibility of analysis when employed in contexts of less (or uneven) conflict. There is an inescapable and uncomfortable tension here: none of the styles of analysis is adequate in and of itself, and yet, applied indiscriminately, the various styles of analysis could well debilitate one another.

A primary concern of this study has been to develop and employ a conceptual framework that allows an observer to distinguish among the various policy contexts, and to anticipate the probable efficacy of the various styles of analysis within those contexts. Arming analysts with such a framework provides a partial resolution to the tension between roles and context: prudent analysts can tailor the practice of analysis to the policy context.

Tailoring analytical practice to context would not be easy. Difficulty may arise over which context actually prevails; the bulk of the analytical contexts fall somewhere between extremes on dimensions of analytical conflict, tractability, and types of fora. Different analysts could quite conceivably perceive these factors differently and therefore adopt and apply incompatible styles of analysis in the same analytical debate. Alternatively, the context may change as the analytical debate wears on, forcing periodic reassessment of the appropriateness of the various analytical styles. It is nonetheless highly likely that most analysts could, particularly in the more extreme cases, discern the major characteristics of the analytical forum. Furthermore, as illustrated in the case studies and chapter 5 in particular, analysts do *as a matter of course* modify their perceptions of the policy context through experience and adjust their styles of analysis accordingly. It was *after* confronting advocacy for the maritime interests on the part of the MarAd analysts that the DOE analyst raised more uncertain issues that would tug the analysis results back in the other direction. And it was *after* repeated experience with OMB analysts doggedly pursuing analytical results that would show a large SPR to be unjustified that analysts from DOE dug in their heels and extracted a concession that permitted them to use their own, superior analytical approach. Thus analysts can and do adjust their roles to context in light of experience. The problem is to determine what the appropriate style would be in a given context.

In my view, the three styles of analysis best correspond to three extremes in the policy context. In combination, flexibly adapted to context, I call them the *prudential style of policy analysis.* In a context in which the issue draws little analytical conflict, when the forum is closed or not widely visible and approximates a professionalized forum, participants should tend toward the objective technician style of analysis. Because of low levels of conflict, participants cannot count on the interests of those aggrieved to readily correct for analysis that neglects or overemphasizes particular dimensions of value or beliefs. Furthermore, the closed or low-profile forum may serve to screen participants that may otherwise have added important dimensions and interests to the debate. The technicians' penchant for comprehensive, neutral analysis, though unlikely to be fully realized in practice,[29] will serve to minimize potential for such distortions.

Sometimes, however, the closed or low-visibility forum will already have a distinctive pattern of expressed interests represented in analysis; analysis may reflect the existence of client politics in which a small group of directly affected beneficiaries have incentives to join the debate while the larger, more diffuse population of those bearing the costs do not. Objective analysis, neutrally applied, could be expected to be folded together with analysis advocating the positions of particular interests, resulting in skewed *aggregate* analysis. In such instances, the issue advocate role is called for, stressing the *costs* of the policy to the broader population.

The issue advocate role is appropriate as well in high conflict debates waged in open fora. In those instances, a variety of interests to the debate can be expected to be well represented by analysis. Because this multiplicity of interests is mobilized, each hammering home its grievances, rights, and expectations, the prudential analyst could well assume the role of partisan efficiency advocate without concern that the structure of values represented to policy elites is unduly distorted.[30]

The practicability of the role of partisan efficiency advocate will often be contingent, of course, on the analyst being subject to only modest levels of organizational allegiance, or working with an uncommitted (or like-minded) client. Because the latter cannot be counted on in high-conflict policy issues, analysts who are subject to significant organizational allegiance may well have to adopt the role of clients' advocate. For high-conflict issues debated in open fora, such a result is not altogether harmful. The tendency of the analytic contribution to such policy contexts to be pluralistic in character would serve to ameliorate advocacy for any particular partisan or position in the aggregate analysis produced. It is well for the analyst to remember, too, that publicly elected or appointed elites have at least an indirect legitimacy in the positions they take by virtue of representative electoral politics. Finally, service of the clients' interests, consonant with the prevailing analytical tractability of the issue at hand, may be necessary in order to maintain the clients' sympathetic ear on other issues. For these reasons, the prudential analyst will on occasion—though with some discomfort—assume the role of client's advocate.

Demands for service of the client's interest may become unreasonable, however. In particular, the demand that analysis be shaded in the client's

---

[29] See section 3.1, chapter 3.

[30] See section 3.2, chapter 3.

interest to a degree that departs from prevailing analytic consensus on the question cannot be met in good conscience.[31] In those instances, should the exercise of voice not modify the demand, the analyst may be compelled to employ exit.[32]

The application of the range of styles of analysis—knowing when each is appropriate and what are their limits—would require considerable judgment on the part of the analyst. As is true of other professions, such choices can be hard choices. Nonetheless, such a prudential style of analysis is practical as a general guide for the roles adopted by analysts within the contingencies of the highly variable policy context. Analysis as a process has had to adapt to that context; I believe that the prudential style of policy analysis offers the best prospect for a *reasoned* adaptation of the professional role of the policy analyst, and one that facilitates the realization of some of the promise of the policy analysis paradigm consonant with the norms of democratic politics.

---

[31] One analyst, Jerry Blankenship, director of the Office of Energy Security at DOE, employed a particularly creative and effective strategy when confronted with a situation of this sort. When in late 1982 the energy secretary's office requested analysis that would show that a large SPR was no longer necessary because of changed world circumstances, Blankenship balked. First he submitted analysis showing that, even under then current circumstances, the SPR appeared justified when a reasonable set of assumptions regarding oil prices and probabilities of future oil market states were employed. The secretary's office again demanded analysis that would justify a reduced SPR. Finally, Blankenship prepared an analysis that assembled the alternative collections of assumptions *that would need to be made* to justify that position. Such assumptions were necessarily extreme; in particular, the assumption of very small probabilities of the occurrence of future oil supply disruptions was required. The analysis was careful *not* to endorse those assumptions; it merely pointed out that they were necessary to justify the secretary's position. In effect, the analysis told the secretary that such a set of assumptions were implausible given the prevailing analytical consensus on the issue. After that, demands for such analysis ceased and, for a while at least, the secretary continued to officially support the large SPR.

[32] David L. Weimer and Aidan R. Vining also discuss the option of "disloyalty," that is, leaking information disfavorable to one's client to the press. See their *Policy Analysis: Concepts and Practice* (Englewood Cliffs, NJ: Prentice-Hall, 1989), chapter 2.

REFERENCES

AARON, HENRY. *Politics and the Professors: The Great Society in Perspective.* Washington, DC: Brookings Institute, 1978.

ACHEN, CHRISTOPHER. "Mass Political Attitudes and the Survey Response." *American Political Science Review*, vol. 69, no. 3 (Fall 1975), pp. 1218–1231.

ALEXANDER, TOM. "Day of Reckoning for Oil Refiners," *Fortune*, January 12, 1981, pp. 38–41.

ALTENSTETTER, CRISTA, AND BJORKMAN, R. "A Longitudinal Study of Health Care Policy in Several American States." Paper presented at the Annual Meeting of the American Political Science Association, Chicago, September 1976.

AMERICAN PETROLEUM REFINERS ASSOCIATION. *APRA Tax Proposals.* Washington, DC: American Petroleum Refiners Association, July 1980.

APPLEBY, PAUL. *Policy and Administration.* University, AL: University of Alabama Press, 1949.

ARCHIBALD, K. A. "Three Views of the Experts' Role in Policymaking: Systems Analysis, Incrementalism, and the Clinical Approach," *Policy Sciences*, vol. 1 (Spring 1970), pp. 73–86.

ARROW, KENNETH. "The Organization of Economic Activity: Issues Pertinent to the Choice of Market Versus Nonmarket Allocation." *Public Expenditure and Policy Analysis.* 2d ed. Edited by Robert H. Haveman and Julius Margolis. Chicago: Rand McNally, 1977.

ARROW, KENNETH. *Social Choice and Individual Value.* 2d ed. New Haven, CT: Yale University Press, 1963.

ASHFORD, NICHOLAS. "Advisory Committees in OSHA and EPA: Their Use in Regulatory Decisionmaking." *Science, Technology, and Human Values*, vol. 9, issue 1 (Winter 1984), no. 46, pp. 72–82.

AWH, ROBERT Y. *Microeconomics: Theory and Applications.* New York: John Wiley & Sons, 1976.

AXELROD, ROBERT, editor. *Structure of Decision: The Cognitive Maps of Political Elites.* Princeton, NJ: Princeton University Press, 1976.

BACHRACH, PETER. *The Theory of Democratic Elitism: A Critique.* Boston: Little, Brown, 1967.

BACON, FRANCIS. *New Atlantis,* in *Selected Writings of Francis Bacon.* Edited by Hugh G. Dick. New York: The Modern Library, 1955.

BALAS, EGAN. *The Strategic Petroleum Reserve: How Large Should It Be?* Management Science Research Report No. 436. Pittsburgh, PA: Graduate School of Industrial Administration, Carnegie-Mellon University, June 30, 1979.

BANFIELD, EDWARD. "Policy Science as Metaphysical Madness." *Bureaucrats, Policy Analysts, Statesmen: Who Leads?* Edited by Robert Goldwin. Washington, DC: American Enterprise Institute, 1980.

BARDACH, EUGENE. *The Implementation Game.* Cambridge: MIT, 1977.

BARDACH, EUGENE AND PUGLIARESI, LUCIAN. "The Environmental Impact Statement vs. the Real World." *The Public Interest,* vol. 49 (Fall 1977), pp. 22–38.

BARKE, RICHARD. "Technological Change and Regulatory Adjustment: The FCC and Technical Standard Setting." Paper delivered at the meetings of the Association for Policy Analysis and Management, New Orleans, LA, October 1984.

BARRETT, PAUL M. "Price of Pleasure: New Legal Theorists Attach a Dollar Value to the Joys of Living," *Wall Street Journal,* vol. CXIX, no. 114 (December 12, 1988), p. A-1.

BAUM, HOWELL S. "Analysts and Planners Must Think Organizationally," *Policy Analysis,* vol. 6, no. 4 (Fall 1980), pp. 479–494.

BEHN, ROBERT. "Policy Analysis and Policy Politics." *Policy Analysis,* vol. 7, no. 2 (Spring 1981), pp. 199–226.

BELL, DANIEL. *The End of Ideology.* New York: Free Press, 1960.

BELL, DANIEL, AND KRISTOL, IRVING. *The Public Interest,* vol. 1, no. 1 (1965), pp. 3–5.

BENELLO, C. GEORGE AND ROUSSOPOULOS, DIMITRIOS, editors. *The Case for Participatory Democracy.* New York: Grossman, 1971.

BENTHAM, JEREMY. *Fragment on Government.* In *The Collected Works of Jeremy Bentham.* Edited by J. H. Burns and F. Rosen. New York: Oxford University Press, 1983.

BENTHAM, JEREMY. *Introduction to the Principles of Morals and Legislation.* Edited by Burns, J. H., and Hart, H. L. A. London: Athlone Press, 1970.

BENTHAM, JEREMY. *Works of Jeremy Bentham.* Edinburgh: Tait, 1843.

BENVENISTE, GUY. *The Politics of Expertise.* Berkeley, CA: Glendessary Press, 1972.

BERMAN, LARRY. *The Office of Management and Budget and the Presidency 1921–1979.* Princeton, NJ: Princeton University Press, 1979.

BERNSTEIN, MARVER. *Regulating Business By Independent Commission.* Princeton, NJ: Princeton University Press, 1955.

BERRY, BRIAN. *The Liberal Theory of Justice.* Oxford: Clarendon Press, 1973.

BLUHM, WILLIAM T. "Liberalism as the Aggregation of Individual Preferences: Problems of Coherence and Rationality in Social Choice." Paper presented at the Conference on the Crisis of Liberal Democracy, SUNY—Geneseo, NY, October 1983.

BLUHM, WILLIAM T. *Theories of the Political System.* Englewood Cliffs, NJ: Prentice-Hall, 1973.

BOGART, LEO. "No Opinion, Don't Know, Maybe, No Answer." *Public Opinion Quarterly,* vol. 31 (Fall 1967), pp. 332–345.

BOHI, DOUGLAS, AND MONTGOMERY, DAVID. *Oil Prices, Energy Security, and Import Policy.* Washington, DC: Resources for the Future, 1982.

BOORSTIN, DANIEL. *The Republic of Technology.* New York: Harper and Row, 1978.

BRECHT, ARNOLD. *Political Theory: The Foundations of Twentieth Century Political Thought.* Princeton, NJ: Princeton University Press, 1959.

BREWER, GARRY. *Politicians, Bureaucrats, and the Consultant.* New York: Basic Books, 1973.

BREWER, GARRY, AND PETER DELEON. *The Foundations of Policy Analysis.* Pacific Grove, CA: Brooks/Cole, 1983.

BRICKMAN, RONALD. "Science and the Politics of Toxic Chemical Regulation: U.S. and European Contrasts." *Science, Technology, and Human Values,* vol. 9, issue 1 (Winter 1984) no. 46, pp. 107–111.

BROOKS, HARVY. "The Resolution of Technically Intensive Public Policy Disputes." *Science, Technology, and Human Values,* vol. 9, issue 1 (Winter 1984) no. 46, pp. 39–50.

BROWN, ANTHONY, AND JOSEPH STUART, JR., "Competing Advocacy Coalitions, Policy Evolution, and Airline Deregulation." Unpublished manuscript, 1988.

BROWN, PETER. "Ethics and Education for the Public Service in a Liberal State." *Journal of Policy Analysis and Management,* vol. 6, no. 1 (Fall 1986), pp. 56–68.

BURNS, J. H., AND ROSEN, F., editors. *The Collected Works of Jeremy Bentham.* New York: Oxford University Press, 1983.

BUTLER, GERARD; CALTER, JOHN; AND IPPOLITO, PAULINE. "Defending Cost–Benefit Analysis," *Regulation,* vol. 5, no. 2 (March/April 1981), pp. 41–42.

CALLAHAN, D., AND JENNINGS, B., editors. *Ethics, The Social Sciences and Policy Analysis.* New York: Plenum, 1983.

CLOCK, GREG. "Refining, Petrochemical Construction on Upswing," *Oil and Gas Journal,* 78(20) May 19, 1980, pp. 43–46.

COASE, R. H. "The Problem of Social Cost," *Journal of Law and Economics,* vol. 3 (1960), pp. 1–44.

COHEN, RICHARD E. "Maritime Industry Keeps Afloat in Seas That Are Often Stormy." *National Journal,* September 4, 1976, pp. 1252–1258.

COLEMAN, JAMES S. *Policy Research in the Social Sciences.* Morristown, NJ: General Learning Press, 1972.

Congressional Quarterly Almamac: 92nd Congress, 1973. Washington, DC: Congressional Quarterly, 1973.

Congressional Quarterly Almanac: 96th Congress, 1977. Washington, DC: Congressional Quarterly, 1977.

COOPER, MARK. "Commentary." *The Deregulation of Natural Gas,* edited by Edward J. Mitchell. Washington, DC: American Enterprise Institute, 1983.

COOPER, RICHARD. "A Note on the Deregulation of Natural Gas Prices." *Brookings Paper on Economic Activity,* vol. 2. Washington, DC: Brookings Institute, 1982.

The Costs and Benefits to the U.S. Economy of Additional Gas Resulting From 'Old' Gas Decontrol. Houston, TX: Shell Oil Company, May 1983.

CRANDALL, ROBERT, AND LAVE, LESTER, editors. *The Scientific Basis of Health and Safety Regulation.* Washington, DC: Brookings Institute, 1981.

The Dallas Morning News. "Hodel Sees Risks in Oil Price Slide," December 12, 1984, p. D-1.

DAVIS, OTTO A., AND KAMIEN, MORTON I. "Externalities, Information, and Alternative Collective Action." *Public Expenditure and Policy Analysis.* 2d ed. Edited by Robert H. Haveman and Julius Margolis. Chicago: Rand McNally, 1977.

DERTHICK, MARTHA. *Policymaking for Social Security.* Washington, DC: Brookings Institute, 1979.

DERTHICK, MARTHA, AND PAUL QUIRK, *The Politics of Deregulation.* Washington, DC: Brookings Institute, 1984.

DEWEY, JOHN. *The Public and Its Problems.* Chicago: Swallow Press, 1927.

DICK, HUGH G., editor. *Selected Writings of Francis Bacon.* New York: The Modern Library, 1955.

DOWNS, ANTHONY. *Inside Bureaucracy.* Boston: Little, Brown, 1967.

DOWNS, ANTHONY. "Up and Down with Ecology—The Issue Attention Cycle." *The Public Interest,* vol. 28 (Summer 1972), pp. 38–50.

DREITZEL, HANS. "Social Science and the Problem of Rationality: Notes on the Sociology of Technocrats," *Politics and Society,* vol. 2, no. 2 (Winter 1972), pp. 165–182.

DUMONT, ETIENNE. *Bentham's Theory of Legislation.* Translated by Charles Atkinson. London: Oxford University Press, 1914.

EADS, GEORGE. "Harnessing Regulation: Evolving White House Oversight." *Regulation,* vol. 5, no. 3 (May/June 1981), pp. 19–26.

ECKSTEIN, OTTO. "A Survey of Public Expenditure Criteria." *Public Finances: Needs, Sources, and Utilization.* Universities-National Bureau for Economic Research. Princeton, NJ: Princeton University Press, 1961.

EDGEWORTH, FRANCIS. *Mathematical Psychics.* London: Kegan Paul, 1881.

ELLUL, JACQUES. *The Technological Society.* New York: Vintage Books, 1964.

ENTHOVEN, ALAIN, AND SMITH, WAYNE K. *How Much Is Enough?* New York: Harper and Row, 1971.

FALKSON, JOSEPH. "Minor Skirmish in a Monumental Struggle: HEW's Analysis of Mental Health Services." *Policy Analysis,* vol. 2, no. 1 (Winter 1976), pp. 93–119.

FARLIE, HENRY. "Galloping Toward Dead Center." *The New Republic,* vol. 178, no. 4 (April 8, 1978), pp. 18–21.

FESLER, JAMES. *Public Administration.* Englewood Cliffs, NJ: Prentice-Hall, 1980.

FOSTER, JOHN L. "An Advocate Role Model for Policy Analysis," *Policy Studies Journal,* vol. 8, no. 6 (Summer 1980), pp. 958–964.

FRAATZ, J. M. B. "Policy Analysts as Advocates," *Journal of Policy Analysis and Management,* vol. 1, no. 2 (Winter 1982), pp. 273–276.

FREEMAN, A. MYRICK III. "Project Evaluation and Design with Multiple Objectives." *Public Expenditure and Policy Analysis.* 2d ed. Edited by Robert H. Haveman and Julius Margolis. Chicago: Rand McNally, 1977.

FRIEDMAN, LEE S. "Public Policy Economics: A Survey of Current Pedagogical Practice." *Journal of Policy Analysis and Management,* vol. 6, no. 3 (Spring 1987), pp. 503–520.

FRIEDMAN, MILTON. *Essays in Positive Economics.* Chicago: Chicago University Press, 1953.

FRIES, SYLVIA. "Expertise Against Politics: Technology as Ideology on Capitol Hill." *Science, Technology, and Human Values,* vol. 43 (Spring 1983), pp. 6–15.

FRITSCHLER, A. LEE. *Smoking and Politics.* 3rd ed. Englewood Cliffs, NJ: Prentice-Hall, 1983.

GENDRON, BERNARD. *Technology and the Human Condition.* New York: St. Martins Press, 1977.

GERTH, H. H., AND MILLS, C. WRIGHT, editors and translators. *From Max Weber: Essays in Sociology.* New York: Oxford University Press, 1946.

GOLDSTEIN, DONALD J., editor. *Energy and National Security.* Washington, DC: National Defense University Press, 1981.

GOLDSTEIN, MICHAEL S.; MARCUS, ALFRED; AND RAUSCH, NANCY. "The Nonutilization of Evaluation Research." *Pacific Sociological Review,* vol. 21, no. 1 (January 1978), pp. 21–44.

GOLDWIN, ROBERT, editor. *Bureaucrats, Policy Analysts, Statesmen: Who Leads?* Washington, DC: American Enterprise Institute, 1980.

GOROVITZ, SAMUEL, editor. *Utilitarianism with Critical Essays.* Indianapolis, IN: Bobbs-Merrill, 1977.

GORZ, ANDRE. *A Strategy for Labor.* Boston: Beacon Press, 1964.

GREENBERGER, MARTIN; BREWER, GARRY; HOGAN, WILLIAM; AND RUSSELL, MILTON. *Caught Unawares: The Energy Decade in Retrospect.* Cambridge, MA: Ballinger, 1983.

GREENBERGER, MARTIN; CRENSON, MATTHEW; AND CRISSEY, BRIAN. *Models in the Policy Process.* New York: Russell Sage Foundation, 1976.

GROOSE, S. *Evaluations of the War on Poverty.* Washington, DC: General Accounting Office, 1969.

HALCROW, HAROLD; HEADY, EARL; AND COTNER, MELVIN, editors. *Soil Conservation: Policies, Institutions and Incentives.* Ankeny, IA: Soil Conservation Society of America, 1981.

HALEVY, ELIE. *La Formation du radicalisme philosophique.* Paris: Germer Bailliere, 1901.

HAUSMAN, JERRY A. "Exact Consumers' Surplus and Deadweight Loss." Unpublished manuscript, June 1980.

HAVEMAN, ROBERT H. "Policy Analysis and the Congress: An Economist's View." *Policy Analysis,* vol. 2, no. 1 (Spring 1976), pp. 235–250.

HAVEMAN, ROBERT H., AND MARGOLIS, JULIUS, editors. *Public Expenditure and Policy Analysis.* 3rd ed. Chicago: Rand McNally, 1977.

HAWKESWORTH, M. E. *Theoretical Issues in Policy Analysis.* Albany: SUNY Press, 1988.

HAYEK, FREIDRICH A. *The Constitution of Liberty.* Chicago: University of Chicago Press, 1960.

HAYEK, FREIDRICH A. *Individualism and Economic Order.* Chicago: University of Chicago Press, 1948.

HAYEK, FREIDRICH A. *The Road to Serfdom.* Chicago: University of Chicago Press, 1972.

HAZBERLE, STEVEN. "The Institutionalization of the Subcommittee in the U.S. House of Representatives." *Journal of Politics,* vol. 40, no. 4 (November 1978), pp. 1054–1065.

HECLO, HUGH. "Issue Networks in the Executive Establishment." *The New American Political System.* Edited by Anthony King. Washington, DC: American Enterprise Institute, 1978.

HECLO, HUGH. "OMB and the Presidency—The Problem of Neutral Competence." *The Public Interest,* vol. 38 (Winter 1975), pp. 80–89.

HECLO, HUGH. *Social Policy in Britain and Sweden.* New Haven, CT: Yale University Press, 1974.

HEINTZ, H. THEODORE, AND JENKINS-SMITH, HANK. "Advocacy Coalitions and the Practice of Policy Analysis," *Policy Sciences,* vol. 21, nos. 2–3, (1988), pp. 263–277.

HENDERSON, JAMES M., AND QUANDT, RICHARD E. *Microeconomic Theory.* New York: McGraw-Hill, 1958.

HERBERGER, ALLEN. "Monopoly and Resource Allocation." *American Economic Review,* vol. 54 (May 1954), pp. 77–87.

HESS, F. WILLIAM. "Listening to the City: Citizen Surveys." *Urban Affairs Papers,* vol. 2 (Summer 1980), pp. 1–9.

HICKS, J. R. "The Foundations of Welfare Economics." *The Economic Journal,* vol. 49, no. 196 (December 1939), pp. 696–712.

HICKS, J. R. *A Revision of Demand Theory.* London: Clarendon Press, 1956.

HIGGINS, TERRENCE, AND JENKINS-SMITH, HANK. "Analysis of the Economic Effect of the Alaskan Oil Export Ban." *Journal of Operations Research,* vol. 33, no. 6 (November/December 1985), pp. 1173–1202.

HILDENBRAND, W., AND KIRMAN, A. P. *Introduction to Equilibrium Analysis: Variations on Themes by Edgeworth and Walras.* New York: American Elsevier, 1976.

HIRSCHMAN, ALBERT. *Exit, Voice, and Loyalty.* Cambridge: Harvard University Press, 1970.

HOCHMAN, HAROLD M., AND ROGERS, JAMES D. "Pareto Optimal Redistribution," *American Economic Review,* vol. 59, no. 4 (September 1969), pp. 542–557.

HOLCOMBE, RANDALL. "A Method for Estimating GNP Loss from a Future Oil Embargo." *Policy Sciences,* vol. 8, no. 1 (June 1977), pp. 217–234.

HOOS, IDA. *Systems Analysis and Public Policy: A Critique.* Berkeley, CA: University of California Press, 1972.

HOOS, IDA. "Systems Techniques for Managing Society: A Critique." *Public Administration Review,* vol. 33 (March/April 1973), pp. 157–164.

HOROWITZ, IRVING. "Social Science Mandarins: Policymaking as a Political Formula." *Policy Sciences,* vol. 1 (1970), pp. 339–360.

INTRILIGATOR, MICHAEL. *Mathematical Optimation and Economic Theory.* 2d ed. Englewood Cliffs, NJ: Prentice-Hall, 1971.

JANIS, IRVING. *Groupthink.* Boston: Houghton Mifflin, 1983.

JENKINS-SMITH, HANK. "Analytical Debates and Policy Learning: Analysis and Change in the Federal Bureaucracy." *Policy Sciences,* vol. 21, nos. 2–3 (1988), pp. 169–211.

JENKINS-SMITH, HANK. "Professional Roles for Policy Analysts: A Critical Assessment." *Journal of Policy Analysis and Management,* vol. 2, no. 1 (Fall 1982), pp. 88–100.

JENKINS-SMITH, HANK, AND WEIMER, DAVID L. "Analysis as Retrograde Action: The Case of Strategic Petroleum Reserves." *Public Administration Review,* vol. 45, no. 4 (July/August 1985), pp. 485–494.

JENNRICH, JOHN. "DOE Refinery Policy Draws Fire." *Oil and Gas Journal,* vol. 78, no. 33 (August 18, 1980), pp. 66–70.

JEVONS, STANLEY. *Theory of Political Economy.* 4th ed. London: Macmillan, 1911.

JOHNSON, BRUCE. "From Analyst to Negotiator: The OMB's New Role." *Journal of Policy Analysis and Management,* vol. 3, no. 4 (1984), pp. 501–515.

JOHNSON, JAMES. "Decontrol of Natural Gas at the Wellhead." Unpublished paper. Standard Oil Company of Indiana, June 1981.

"Joint Independent Gas Producers Committee—Consumer Federation of America Analysis of Shell Old Gas Study." Washington, DC, May 16, 1983.

JONES, CHARLES O. "Why Congress Can't Do Policy Analysis (or Words to that Effect)." *Policy Analysis,* vol. 2, no. 2 (Spring 1976), pp. 251–264.

KALT, JOSEPH. *The Economics and Politics of Oil Price Regulation: Federal Policy in the Post-Embargo Era.* Cambridge, MA: MIT Press, 1981.

KAPLAN, NATHAN; MORRISON, ANDREA; AND STAMBAUGH, R. J. *The Use of Social Science Knowledge in Policy Decisions at the National Level.* Ann Arbor, MI: University of Michigan, Institute for Social Research, 1975.

KARIEL, HENRY. *The Promise of Politics.* Englewood Cliffs, NJ: Prentice-Hall, 1966.

KAUFMAN, HERBERT. *Administrative Feedback: Monitoring Subordinate's Behavior.* Washington, DC: Brookings Institute, 1973.

KAUFMAN, HERBERT. "Emerging Conflicts in Democratic Public Administration." *American Political Science Review,* vol. 50, no. 4 (December 1956), pp. 1057–1073.

KELEZO, GENEVIVE. *Program Evaluation: Emerging Issues of Possible Legislative Concern Relating to the Conduct and Use of Evaluation in the Congress and Executive Branch.* Washington, DC: Congressional Research Service, Library of Congress, 1974.

KELMAN, STEVEN. "Cost–Benefit Analysis: An Ethical Critique," *Regulation,* vol. 5, no. 1 (January/February 1981), pp. 34–42.

KEUNNE, ROBERT; HIGGINS, GERALD; MICHAELS, ROBERT; AND SUMMERFIELD, MARY. "A Policy to Protect the U.S. Against Oil Embargoes." *Policy Analysis,* vol. 1, no. 4 (Fall 1975), pp. 571–597.

KING, ANTHONY, editor. *The New American Political System.* Washington, DC: American Enterprise Institute, 1978.

KINGDON, JOHN. *Agendas, Alternatives and Public Policies.* Boston: Little, Brown, 1984.

KINGDON, JOHN. *Congressmen's Voting Decisions.* New York: Harper and Row, 1973.

KLEIN, RUDOLF. "The Rise and Decline of Policy Analysis: The Strange Case of Health Policymaking in Britain." *Policy Analysis,* vol. 2, no. 3 (Summer 1976), pp. 459–475.

KNIGHT, F. H. "Some Fallacies in the Interpretation of Social Cost." *Quarterly Journal of Economics,* vol. 38 (1924), pp. 582–606.

KOURILSKY, MARILYN. "An Adversary Model for Educational Evaluation." *Evaluation Comment,* vol 4, no. 2 (June 1973), pp. 3–6.

KRASNOW, ERWIN, AND LONGLEY, LAWRENCE. *The Politics of Broadcast Regulation.* New York: St. Martins, 1978.

KUHN, THOMAS. *The Structure of Scientific Revolutions.* 2d ed. Chicago: University of Chicago Press, 1970.

LADD, EVERETT. "Question Wording Makes a Difference: German Public Attitudes Toward Deployment." *Public Opinion,* vol. 6, no. 6 (December/January 1984), pp. 38–39.

LAKOTOS, IMRE. "History of Science and its Rational Reconstruction." *Boston Studies in the Philosophy of Science,* no. 8 (1971), pp. 42–134.

LANDAU, MARTIN. "The Proper Domain of Policy Analysis." *American Journal of Political Science,* vol. 21 (May 1977), p. 419.

LASSWELL, HAROLD. "The Policy Orientation." *The Policy Sciences.* Edited by Max Lerner and Harold Lasswell. Palo Alto, CA: Stanford University Press, 1951.

LEFFLER, WILLIAM. *Petroleum Refining for the Non-Technical Person.* Tulsa, OK: Pennwell, 1974.

LEMAN, C. K. "Political Dilemmas in Evaluating and Budgeting Soil Conservation Programs: The RCA Process." *Soil Conservation: Policies, Institutions, and Incentives.* Edited by Harold Halcrow, Earl Heady, and Melvin Cotner. Ankeny, IA: Soil Conservation Society of America, 1982.

LEMAN, C. K. "Some Benefits and Costs of the Proliferation of Analysis in Natural Resource Budgeting." Discussion paper D-101. Washington, DC: Resources for the Future, December 1982.

LEMAN, C. K., AND NELSON, R. H. "Ten Commandments for Policy Economists." *Journal of Policy Analysis and Management,* vol. 1, no. 1 (Fall 1981), pp. 97–117.

LERNER, MAX, AND LASSWELL, HAROLD, editors. *The Policy Sciences.* Palo Alto, CA: Stanford University Press, 1951.

LEVINE, MURRAY. "Scientific Method and the Adversary Model: Some Preliminary Suggestions." *Evaluation Comment,* vol. 4, no. 2 (June 1973), pp. 1–3.

LINDBLOM, CHARLES. *The Policy-Making Process.* Englewood Cliffs, NJ: Prentice-Hall, 1968.

LINDBLOM, CHARLES. "The Science of Muddling Through." *Public Administration Review,* vol. 19, no. 2 (Spring 1959), pp. 79–88.

LINDBLOM, CHARLES, AND BAYBROOKE, DAVID. *A Strategy of Decision.* New York: Free Press, 1963.

LINDBLOM, CHARLES, AND COHEN, DAVID. *Usable Knowledge.* New Haven, CT: Yale University Press, 1979.

LITTLE, I. M. D. *A Critique of Welfare Economics.* London: Clarendon Press, 1957.

LONG, DAVID; MALLAR, CHARLES; AND THORNTON, CRAIG. "Evaluating the Benefits and Costs of the Job Corps." *Journal of Policy Analysis and Management,* vol. 1, no. 1 (Fall 1981), pp. 55–56.

LYNN, LAURENCE, editor. *Knowledge and Policy: The Uncertain Connection.* Washington, DC: The National Research Council, 1978.

MACRAE, DUNCAN, JR. "Policy Analysis as an Applied Social Science Discipline." *Administration and Society,* vol. 6, no. 4 (February 1975), pp. 363–388.

MACRAE, DUNCAN, JR., AND DALE WHITTINGTON. "Assessing Preferences in Cost–Benefit Analysis: Reflections on Rural Water Supply Evaluations in Haiti." *Journal of Policy Analysis and Management,* vol. 7, no. 2 (Winter 1988), pp. 246–263

MACRAE, DUNCAN, JR., AND DALE WHITTINGTON. "The Issue of Standing in Cost–Benefit Analysis." *Journal of Policy Analysis and Management,* vol. 5, no. 4 (Summer 1986), pp. 665–682.

MADISON, CHRISTOPHER. "The Minors Fear for Their Lives When Federal Controls are Gone," *National Journal,* July 19, 1980, pp. 1172–1176.

MADISON, JAMES. *Federalist No. 10,* in *The Federalist Papers.* Alexander Hamilton, James Madison, and John Jay. New York: New American Library, 1961.

MAJONE, GIANDOMENICO. "Policies as Theories," *Omega,* no. 8 (1980), pp. 151–162.

MALBIN, MICHAEL. "Congress, Policy Analysis, and Natural Gas Regulation: A Parable About Fig Leaves." *Bureaucrats, Policy Analysts, Statesmen: Who Leads?* Edited by Robert Goldwin. Washington, DC: American Enterprise Institute, 1980.

MALBIN, MICHAEL. *Unelected Representatives: Congressional Staff and the Future of Representative Government.* New York: Basic Books, 1980.

MANNHEIM, KARL. *Man and Society in an Age of Reconstruction.* London: Paul, Trench, Trubner, 1940.

MARANISS, DAVID. "Competing Interests Snarl Gas Debate," *Washington Post.* June 6, 1983, p. A-14.

MARCUSE, HERBERT. *One Dimensional Man.* Boston: Beacon Press, 1964.

MARGOLIS, HOWARD. *Technical Advice on Policy Issues.* Newbury Park, CA: Sage, 1973.

MARGOLIS, JULIUS. "Shadow Prices for Incorrect or Nonexistent Market Values." *Public Expenditure and Policy Analysis.* 2d ed. Edited by Robert H. Haveman and Julius Margolis. Chicago: Rand McNally, 1977.

MARSHALL, ALFRED. *Principles of Economics.* London: Macmillan, 1890.

MARVER, JAMES. *Consultants Can Help: The Use of Outside Experts in the U.S. Office of Child Development.* Lexington, MA: Lexington Books, 1979.

MATTHEWS, C. S. *Increase in United States "Old Gas" Reserves Due to Deregulation.* Houston, TX: Shell Oil Company, April 1983.

MCKEAN, ROLAND. "The Unseen Hand in Government." *American Economic Review,* vol. 55 (June 1965), pp. 496–505.

MELTSNER, ARNOLD. *Policy Analysts in the Bureaucracy.* Berkeley, CA: University of California Press, 1976.

MENGER, CARL. *Grundsatze der Volkswirtschaftslehre.* Vienna: Braumuller, 1871.

MEYNAUD, JEAN. *Technocracy.* Translated by Paul Barns. New York: The Free Press, 1969.

MILL, J. S. *Utilitarianism,* in *Utilitarianism, Liberty, and Representative Government.* New York: E. P. Dutton, 1951.

MILLER, JAMES C., III, AND YANDLE, BRUCE, editors. *Benefit–Cost Analysis of Social Regulation.* Washington, DC: American Enterprise Institute, 1979.

MISHAN, E. J. *Cost–Benefit Analysis.* 3rd ed. Boston: George, Allen and Unwin, 1982.

MITCHELL, EDWARD, editor. *The Deregulation of Natural Gas.* Washington, DC: American Enterprise Institute, 1983.

Monthly Energy Review. Washington, DC: Energy Information Agency, U.S. Department of Energy, May 1984.

MOORE, MARK. "Statesmanship in a World of Particular Substantive Choices." *Bureaucrats, Policy Analysts, Statesmen: Who Leads?* Edited by Robert Goldwin. Washington, DC: American Enterprise Institute, 1980.

MOSHER, FREDERICK. *Democracy and the Public Service.* New York: Oxford Press, 1968.

MUSGRAVE, RICHARD. *The Theory of Public Finance.* New York: McGraw-Hill, 1959.

NACHMIAS, DAVID. *Public Policy Evaluation: Approaches and Methods.* New York: St. Martins Press, 1979.

NELSON, RICHARD. *The Moon and the Ghetto.* New York: W. W. Norton, 1977.

NELSON, ROBERT. "The Economics Profession and the Making of Public Policy." *Journal of Economic Literature,* vol. 25 (March 1987), pp. 42–84.

NEUSTADT, RICHARD, AND FINEBERG, HARVEY. *The Swine Flu Affair.* Washington, DC: U.S. Department of Health, Education and Welfare, 1978.

NIEMAN, MAX. "The Ambiguous Role of Policy Analysis and an Illustrative Look at Housing Policy." Paper presented at the annual meeting of the Western Political Science Association, Sacramento, CA, April 1984.

NISBIT, ROBERT. "Defending Cost–Benefit Analysis." *Regulation,* vol. 5, no. 2 (March/April 1981), pp. 42–43.

NISKANEN, WILLIAM. "Bureaucrats and Politicians." *Journal of Law and Economics,* vol. 18, no. 3 (December 1975), pp. 617–643.

NOLL, ROGER G. *Reforming Regulation: An Evaluation of the Ash Council Proposals.* Washington, DC: Brookings Institute, 1971.

NOZICK, ROBERT. *Anarchy, State and Utopia.* New York: Basic Books, 1974.

Oil and Gas Journal. "North Slope Oil: A Bargain for Lower 48 Refiners," vol. 78, no. 16 (April 21, 1980), p. 28.

OKUN, ARTHUR. *Equality and Efficiency: The Big Tradeoff*. Washington, DC: Brookings Institute, 1975.

OLSON, MANCUR. *The Logic of Collective Action*. Cambridge, MA: Harvard University Press, 1965.

ORNSTEIN, NORMAN. "Causes and Consequences of Congressional Change: Subcommittee Reform in the House of Representatives, 1970–1973." *Congress in Change: Evolution and Reform*. Edited by Norman Ornstein. New York: Praeger, 1975.

ORNSTEIN, NORMAN, editor. *Congress in Change: Evolution and Reform*. New York: Praeger, 1975.

OSER, JACOB, AND BLANCHFIELD, WILLIAM C. *The Evolution of Economic Thought*. 3rd ed. New York: Harcourt, Brace, Jovanovich, 1975.

PARETO, VILFREDO. *Manuale di economia politica*. Milan: Piccola Biblioteca Scientifica, 1919.

PARIS, DAVID, AND REYNOLDS, JAMES. *The Logic of Policy Inquiry*. New York: Longman, 1983.

PATEMAN, CAROLE. *Participation and Democratic Theory*. Cambridge: Cambridge University Press, 1970.

PECHMAN, JOSEPH A., AND TIMPANE, P. MICHAEL, editors. *Work Incentives and Income Guarantees: The New Jersey Negative Income Tax Experiment*. Washington, DC: Brookings Institute, 1975.

PELTZMAN, SAM. "Toward a More General Theory of Regulation," *Journal of Law and Economics*, vol. 19, no. 2 (August 1976), pp. 211–240.

Petroleum Intelligence Weekly. "Alaskan Oil Earning Tidy Profit," vol. 20, no. 11 (March 16, 1981), pp. 3–4.

PHILLIPS, D. C. "When Evaluators Disagree: Perplexities and Perspectives," *Policy Sciences*, vol. 8 (1977), pp. 147–159.

PLETT, ROBERT AND ASSOCIATES. *Analytical History of the Entitlements Program*. Washington, DC: DOE/RG/10572-1, 1982.

RAWLS, JOHN. *A Theory of Justice*. Cambridge, MA: Harvard University Press, 1971.

REDFORD, EMMETTE. *Democracy in the Administrative State*. New York: Oxford University Press, 1969.

REIN, MARTIN, AND WHITE, SHELDON. "Can Policy Research Help Policy?" *The Public Interest*, vol. 49 (Fall 1977), pp. 119–136.

REIN, MARTIN, AND WHITE, SHELDON. "Policy Research: Belief and Doubt." *Policy Analysis*, vol. 3, no. 2 (Spring 1977), pp. 239–271.

RHOAD, STEVEN. *The Economist's View of the World*, New York: Cambridge University Press, 1985.

RIKER, WILLIAM H. "The Heresthetics of Constitution-Making: The Presidency of 1787, with Comments on Determinism and Rational Choice." *American Political Science Review*, vol. 78, no. 1 (March 1984), pp. 1–16.

RIKER, WILLIAM H. *Liberalism Against Populism*. San Francisco: Freeman, 1982.

RIKER, WILLIAM H., AND ORDESHOOK, PETER C. *An Introduction to Positive Political Theory*. Englewood Cliffs, NJ: Prentice-Hall, 1973.

RIVLIN, ALICE. *Systematic Thinking for Social Action.* Washington, DC: Brookings Institute, 1971.

ROBINSON, JOHN B. "Apples and Horned Toads: on the Framework-Determined Nature of the Energy Debate." *Policy Sciences,* vol. 15 (1982), pp. 23–45.

ROWAN, HENRY. "The Role of Cost–Benefit Analysis in Policymaking." *Public Expenditure and Policy Analysis.* 2d ed. Edited by Robert H. Haveman and Julius Margolis. Chicago: Rand McNally, 1977.

RULE, JAMES B. "The Problem with Social Problems." *Politics and Society,* vol. 2, no. 2 (Fall 1971), pp. 47–56.

RUSHEFSKY, MARK. "The Misuse of Science in Governmental Decision Making," *Science, Technology, and Human Values,* vol. 9, issue 3 (Summer 1984) no. 48, pp. 47–59.

SABATIER, PAUL. "An Advocacy Coalition Framework of Policy Change and the Role of Policy-Oriented Learning Therein," *Policy Sciences,* vol. 21, nos. 2–3 (1988), pp. 129–168.

SABATIER, PAUL, AND HANK JENKINS-SMITH, editors. "Policy Change and Policy-Oriented Learning: Exploring an Advocacy Coalition Framework." *Policy Sciences,* vol. 21, nos. 2–3 (1988).

SAINT-SIMON, HENRI DE. *Social Organization, the Science of Man and Other Writings.* Edited and Translated by Felix Markham. New York: Harper and Row, 1964.

SALANT, STEPHEN W. "Exhaustible Resources and Industrial Structure: A Nash-Cournot Approach to the World Oil Market." *Journal of Political Economy,* vol. 84, no. 5 (1976), pp. 1079–1093.

SAMUELSON, PAUL A. *Foundations of Economic Analysis.* Cambridge, MA: Harvard University Press, 1947.

SANDERS, M. ELIZABETH. *The Regulation of Natural Gas: Policy and Politics, 1938–1978.* Philadelphia: Temple Press, 1981.

SARTORI, GIOVANNI. *Democratic Theory.* Detroit, MI: Wayne State University Press, 1962.

SCHANTZ, JOHN J. *Oil and Gas Resources—Welcome to Uncertainty.* Reprint No. 58, Washington, DC: Resources for the Future, 1978.

SCHEFLER, ISRAEL. *Science and Subjectivity.* Indianapolis, IN: Bobbs-Merrill, 1967.

SCHICK, ALLEN. "A Death in the Bureaucracy: The Demise of Federal PPB." *Public Expenditure and Policy Analysis.* 2d ed. Edited by Robert H. Haveman and Julius Margolis. Chicago: Rand McNally, 1977.

SCHICK, ALLEN, editor. *Perspectives on Budgeting.* Washington, DC: American Society for Public Administration, 1980.

SCHICK, ALLEN. "The Road to PPB: The Stages of Budget Reform." *Perspectives on Budgeting.* Edited by Allen Schick. Washington, DC: American Society for Public Administration, 1980.

SCHULER, HENRY. *The National Security Implications of Increased Reliance Upon Importation of Refined Products.* Washington, DC: Conant and Associates, 1979.

SCHULTZE, CHARLES. *The Politics and Economics of Public Spending.* Washington, DC: Brookings Institute, 1968.

SCITOVSKY, T. "Two Concepts of External Economics." *Journal of Political Economy*, vol. 62 (1954), pp. 143–151.

SEIDMAN, DAVID. "The Politics of Policy Analysis: Protection or Overprotection in Drug Regulation?" *Regulation*, vol. 1, no. 1 (July/August 1977), pp. 22–37.

SIMON, HERBERT. *Models of Thought*. New Haven, CT: Yale University Press, 1979.

SIMON, HERBERT. *The Science of the Artificial*. Cambridge, MA: MIT Press, 1969.

SMART, J. J. C., AND WILLIAMS, BERNARD, editors. *Utilitarianism: For and Against*. Cambridge: Cambridge University Press, 1973.

SMITH, V. KERRY, editor. *Environmental Policy Under Reagan's Executive Order 12291: The Role of Benefit–Cost Analysis*. Chapel Hill, NC: University of North Carolina Press, 1984.

SOLOW, ROBERT M. "Defending Cost–Benefit Analysis." *Regulation*, vol. 5, no. 2 (March/April 1981), p. 41.

STEINER, PETER O. "The Public Sector and the Public Interest." *Public Expenditure and Policy Analysis*. 2d ed. Edited by Robert H. Haveman and Julius Margolis. Chicago: Rand McNally, 1977.

STIGLER, GEORGE. *The Development of Utility Theory*. In *Essays in the History of Economics*. Chicago: University of Chicago Press, 1965.

STIPAK, BRIAN. "Local Government's Use of Citizen Surveys." *Public Administration Review*, vol. 40 (September/October 1980), pp. 521–525.

STOKES, DONALD. "Political and Organizational Analysis of the Policy Curriculum." *Journal of Policy Analysis and Management*, vol. 6, no. 1 (Fall 1986), pp. 45–55.

STOKEY, EDITH, AND ZECKHAUSER, RICHARD. *A Primer for Policy Analysis*. New York: W. W. Norton and Co., 1978.

STRAUSSMAN, JEFFREY. *The Limits of Technocratic Politics*. New Brunswick, NJ: Transaction Books, 1978.

SUTTON, JOHN F. "The American Bar Association Code of Professional Responsibility: An Introduction." *Texas Law Review*, vol. 48, no. 2 (January, 1970), pp. 255–266.

TAYLOR, F. W. *The Principles of Scientific Management*. New York: Harper and Row, 1947.

TEISBERG, THOMAS. "A Dynamic Programming Model of the U.S. Strategic Petroleum Reserve." *Bell Journal of Economics*, vol. 12, no. 2 (Autumn 1981), pp. 526–546.

TEISBERG, THOMAS. "A Model for Simulating World Oil Market Arbitrage During Embargos." Working Paper. Cambridge, MA: Massachussetts Institute of Technology, November 26, 1979.

TESSER, ABRAHAM. "Self Generated Attitude Change." *Advances in Experimental Psychology*, no. 11 (1978), pp. 289–338.

TOLCHIN, SUSAN. "Presidential Power and the Politics of RARG," *Regulation*, vol. 3, no. 4 (July/August 1979), pp. 44–49.

TREXLER, MARK. *Export Restrictions on Domestic Oil: A California Perspective*. Sacramento, CA: California Energy Commission, November 1982.

TRIBE, LAURENCE. "Policy Science: Analysis or Ideology?" *Philosophy and Public Affairs*. vol. 2 (Fall 1972), pp. 67–110.

TRIBE, LAURENCE. "Trial by Mathematics: Precision and Ritual in the Legal Process." *Harvard Law Review,* vol. 84 (1971), pp. 1361–1365.

U.S. CONGRESS. "Export Administration Act." Public Law 95-52, June 22, 1977, 91 Stat. 235.

U.S. CONGRESS. HOUSE OF REPRESENTATIVES. SUBCOMMITTEE ON FOSSIL AND SYNTHETIC FUELS. "Cost to Consumers of Producing Added 52 TCF of Old Gas Reserves Under Deregulation." Unpublished staff analysis. Washington, DC, May 6, 1983.

U.S. CONGRESS. "Merchant Marine Act of 1920." June 5, 1920, Ch. 250, 41 Stat. 988.

U.S. CONGRESS. "Merchant Marine Act of 1936." June 29, 1936, Ch. 858, 49 Stat. 1985.

U.S. CONGRESS. "National Environmental Policy Act." Public Law 91-190, December 22, 1970.

U.S. CONGRESS. SENATE. See the testimony of Jack O'Leary, Deputy Secretary of Energy, in U.S. Senate, *Domestic Refinery Development and Improvement Act,* Part I. Hearing before the Subcommittee on Energy Regulations, Committee on Energy and Natural Resources. Washington, DC: U.S. Government Printing Office, September 11, 1979.

U.S. CONGRESS. SENATE. COMMITTEE ON FINANCE. *Incentives for Domestic Refining.* Hearing before the Subcommittee on Energy and Agricultural Taxation. Washington, DC: U.S. Government Printing Office, March 27, 1981.

U.S. CONGRESS. SENATE. COMMITTEE ON FOREIGN RELATIONS. *Export of Alaskan Oil.* Hearings before the Subcommittee on East Asian and Pacific Affairs. Washington, DC: U.S. Government Printing Office, July 19–20, 1983.

U.S. CONGRESS. "Windfall Profits Tax Act." Public Law 96-223, April 2, 1980, 94 Stat. 230.

U.S. DEPARTMENT OF ENERGY. "Action Memorandum: Refinery Policy." Unpublished memorandum from Lynn Coleman, General Council, U.S. Department of Energy to William Lewis, Policy and Evaluation, U.S. Department of Energy, Washington, DC, March 3, 1980.

U.S. DEPARTMENT OF ENERGY. "Analysis of the Costs and Benefits of a Protective Tariff on Refined Petroleum Products." Unpublished memorandum from William Lewis, Policy and Evaluation, U.S. Department of Energy to the Secretary and Deputy Secretary of the U.S. Department of Energy, Washington, DC, December 31, 1979.

U.S. DEPARTMENT OF ENERGY. "Discussion of Whether Federal Subsidies Should Be Provided to Encourage Domestic Refineries to Upgrade Existing Capacities." Unpublished memorandum from R. Dobie Langenkamp, Resource Development and Operation, Resource Applications, U.S. Department of Energy, to William Lewis, Policy and Evaluation, U.S. Department of Energy, Washington, DC, April 11, 1980.

U.S. DEPARTMENT OF ENERGY. "Exports/Exchanges of Alaskan Oil." Unpublished memorandum, Washington, DC, June 30, 1981.

U.S. DEPARTMENT OF ENERGY. "Issue Paper: Alaskan Crude Oil Exports." Unpublished paper, Washington, DC, July 31, 1981.

U.S. DEPARTMENT OF ENERGY. "Refinery Investment." Unpublished memorandum from William Lewis, Policy and Evaluation, U.S. Department of Energy to the Secretary and Deputy Secretary of Energy, U.S. Department of Energy, Washington, DC, June 4, 1980.

U.S. DEPARTMENT OF ENERGY. "Refinery Policy—Previous FEA/DOE Positions." Unpublished memorandum from Craig Bamburger, General Council, U.S. Department of Energy to William Lewis, Policy and Evaluation, U.S. Department of Energy, Washington, DC, April 15, 1980.

U.S. DEPARTMENT OF ENERGY. "Release of Policy and Evaluation Protective Tariff/Refinery Study." Unpublished memorandum from Undersecretary of Energy, U.S. Department of Energy to Secretary of Energy, U.S. Department of Energy, Washington, DC, January 14, 1980.

U.S. DEPARTMENT OF ENERGY. DIVISION OF OIL AND GAS. OFFICE OF ENERGY SOURCE ANALYSIS. "The Natural Gas Market Under the Natural Gas Policy Act." By Mary Carlson, Nancy Ody, Richard O'Neill, Mark Rudekohr, Phil Shambaugh, Richard Throsser, and William Trapmann. Unpublished paper, Washington, DC: Energy Information Administration, June 1981.

U.S. DEPARTMENT OF ENERGY. OFFICE OF ENERGY EMERGENCIES, ENVIRONMENTAL PROTECTION, SAFETY AND EMERGENCY PREPAREDNESS. "Issues and Analysis of the Use of the Strategic Petroleum Reserve: Staff Paper on the Department of Energy Approaches and Current Status of Studies." Unpublished paper, Washington, DC: DOE/EP-0075, December 1, 1982.

U.S. DEPARTMENT OF ENERGY. OFFICE OF POLICY AND EVALUATION. "An Analysis of Acquisition and Drawdown Strategies for the Strategic Petroleum Reserve." By Glen Sweetnam, George Horwich, and Steve Minihan. Unpublished paper, Washington, DC, December 1979.

U.S. DEPARTMENT OF ENERGY. OFFICE OF POLICY AND EVALUATION. "Comments on the Refinery Policy Study/Summary of Analysis." Unpublished paper, Washington, DC, August 1980.

U.S. DEPARTMENT OF ENERGY. OFFICE OF POLICY AND EVALUATION. "Costs and Benefits of a Protective Tariff on Refined Petroleum Products After Crude Oil Decontrol." Unpublished paper, Washington, DC: DOE/PE-0028, December 1980.

U.S. DEPARTMENT OF ENERGY. OFFICE OF POLICY, PLANNING AND ANALYSIS. "Issues in the Debate Over the Natural Gas Policy Act of 1978." By Catherine Abbott. Unpublished paper, Washington, DC, November 13, 1981.

U.S. DEPARTMENT OF ENERGY. OFFICE OF POLICY, PLANNING AND ANALYSIS. "Supplemental Analysis of Natural Gas Consumer Regulatory Reform." Unpublished paper, Washington, DC, May 1983.

U.S. DEPARTMENT OF TREASURY, OFFICE OF TAX ANALYSIS AND U.S. DEPARTMENT OF ENERGY, OFFICE OF POLICY AND EVALUATION. "Evaluation of Certain Proposals to Aid Domestic Refiners." Unpublished paper, Washington, DC, January 16, 1981.

U.S. MARITIME ADMINISTRATION. "The Impact of Exporting Alaskan North Slope Oil on U.S. Flag Tanker Employment." Unpublished paper, Washington, DC, August 14, 1981.

U.S. OFFICE OF THE PRESIDENT. CABINET COUNCIL ON NATURAL RESOURCES AND THE ENVIRONMENT. Unpublished working paper, final draft, Washington, DC, November 5, 1981.

UNIVERSITIES-NATIONAL BUREAU FOR ECONOMIC RESEARCH. *Public Finances: Needs, Sources, and Utilization.* Princeton, NJ: Princeton University Press, 1961.

VEATCH, ROBERT M. *Professional Ethics: New Principles for Physicians?* Hastings-On-Hudson: Hastings Center, 1980.

VEBLEN, THORSTEIN. *The Engineers and the Price System.* New York: The Viking Press, 1954.

WALRAS, LEON. Elements d'economie politique pure. Paris: Pichon and Durand-Auzais, 1926.

WAMSLEY, GARY. "Policy Subsystems as a Unit of Analysis in Implementation Studies." Paper presented at Erasmus University, Rotterdam, June 1983.

WEBBER, DAVID. "Obstacles to the Utilization of Systematic Policy Analysis: Conflicting World Views and Competing Disciplinary Matrices." *Knowledge: Creation, Diffusion, Utilization,* vol. 4, no. 4 (June 1983), pp. 534–560.

WEBER, MAX. *Structures of Power.* In *From Max Weber: Essays in Sociology.* Edited and Translated by H. H. Gerth and C. Wright Mills. New York: Oxford University Press, 1946.

WEIDENBAUM, MURRAY L. "Economic Policymaking in the Reagan Administration." *Presidential Studies Quarterly,* vol. XII (Winter 1982), pp. 95–99.

WEIMER, DAVID. *The Strategic Petroleum Reserve: Planning, Implementation, and Analysis.* Westport, CT: Greenwood Press, 1982.

WEIMER, DAVID L., AND AIDAN R. VINING, *Policy Analysis: Concepts and Practice.* Englewood Cliffs, NJ: Prentice-Hall, 1989.

WEISS, CAROL. *Evaluation Research: Methods of Assessing Program Effectiveness.* Englewood Cliffs, NJ: Prentice-Hall, 1972.

WEISS, CAROL. "Ideology, Interests, and Information: The Basis of Policy Positions." *Ethics, The Social Sciences, and Policy Analysis.* Edited by D. Callahan and B. Jennings. New York: Plenum, 1983.

WEISS, CAROL. "Research for Policy's Sake: The Enlightenment Function of Social Research." *Policy Analysis,* vol. 3, no. 4 (Fall 1977), pp. 531–545.

WEST, WILLIAM. "Institutionalizing Rationality in Regulatory Administration." *Public Administration Review,* vol. 43, no. 4 (August 1983), pp. 326–334.

WEYANT, JOHN. "A Decade of Natural Gas Policy Analyses: Economic Foundations, Political Orientations and Organizational Designs." Discussion paper. Energy Modeling Forum, Stanford University, Palo Alto, CA, September 1983.

WEYANT, JOHN. "Is There Policy-Oriented Learning in the Analysis of Natural Gas Policy Issues?" *Policy Sciences,* vol. 21, nos. 2–3 (1988), pp. 239–262.

WILDAVSKY, AARON. "The Analysis of Issue Contexts in the Study of Decision-Making." *The Journal of Politics,* vol. 24 (1962), pp. 717–732.

WILDAVSKY, AARON. "The Political Economy of Efficiency: Cost–Benefit Analysis, Systems Analysis, and Program Budgeting." *Public Administration Review,* vol. 26, no. 4 (December 1966), pp. 292–310.

WILDAVSKY, AARON. *The Politics of the Budgetary Process.* 3rd ed. Boston: Little Brown, 1979.

WILDAVSKY, AARON. *Principles for a Graduate School of Public Policy.* Berkeley, CA: University of California at Berkeley, 1977.

WILDAVSKY, AARON. "The Self-Evaluating Organization." *Public Administration Review,* vol. 32, no. 5 (September/October 1973), pp. 509–520.

WILDAVSKY, AARON. *Speaking Truth to Power.* Boston: Little, Brown, 1979.

WILDAVSKY, AARON, AND TENENBAUM, ELLEN. *The Politics of Mistrust: Estimating American Oil and Gas Reserves.* Newbury Park, CA: Sage, 1981.

WILLIAMS, ALLAN. "Cost–Benefit Analysis: Bastard Science? And/Or Insidious Poison in the Body Politick?" *Public Expenditure and Policy Analysis.* 2d ed. Edited by Robert H. Haveman and Julius Margolis. Chicago: Rand McNally, 1977.

WILLIG, R. D. "Consumers' Surplus Without Apology." *American Economic Review,* vol. 66 (September 1976), pp. 589–597.

WILSON, JAMES Q., editor. *The Politics of Regulation.* New York: Basic Books, 1980.

WILSON, WOODROW. "The Study of Administration." *Political Science Quarterly,* (June 1887), pp. 197–222.

WINNER, LANGDON. *Autonomous Technology: Technics Out-of-Control as a Theme in Political Thought.* Cambridge, MA: MIT Press, 1977.

YATES, DOUGLAS. *Bureaucratic Democracy.* Cambridge, MA: Harvard University Press, 1982.

YOUNG, A. A. "Pigou's Wealth and Welfare." *Quarterly Journal of Economics,* vol. 27 (1913), pp. 672–686.

ZECKHAUSER, RICHARD. "Procedures for Valuing Lives." *Public Policy,* vol. 23, no. 4 (Fall 1975), pp. 419–464.

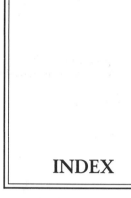

INDEX

Note: key definitions and concepts are indicated by bold page numbers.